THE DRAKE GUIDE TO
OSCAR WILDE

THE
DRAKE GUIDE TO
Oscar Wilde

By MICHAEL HARDWICK

DRAKE PUBLISHERS INC NEW YORK

ISBN 0-87749-544-0
LCCCN 73-4850

PUBLISHED IN 1973 BY
DRAKE PUBLISHERS INC
381 PARK AVENUE SOUTH
NEW YORK, N.Y. 10016

Printed in Great Britain

Contents

Introduction

OSCAR WILDE is not easily summed up in a phrase, either as artist or man; therefore a good deal of what has been selected to appear in this book has been chosen because it seems to reflect facets of his character, as well as demonstrating his art. But a word of warning is necessary: he was not one for taking things seriously, and often when he appears to be striving for profoundity or intense effect he is probably at his most facile; he may even be plagiarizing. Conversely, he often goes deepest when he merely seems to be skating the surface of flippancy. Much of what he wrote, as will be seen, originated in the table-talk at which he excelled; but that table-talk was carefully planned, even rehearsed. Many of the brightest and most lightly tossed-off quips had been thought up in advance and saved for exactly the right cue: a more good-natured equivalent of A. E. Housman's practice of hoarding his sarcastic barbs in notebooks.

Wilde's detractors have urged that but for his personal notoriety he would now be forgotten. Undoubtedly, his scandal has brought him to the curious notice of many who otherwise would not have encountered him. But not on the strength of this alone has he achieved his enduring and world-wide reputation. *The Importance of Being Earnest* is manifestly one of the funniest plays ever written, and the other three social comedies are still quite often performed. There are admirable things sprinkled throughout the shorter prose works and the poetry, while *The Ballad of Reading Gaol* is something of a classic. *Salomé* lives obliquely as the basis of Richard Strauss's music drama, to the popularity of which the number of complete recordings listed here in the Discography bears witness.

Wilde tried his hand at many literary forms, and in them all succeeded to a greater or lesser degree. The lack of consistency in

his work, or of any steady development towards a supreme
style – he was quite capable of following *The Importance of Being
Earnest* with some fragment of perfumed affectation – must be
put down to his too-conscious cleverness, his attitudinizing, his
delight in startling, shocking or making fun of critics and public.
His erratic personal life also must have helped to retard his
achievement. One's attitude towards Oscar Wilde the artist
as well as the man may largely depend on one's attitude to
homosexuality.

I am not a homosexual and have no particular sentiments about
it, apart from its use to exploit or corrupt the unwitting and
ingenuous. Much great art is undoubtedly attributable to homosexuals, perhaps to their homosexuality. Now that they have been
emancipated – in Great Britain, at least – one should surely be
free to discuss detectable trends when reviewing their work,
as in the case of artists of known political or religious bias; but it
will be some time before critics will feel enough assurance to do
so. Things are different for the unlucky dead: on them we may
deliver judgments from which they have no appeal.

In any case, this volume is a 'guide' to Oscar Wilde, not a
biography or a work of detailed criticism. As with the companion
volumes in this series I have tried to convey something of the
nature of his writings, in their varying styles, and to include
sufficient facts about them and his life to add up to ready reference,
pleasurable browsing, and dispassionate introduction for those
readers who come quite new to him. As ever, a great deal has had
to be omitted: one could fill an extra volume with 'Oscarisms',
true and apocryphal. I have tried to avoid quoting for quoting's
sake, and have only done so to carry along a story-line or give a
taste of a distinctive flavour.

The taste I myself retain predominantly is an agreeable one – a
subtle blend of bitter-sweet, with the final hint of *The Importance
of Being Earnest* lingering to make me wish there were more to
come. If a personal summing-up of Oscar Wilde may be permitted,
it is that he was a mother-spoiled, too-precocious, brilliant,
witty, charming, vain, indolent and foolish ass, who, unlike

many of smaller ability and achievement who grew to be their own worst enemies and got away with it, defeated himself.

Michael Hardwick

The Life of Oscar Wilde

OSCAR FINGAL O'FLAHERTIE WILLS WILDE was born on 16 October 1854 at 21 Westland Row, Dublin. His parents were a young doctor, William Wilde, notable for his tiny stature and biting wit, and notorious for his insatiable sexuality – Oscar Wilde had only one legitimate brother, but a countless brood of half-brothers and sisters – and a strikingly large, commanding and romantically-idealist girl, formerly Jane Francesca Elgee, widely known by the pen-name 'Speranza' with which she signed patriotic verse and other writings. William Wilde would soon become noted and prosperous as an eye specialist, being granted a knighthood in 1864 and dying in 1876: 'Speranza' was to outlive him by twenty years of increasing eccentricity.

What they lacked in uniformity of stature they shared in avidity for culture and bohemian hospitality. Unlike most Victorian children, Oscar and his elder brother Willie were allowed to mix freely with the adult guests, many of whom were literary people and classicists. But by the time Oscar was ready to be sent away to school the family home had begun to break up, largely owing to Sir William's costly indiscretions with a demented girl who blackmailed him. From little more than infancy Oscar was his mother's boy – she petted and idolized him and dressed him in her clothes beyond the age when it was customary for Victorian boy children to wear frocks.

The life of a boarder at Portora Royal School, Enniskillen, must have come as an uncomfortable contrast to this mother–adoration. Oscar made little attempt to integrate with the other pupils; he resisted all forms of sport, read widely, and delighted in an ability in Latin and Greek that even the oldest of his schoolfellows could not match. His mother, who had grounded him in the classics, had also introduced him to English, French and Italian literature, especially poetry. One of his favourite English prose authors, though by no means in the front rank, was Benjamin Disraeli, whose literary and sartorial mannerisms and gift of witty repartee are often reflected in his own life and work. But Disraeli's writing was to be far from the only influence on Wilde's style. His facility for reproducing the styles of others he admired was acquired early and never left him; it marred his development as an original artist and provided his critics with welcome ammunition.

In 1871 Wilde moved on to Trinity College, Dublin, where he came under the more direct influence of the Rev. John Pentland Mahaffy, Ireland's leading Greek scholar and a brilliant conversationalist moving widely in fashionable Dublin society. Mahaffy not only rounded off Wilde as a scholar – he won the Berkeley Gold Medal for Greek and other awards – but developed his gifts as talker and raconteur. An interesting sidelight on Wilde at Trinity, which does something to offset the effeminate image too easily attributed to him, is the story of his soundly beating a tough fellow student who had sneered at him for declaiming his poetry. This incident was to have its parallel at Oxford when a group of hearties set forth to beat up Wilde for his aesthetic attitudinizing and smash the blue and white china he treasured in his rooms: he threw the lot of them out by main force. He held a lifelong aversion to physical exercise, which in the days of his professional success he was to carry to the extreme of spending much of each day in bed and the rest of it at a restaurant table, never walking between the two if possible and consequently growing gross and bloated. In young manhood, however, he was a strapping figure, over six feet in height, handsomely though somewhat exotically featured, and able to overcome by sheer good nature the prejudice of many university men against students who preferred brain to brawn. Although his subsequent downfall was attributable to homosexuality, he flirted with girls in his undergraduate days, subsequently married and fathered two children, and when he turned to homosexuality it was in the dominant role.

In 1874, when he was twenty, Wilde entered Magdalen College, Oxford, and proceeded to establish himself as an Original in an institution where wealth and rank counted as highly as academic brilliance. Consummately self-assured in scholarship and poise, he nonchalantly ignored his detractors, dressed in loud suitings that ensured personal recognition, and patronized the stuffier dons, preferring to ally himself with the then Slade Professor of Art, John Ruskin, and Walter Pater, Fellow of Brasenose, both sexually inadequate men who had opted for the notion that beauty, expressed through the arts and religion, was the essence of life.

Wilde left Oxford in 1878 with a triumphant flourish of academic and poetic distinction (see *Poetry*) and set himself up in rooms in London, off the Strand, with an Oxford friend, Frank Miles, who was already making a name as a pencil portraitist of the most beautiful women of the day. He cultivated their acquaintance, flattered them, wrote poems to them, and became familiar in theatrical society through the friendships he easily struck up with such celebrated figures as Lillie Langtry, Ellen Terry, Helena Modjeska, Sarah Bernhardt, and, on the male side, Henry Irving. Though he had little money, he got himself invited to fashionable and aristocratic houses, achieved general notice and amused notoriety by dressing in an outrageously 'aesthetic' manner, and, like the young Disraeli, was given the invaluable advertisement of being caricatured in *Punch*. He did not start the 'Aesthetic Movement'. No such thing existed in precise terms: it was a trend against the dullness and materialism of Victorian values to which Ruskin, Pater, James McNeill Whistler and others had made their varying contributions before ever Oscar Wilde appeared upon the scene; but by sheer self-advertisement Wilde came to epitomize it in the eyes of the Press and public. He would continue to utter upon the subject of 'art for art's sake' for the rest of his life, but it may be confidently asserted that only at certain times, and in certain moods and circumstances, did he really believe in it. He was manifestly unfaithful to that ideal in many phases of his life and work, though at times he blemished both by a too-ardent pursuit of it. In those early days, at least, he was conducting a calculated campaign towards 'getting on' and attaining the fame which he knew to be his right but whose form he could not envisage in clear outline.

His great moment came when W. S. Gilbert and Arthur Sullivan created their comic opera, *Patience*, in 1881. This amusing and winningly musical satire on the 'Aesthetic Movement' was not, as has been widely believed, composed with Oscar Wilde as its butt. Gilbert and Sullivan satirized many long-established British institutions – the Law, the Royal Navy, Parliament, the Peerage – but the target of the Aesthetics was too topically tempting to be ignored, and they hit it with consummate accuracy. Moreover, Gilbert and Sullivan were only two of a triumvirate, the third member of which was an astute entrepreneur and, as it happened, lecture agent, Richard D'Oyly Carte. It occurred to Carte that the American success of *Patience* would be notably enhanced if the Aesthete of Aesthetes could be persuaded to show himself over there in person, and he invited Wilde to undertake a lecture tour. Wilde accepted, and played his role to perfection. From the moment he stepped ashore in New York on 2 January 1882 and, in answer to the Customs ritual, stated that he had nothing to declare except his genius, he was the talk of America. But it was on his own terms that he made his gimmick-conceived undertaking a success. He spoke on 'The English Renaissance' and similar themes with a wit and intellectual percipience that won over his audiences. The less serious elements of the Press made great fun over him and fulfilled Carte's purpose; but Wilde's visit to America made him many serious friends there and gained him the admiration of such notable figures as Oliver Wendell Holmes Sen., Henry Wadsworth Longfellow, Louisa M. Alcott and Walt Whitman.

Thus, through academic attainment, sure-footed social climbing and the ability to achieve and make the most of personal publicity, Oscar Wilde had made his name known on both sides of the Atlantic, and to some extent in Europe, well before his thirtieth birthday. Up to that time his only publication of any substance had been the *Poems* in 1881. They had sold unusually well but had brought in little hard cash. In 1884 Wilde married Constance Lloyd, and three years later was still without a literary income, so that he was glad to take on the editorship of a monthly magazine, *Woman's World*. He took the work seriously, did it for a year with great panache, and went through a period of literary invigoration that resulted in his writing down the *Fairy Tales* some of the essays, *The Picture of Dorian Gray* and other short pieces.

The evolution of these works emerges as this present volume goes forward, and needs no further discussion here. Nevertheless, it remains sadly necessary to mention the sordid and dramatic sequence of events which brought him to imprisonment, ruin and premature death. Numerous books have been written about the downfall of Oscar Wilde, and those who wish to pursue the unpleasant yet fascinating details will find some of their titles listed in my Selected Bibliography. The brief particulars are as follows.

It is not known when Wilde had his first homosexual experience, nor when he began to indulge himself with any frequency. Many of his closest friends, both at Oxford and after, were homosexuals in varying degrees; and the homosexual relationship, with its classical precedents, was a traditional corollary to the pursuit of the aesthetic ideal. The names of several of these men are little known except for their association with Wilde: one or two were sincere enough to stand by him through the worst of his troubles and to help him after his imprisonment. The names of too many others merely flit through the accounts of his life and his correspondence – male prostitutes, casual acquaintances, compliant youths of various nationalities picked up on holidays abroad and in the last years of exile – and there is no doubt that there were countless others whose names are unrecorded, for Wilde appears to have set no limit to his appetite for young men, any more than he did for drink or rich food; and it is a major factor of his tragedy (and a trenchant comment on the society that could imprison him for two years, without remission, for not keeping his sexual practices private) that prison did nothing to reform him, but reduced him to that abject state of defiant resignation in which there seems nothing more to be lost by complete surrender to the appetites.

From among this named and nameless host one person is most notoriously associated with Wilde: Lord Alfred Douglas, third son of the eighth Marquess of Queensberry and sixteen years Wilde's junior. They appear to have been introduced in 1891 when Douglas was still an undergraduate at Wilde's old college, Magdalen, and virtually from then onward their story is one of the older man's infatuation with this youth of notable beauty, poetic gifts and indolent disposition, known to his friends as 'Bosie', a variant of his mother's baby-name for him, 'Boysie'. Although each indulged quite overtly in *affaires* with other males, and many bitter quarrels rent them apart from time to time, Wilde and Bosie seem to have remained mutually attracted. Writing out his self-pity in *De Profundis* in gaol, Wilde accused Douglas of having ruined him financially and professionally by his selfish demands upon his purse and time, giving little in return; but on his release he was quick to return to his 'darling boy'. The homosexual relationship, being unnatural, however artistic in the view of its participants, is difficult to sustain with equanimity. That of Wilde and Douglas, though the most publicized of all such associations, must, one imagines, fairly typify countless others through the ages.

The main untypical element was Douglas's father, Queensberry, an eccentric, a bully, a wastrel, and in some degree a madman, whose name has lived in the disparate connections of the Oscar Wilde scandal and the sport of boxing, of which it was he who initiated the 'Queensberry Rules'. At the time of the Wilde–Douglas association Queensberry was divorced from his wife, with whom Bosie continued to live; but the attachment between the two men inevitably reached his notice and he made a series of attempts to persuade Bosie to break it off which began with appeals and rose in a crescendo of violent threats and warnings of physical violence itself. These culminated, in 1895, in Queensberry's planning to create a disturbance at the first night of *The Importance of Being Earnest*, being refused admission to the theatre, and three days later leaving his card at Wilde's club bearing the inscription 'To Oscar Wilde posing as a somdomite' (*sic*).

After consulting with his friends, Wilde unwisely decided to prosecute Queensberry for libel. When asked by his high-minded counsel, Sir Edward Clarke, whether there was any truth in the accusation, he lied to him; this was even more unwise, for he was aware that many people in London knew of his proclivities and that some of his letters to Douglas, written in extravagantly affectionate language that could scarcely be misconstrued, were circulating in the blackmail market.

Queensberry was duly arrested and tried. His agents had no trouble in assembling a corps of witnesses prepared to testify to Wilde's behaviour. Ironically, it was Edward Carson, a former fellow student of Wilde's at Trinity College, Dublin, who was briefed to appear against him. Some of Wilde's friends tried to persuade him to abandon the case and leave the country for a time; but, egged on as he was by Douglas who longed to see his detested father humiliated, his own vanity and his view of himself as a martyr would not allow him to follow wise counsel. The outcome needs no re-telling: despite a brilliant display of argument and wit from the witness-box, Wilde, whose counsel's withdrawal on the third day was tantamount to an admission, lost his case. He seems to have been given the opportunity still to leave the country, but he would not go. Predictably, Queensberry demanded his arrest: he was refused bail and kept in gaol for three weeks until his trial, at which the jury disagreed. A brief period on bail, during which he yet again refused to leave the country, was followed by his second trial, a verdict of Guilty, and the savage sentence of two years' hard labour.

The rest is sadness. He suffered mentally and physically in gaol, was made bankrupt, was divorced and deprived of his children, and served his full term in the knowledge that he would never again enjoy public esteem: indeed, so great was the opprobrium now attached to his name that even his innocent wife and his children were asked to leave an hotel in Switzerland when their identity became known.

He wrote the long, self-pitying, but in many ways impressive essay *De Profundis*, in the form of a long letter to Lord Alfred Douglas, shortly before his release from Reading Gaol, and, subsequently, his best and most famous poem, *The Ballad of Reading Gaol*. Otherwise he was finished. Post-prison attempts to write soon petered out. He lived abroad on a small allowance from his ex-wife and gifts and loans from friends and a few sincere admirers of his works. He called himself 'Sebastian Melmoth', probably a symbolical combination of the names of the martyred Saint Sebastian and Melmoth the Wandering Jew of a play by his great-uncle Charles Robert Maturin. The symbolism was apt, for the last three years of his life were occupied in restless movement about the Continent, existing always beyond his slender means, sometimes accompanied by Bosie but more and more frequently resorting to the casual pick-up of youths in public places. His wanderings came to their end in a Paris hotel on 30 November 1900 when he died in agony of an ear infection, possibly cerebral meningitis, which may have had a syphilitic origin. He was buried simply at Bagneux, but in 1909 his remains were transferred to Père-Lachaise, Paris, where his tomb, with its impressive monument by Epstein, is one of the most-visited in that celebrated resting-place of great people.

The Characters

AGATHA, LADY: Lord Henry Wotton's aunt, presumably a sister of Lord Fermor. A society hostess, but something of a philanthropist, on whose behalf Dorian Gray had intended to do good works before his corruption. *'She told me she had discovered a wonderful young man, who was going to help her in the East End, and that his name was Dorian Gray. I am bound to state that she never told me he was good-looking. Women have no appreciation of good looks; at least, good women have not. She said that he was very earnest, and had a beautiful nature. I at once pictured to myself a creature with spectacles and lank hair, horribly freckled, and tramping about on huge feet.'* (Lord Henry, *Picture of Dorian Gray*)

ALBUQUERQUE, DUCHESS OF: Companion to the Infanta of Spain. *Even the Duchess – the Camerera-Mayor as she was called – a thin, hard-featured woman with a yellow ruff, did not look quite so bad-tempered as usual, and something like a chill smile flitted across her wrinkled face and twitched her thin bloodless lips.* (Fairy Tales: 'The Birthday of the Infanta')

ALEXIS, CZAREVITCH: A member of the Nihilists under the alias of Alexis Ivanacievitch, a medical student, he succeeds his father as Czar. Vera, whom he loves, sacrifices herself to save him from her fellow-Nihilists. *You think I am a traitor, a liar, a king? I am, for love of you. Vera, it was for you I broke my oath and wear my father's crown. I would lay at your feet this mighty Russia, which you and I have loved so well; would give you this earth as your footstool; set this crown on your head. The people will love us. We will rule them by love, as a father rules his children. There shall be liberty in Russia for every man to think as his heart bids him; liberty for men to speak as they think.* (*Vera*)

ALICE: Mrs Arbuthnot's maid (*Woman of No Importance*)

ALLONBY, MRS: A guest at Lady Hunstanton's. *Mrs Allonby is
very well born. She is a niece of Lord Brancaster's. It is said, of course,
that she ran away twice before she was married. But you know how
unfair people often are. I myself don't believe she ran away more than
once.* (Lady Caroline, *Woman of No Importance*)

ALROY, LADY: A beautiful woman loved by Lord Murchison,
who repudiates her on the point of proposing to her because of
his suspicions of her. She dies soon afterwards. *It seemed to me
the face of some one who had a secret, but whether that secret was good
or evil I could not say. Its beauty was a beauty moulded out of many
mysteries – the beauty, in fact, which is psychological, not plastic –
and the faint smile that just played across the lips was far too subtle
to be really sweet.* ('The Sphinx Without a Secret')

ARBUTHNOT, GERALD: Illegitimate son of Rachel Arbuthnot
and Lord Illingworth, whose proposal to advance Gerald's
career by making him his secretary she vehemently contests.
He is loved by the puritanical Hester Worsley. *Mr. Arbuthnot
has a beautiful nature! He is so simple, so sincere. He has one of the
most beautiful natures I have ever come across. It is a privilege to
meet him.* (Hester Worsely, *Woman of No Importance*)

ARBUTHNOT, MRS RACHEL: A neighbour of Lady Hunstan-
ton; mother (unmarried) of Gerald Arbuthnot by Lord
Illingworth when he was George Harford. *Oh, she is very
feminine, Caroline, and so good, too. You should hear what the
Archdeacon says of her. He regards her as his right hand in the parish.*
(Lady Hunstanton, *Woman of No Importance*)

ARNHEIM, THE LATE BARON: An international manipulator,
he had persuaded Sir Robert Chiltern, when a young politician,
to part with a Cabinet secret for the money with which to
achieve success. Later a lover of Mrs Cheveley, who had
obtained from him the compromising letter with which she
attempts to blackmail Chiltern.

LORD GORING: *Damned scoundrel!*

CHILTERN: *No; he was a man of a most subtle and refined intellect. A man of culture, charm, and distinction. One of the most
intellectual men I ever met.*

LORD GORING: *Ah! I prefer a gentlemanly fool any day.*
> (*Ideal Husband*)

BARDI, PRINCE GUIDO: Only son of the ruler of Florence. About to seduce Bianci, he is killed by her husband, Simone.

SIMONE: . . . *your father*
> *When he is childless will be happier.*
> *As for the State, I think our state of Florence*
> *Needs no adulterous pilot at its helm.*
> *Your life would soil its lilies.* (*Florentine Tragedy*)

BARDI, TADDEO; PETRUCCI, MAFFIO; VITELLOZZO, JEPPO. Gentlemen of the Duke of Padua's household.

DUKE: *Why, every man among them has his price,*
> *Although, to do them justice, some of them*
> *Are quite expensive.* (*Duchess of Padua*)

BASILDON, OLIVIA, COUNTESS OF, and MARCHMONT, MRS MARGARET. Friends of Gertrude Chiltern. *Two very pretty women. . . . They are types of exquisite fragility. Their affectation of manner has a delicate charm. Watteau would have loved to paint them.* (Stage direction in *Ideal Husband*)

BEATRICE: Duchess of Padua. She kills her husband, Simone Gesso, for love of Guido Ferranti, and subsequently takes poison. *She is worse than ugly, she is good.* (Duke, *Duchess of Padua*)

BEAUCHAMP, LADY CLEMENTINA: Lord Arthur Savile's elderly second cousin, whom he tries to poison in order to accomplish the murder read in his palm by Mr Podgers. '*Here I am, a poor rheumatic creature, with a false front and a bad temper.*
> ('Lord Arthur Savile's Crime')

BERWICK, DUCHESS OF: A member of the Windermeres' social circle. Mother of Lady Agatha Carlisle and sister to Lord Augustus Lorton. *I assure you, my dear, that on several occasions after I was first married, I had to pretend to be very ill, and was obliged to drink the most unpleasant mineral waters, merely to get Berwick out of town. He was so extremely susceptible. Though I am bound to say he never gave away any large sums of money to anybody.* (*Lady Windermere's Fan*)

BIANCA: Simone's wife, being courted by Guido Bardi when her husband returns home.

> SIMONE: . . . *I trust my honest wife,*
> *Most honest if uncomely to the eye,*
> *Hath not with foolish chatterings wearied you,*
> *As is the wont of women.*
>
> *(Florentine Tragedy)*

BRACKNELL, LADY: Mother of Gwendolen Fairfax; Algernon Moncrieff's Aunt Augusta. *I don't really know what a gorgon is like but I am quite sure that Lady Bracknell is one. In any case, she is a monster, without being a myth, which is rather unfair.* (John Worthing, *The Importance of Being Earnest*)

BRANDON, LADY: A garrulous Society figure who introduces Basil Hallward to Dorian Gray. '*She tried to found a salon, and only succeeded in opening a restaurant.*' (Lord Henry, *Picture of Dorian Gray*)

BUNBURY: A fictitious permanent invalid invented by Algernon Moncrieff, who accounts for his absences from town on romantic and other errands by saying that he has had to visit Bunbury.

> ALGERNON: *Bunbury is perfectly invaluable. If it wasn't for Bunbury's extraordinary bad health, for instance, I wouldn't be able to dine with you at Willis's to-night, for I have been really engaged to Aunt Augusta for more than a week.*
>
> JACK: *I haven't asked you to dine with me anywhere to-night.*
>
> ALGERNON: *I know. You are absolutely careless about sending out invitations.* (Importance of Being Earnest)

BURDON, SIR THOMAS: A Radical member of Parliament lunching at Lord Henry Wotton's Aunt Agatha's. *Followed his leader in public life, and in private life followed the best cooks, dining with the Tories, and thinking with the Liberals, in accordance with a wise and well-known rule.* (Picture of Dorian Gray)

CAMPBELL, ALAN: A scientist and amateur musician, formerly a friend of Dorian Gray who led him into corrupt ways. He commits suicide not long after being blackmailed by Gray into disposing, by chemical means, of the body of Basil Hallward. *To him, as to many others, Dorian Gray was the type of everything that is wonderful and fascinating in life. Whether or not a quarrel had taken place between them no one ever knew. But suddenly people remarked that they scarcely spoke when they met, and that Campbell seemed always to go away early from any party at which Dorian Gray was present. (Picture of Dorian Gray)*

CANTERVILLE, LORD: Vendor of Canterville Chase, his ancestral home, to Hiram B. Otis. *'We have not cared to live in the place ourselves,' said Lord Canterville, 'since my grand-aunt, the Dowager Duchess of Bolton, was frightened into a fit, from which she never really recovered, by two skeleton hands being placed on her shoulders as she was dressing for dinner.'* ('The Canterville Ghost')

CANTERVILLE GHOST, THE: The spirit of Sir Simon de Canterville, who had murdered his wife, Lady Eleanore de Canterville in 1575 and suddenly disappeared, in mysterious circumstances, nine years later, to haunt Canterville Chase for three centuries until released by Virginia Otis. *He was simply but neatly clad in a long shroud, spotted with churchyard mould, had tied up his jaw with a strip of yellow linen, and carried a small lantern and a sexton's spade. In fact, he was dressed for the character of 'Jonas the Graveless, or the Corpse-Snatcher of Chertsey Barn,' one of his most remarkable impersonations.* ('Canterville Ghost')

CARDEW, CECILY: John Worthing's ward, in love with Algernon Moncrieff.

LADY BRACKNELL: *The two weak points in our age are its want of principle and its want of profile. The chin a little higher, dear. Style largely depends on the way the chin is worn. They are worn very high, just at present. Algernon!*

ALGERNON: *Yes, Aunt Augusta!*

LADY BRACKNELL: *There are distinct social possibilities in Miss Cardew's profile.*

ALGERNON: *Cecily is the sweetest, dearest, prettiest girl in the whole world. And I don't care twopence about social possibilities.*

LADY BRACKNELL: *Never speak disrespectfully of Society,*

Algernon. Only people who can't get into it do that. (*Importance of Being Earnest*)

CARLISLE, LADY AGATHA: Gauche daughter of the Duchess of Berwick, courted by Mr Hopper. *Dear girl! She is so fond of photographs of Switzerland. Such a pure taste, I think.* (Duchess of Berwick, *Lady Windermere's Fan*)

CAVALCANTI, BERNARDO: Lord Justice of Padua, presiding at Guido Ferranti's trial.

>   LORD JUSTICE: *Madam, it were a precedent most evil*
>   *To wrest the law from its appointed course,*
>   *For, though the cause be just, yet anarchy*
>   *Might on this licence touch these golden scales*
>   *And unjust causes unjust victories gain.*
>
>   (*Duchess of Padua*)

CAVERSHAM, EARL OF, K.G.: A senior member of the Government Party, aged seventy. Father of Viscount Goring. *Never go anywhere now. Sick of London Society. Shouldn't mind being introduced to my own tailor; he always votes on the right side. But object strongly to being sent down to dinner with my wife's milliner. Never could stand Lady Caversham's bonnets.* (*Ideal Husband*)

CHAPMAN, LADY ALICE: Lady Narborough's daughter, present with her husband at her mother's dinner party attended by Dorian Gray. *A dowdy dull girl, with one of those characteristic British faces, that, once seen, are never remembered; and her husband, a red-cheeked, white-whiskered creature who, like so many of his class, was under the impression that inordinate joviality can atone for an entire lack of ideas.* (*Picture of Dorian Gray*)

CHASUBLE, THE REV. CANON FREDERICK, D.D.: Rector of Woolton, Hertfordshire, where John Worthing has his home. Admirer of, and admired by, Miss Prism.

>   MISS PRISM: *You are too much alone, dear Dr Chasuble. You should get married. A misanthrope I can understand – a woman-thrope, never!*
>
>   CHASUBLE: *Believe me, I do not deserve so neologistic a phrase. The precept as well as the practice of the Primitive Church was distinctly against matrimony.*

MISS PRISM: *That is obviously the reason why the Primitive Church has not lasted up to the present day. And you do not seem to realise, dear Doctor, that by persistently remaining single, a man converts himself into a permanent temptation. Men should be more careful; this very celibacy leads weaker vessels astray.*

CHASUBLE: *But is a man not equally attractive when married?*

MISS PRISM: *No married man is ever attractive except to his wife.*

CHASUBLE: *And often, I've been told, not even to her.*

MISS PRISM: *That depends on the intellectual sympathies of the woman. Maturity can always be depended on. Ripeness can be trusted. Young women are green. I spoke horticulturally. My metaphor was drawn from fruit.* (*Importance of Being Earnest*)

CHESHIRE, DUKE OF: Youthful admirer of Virginia E. Otis, and ultimately her husband. *Proposed to her on the spot, and was sent back to Eton that very night by his guardians in floods of tears.* ('Canterville Ghost')

CHEVELEY, MRS LARUA: An unscrupulous schemer, once at school with Gertrude Chiltern whose husband she attempts to blackmail into using his political influence to her advantage. She also tries to force Lord Goring, who had once loved her, into marrying her. *I should fancy Mrs Cheveley is one of those very modern women of our time who find a new scandal as becoming as a new bonnet, and air them both in the Park every afternoon at five-thirty.* (Lord Goring, *Ideal Husband*)

CHICHESTER, DEAN OF: Father of Jane Percy and uncle of Lord Arthur Savile, who tries to blow him up in order to accomplish the murder read in his palm by Mr Podgers. *The Dean, who was a man of great culture and learning, was extremely fond of clocks, and had a wonderful collection of timepieces, ranging from the fifteenth century to the present day, and it seemed to Lord Arthur that this hobby of the good Dean's offered him an excellent opportunity for carrying out his scheme. Where to procure an explosive machine was, of course, quite another matter.* ('Lord Arthur Savile's Crime')

CHILTERN, LADY GERTRUDE: Sir Robert Chiltern's wife, aged about 27. She had been at school with Laura Cheveley, her husband's would-be blackmailer. *A woman of grave Greek beauty.* (Stage direction in *Ideal Husband*)

CHILTERN, MABEL: Sir Robert Chiltern's sister. Partly by flirting with Tommy Trafford, she achieves a declaration from Lord Goring. *A perfect example of the English type of prettiness, the apple-blossom type. . . . She has the fascinating tyranny of youth, and the astonishing courage of innocence. To sane people she is not reminiscent of any work of art. But she is really like a Tanagra statuette, and would be rather annoyed if she were told so.* (Stage direction in *Ideal Husband*)

CHILTERN, SIR ROBERT, BART: Under-Secretary for Foreign Affairs, whom his wife's former schoolfellow, Laura Cheveley, attempts to blackmail over a political misdemeanour in his early career. *A man of forty, but looking somewhat younger. . . . Not popular – few personalities are. But intensely admired by the few, and deeply respected by the many. The note of his manner is that of perfect distinction, with a slight touch of pride. One feels that he is conscious of the success he has made in life.* (Stage direction in *Ideal Husband*)

CLOUSTON, SIR GEOFFREY: Brother of the Duchess of Monmouth. A fellow guest of hers at Dorian Gray's cointry home, where he accidentally kills James Vane. '*Why on earth don't you keep your men back? Spoiled my shooting for the day.*' (*Picture of Dorian Gray*)

COWPER-COWPER, MRS: A guest at Lady Windermere's coming-of-age party. (*Lady Windermere's Fan*)

CRISTOFANO, ASCANIO: Guido Ferranti's closest friend, whom he repudiates on Count Moranzone's instructions when his work of vengeance begins.

> ASCANIO: *I thought the friendship of the antique world*
> *Was not yet dead, but that the Roman type*
> *Might even in this poor and common age*
> *Find counterparts of love; then by this love*
> *Which beats between us like a summer sea,*
> *Whatever lot has fallen to your hand*
> *May I not share it?*   (*Duchess of Padua*)

DAMPIER, REV. AUGUSTUS: Fellow of King's College, Cambridge, and rector of the parish in which Canterville Chase stands. He conducts the ghost's funeral service. ('Canterville Ghost')

DARLINGTON, LORD: Lady Windermere's would-be admirer; a self-professed cynic. *I shouldn't like you at all if I thought you were what most other men are. Believe me, you are better than most other men, and I sometimes think you pretend to be worse.* (Lady Windermere, *Lady Windermere's Fan*)

DAUBENY, VEN. ARCHDEACON, D. D.: Lady Hunstanton's local rector; possessor of a determinedly ailing wife. *Her deafness is a great privation to her. She can't even hear my sermons now.* (*Woman of No Importance*)

DE KOLOFF, MONSIEUR: Russian Ambassador, present at Lady Windermere's when Mr Podgers is reading palms. *Nothing that Lady Windermere could do would induce Monsieur de Koloff, the Russian Ambassador, even to take his gloves off.* ('Lord Arthur Savile's Crime')

DEVEREUX, LADY MARGARET: Dorian Gray's late mother, daughter of the last Lord Kelso. A beautiful girl who could have had her pick of London's most eligible bachelors, she ran away with, and married, a penniless young army officer. *'The poor chap was killed in a duel at Spa, a few months after the marriage. There was an ugly story about it. They said Kelso got some rascally adventurer, some Belgian brute, to insult his son-in-law in public; paid him, sir, to do it, paid him; and that the fellow spitted his man as if he had been a pigeon. The thing was hushed up, but, egad, Kelso ate his chop alone at the club for some time afterwards. He brought his daughter back with him, I was told, and she never spoke to him again. Oh yes; it was a bad business. The girl died too; died within a year.'* (Lord Fermor, *Picture of Dorian Gray*)

DON PEDRO OF ARAGON: Brother of the King of Spain and uncle of the Infanta. *Whose cruelty, even in Spain, was notorious, and who was suspected by many of having caused the Queen's death by means of a pair of poisoned gloves.* (*Fairy Tales:* 'The Birthday of the Infanta')

DUMBY, MR: A member of the Windermeres' social circle. *I am the only person in the world I should like to know thoroughly; but I don't see any chance of it just at present.* (*Lady Windermere's Fan*)

DWARF, THE LITTLE: The grotesque son of a poor charcoal-burner, he delights the Infanta with his dancing at her birthday party, then dies of a broken heart after seeing himself for the first time in a mirror and realizing why she had found him so amusing. *Perhaps the most amusing thing about him was his complete unconsciousness of his own grotesque appearance. Indeed he seemed quite happy and full of the highest spirits. When the children laughed, he laughed as freely and as joyously as any of them, and at the close of each dance he made them each the funniest of bows, smiling and nodding at them just as if he was really one of themselves, and not a little misshapen thing that Nature, in some humorous mood, had fashioned for others to mock at.* (*Fairy Tales:* 'The Birthday of the Infanta')

ERLYNNE, MRS: Suspected by Society of being Lord Windermere's mistress, she is actually his wife's disgraced mother. She accepts the hand of Lord Augustus Lorton. *Looks like an* edition de luxe *of a wicked French novel, meant specially for the English market.* (Dumby, *Lady Windermere's Fan*)

A Mrs Erlynne, described as 'a pushing nobody, with a delightful lisp', is among Lady Narborough's dinner guests in *Dorian Gray*.

ERSKINE, HUGHIE: The generous-natured friend of the artist Alan Taylor, who empties his pockets for the artist's 'poor' model, who turns out to be the fabulously wealthy Baron Hausberg. Erskine's gesture is suitably rewarded when he marries Laura Merton. *He was as popular with men as he was with women, and he had every accomplishment except that of making money. . . . He had tried everything. He had gone to the Stock Exchange for six months; but what was a butterfly to do among bulls and bears? He had been a tea-merchant for a little longer, but had soon tired of pekoe and souchong. Then he had tried selling dry sherry. That did not answer; the sherry was a little too dry. Ultimately he became nothing, a delightful, ineffectual young man with a perfect profile and no profession.* ('Model Millionaire')

ERSKINE OF TREADLEY, MR: A luncheon guest at Lord Henry Wotton's Aunt Agatha's. *An old gentleman of considerable charm and culture, who had fallen, however, into bad habits of silence, having, as he explained once to Lady Agatha, said everything that he had to say before he was thirty. (Picture of Dorian Gray)*

FAIRFAX, THE HON. GWENDOLEN: Lady Bracknell's daughter and Algernon Moncrieff's first cousin. She becomes engaged to John Worthing, believing him to be his fictitious brother Ernest, to whom Cecily Cardew believes herself to be engaged.

> CECILY: *Do you suggest, Miss Fairfax, that I entrapped Ernest into an engagement? How dare you? This is no time for wearing the shallow mask of manners. When I see a spade I call it a spade.*

> GWENDOLEN: *I am glad to say that I have never seen a spade. It is obvious that our social spheres have been widely different.*

> *(Importance of Being Earnest)*

FARQUHAR: Lady Hunstanton's butler. (*Woman of No Importance*)

FAUDEL, LORD: A luncheon guest at Lord Henry Wotton's Aunt Agatha's. *A most intelligent middle-aged mediocrity, as bald as a Ministerial statement in the House of Commons. (Picture of Dorian Gray)*

FERMOR, GEORGE, LORD: Lord Henry Wotton's uncle. *A genial if somewhat rough-mannered old bachelor, whom the outside world called selfish because it derived no particular benefit from him, but who was considered generous by Society as he fed the people who amused him. . . . His principles were out of date, but there was a good deal to be said for his prejudices. (Picture of Dorian Gray)*

FERMOR, LADY: One of Lady Windermere's guests whose palm is read by Mr Podgers. *When he told poor Lady Fermor, right out before every one that she did not care a bit for music, but was extremely fond of musicians, it was generally felt that cheiromancy was a most dangerous science, and one that ought not to be encouraged, except in a tête-à-tête.* ('Lord Arthur Savile's Crime')

FERRANTI, GUIDO: Son of the late Duke Lorenzo of Parma, who had been betrayed by Simone Gesso and put to death.

Persuaded by Count Moranzone to avenge his father, Guido falls in love with Gesso's wife, Beatrice, but both die in Guido's cell after his supposed murder of Gesso.

MORANZONE: *Nay, nay, I trust thee not: your hot young blood,*
Undisciplined nature, and too violent rage
Will never tarry for this great revenge,
But wreck itself on passion.

(Duchess of Padua)

FISHERMAN, THE YOUNG: A youth who banishes his Soul for the love of a Mermaid. '*Of what use is my soul to me? I cannot see it. I may not touch it. I do not know it. Surely I will send it away from me, and much gladness shall be mine.*' (*Fairy Tales:* 'The Fisherman and his Soul')

FLORA, LADY: Daughter of the Duchess of Paisley, she is one of the guests at Lady Windermere's whose palm is read by Mr Podgers. *A tall girl, with sandy Scotch hair, and high shoulder-blades, stepped awkwardly from behind the sofa, and held out a long, bony hand with spatulate fingers.* '*Ah, a pianist! I see,*' *said Mr Podgers,* '*an excellent pianist, but perhaps hardly a musician.*' ('Lord Arthur Savile's Crime')

FRANCIS: Lady Hunstanton's footman. (*Woman of No Importance*)

GESSO, SIMONE: Duke of Padua. Malicious husband of Beatrice, who murders him for love of Guido Ferranti.

DUKE: *See thou hast enemies.*
Else will the world think very little of thee.

(Duchess of Padua)

GIANT, THE SELFISH: Owner of the garden where the children come to play. '*My own garden is my own garden,*' *said the Giant;* '*anyone can understand that, and I will allow no one to play in it but myself.*' (*Fairy Tales:* 'The Selfish Giant')

GORING, ARTHUR, VISCOUNT: Son of the Earl of Caversham. He is instrumental in saving his friend Sir Robert Chiltern from the machinations of Mrs Cheveley. He proposes, after long delay, to Mabel Chiltern, and is accepted. *Thirty-four, but always says he is younger. . . . A flawless dandy, he would be annoyed if he were considered romantic. He plays with life, and is on*

*perfectly good terms with the world. He is fond of being misunderstood.
It gives him a post of vantage.* (Stage direction in *Ideal Husband*)

GRAHAM, CECIL: A member of Lord Darlington's circle. *My
own business always bores me to death. I prefer other people's.*
(*Lady Windermere's Fan*)

GRAY, DORIAN: The 20-year-old orphaned son of a runaway
marriage between Lady Margaret Devereux and a penniless
young army officer. He is under the guardianship of Lord and
Lady Radley when he meets Basil Hallward, whose painting
of him causes Dorian Gray to sacrifice his soul in order to retain
his youthful beauty; a transaction which leads to corruption,
murder and a strange form of suicide. *Yes, he was certainly
wonderfully handsome, with his finely-curved scarlet lips, his frank
blue eyes, his crisp gold hair. There was something in his face that
made one trust him at once. All the candour of youth was there, as
well as all youth's passionate purity. One felt that he had kept himself
unspotted from the world.* (*Picture of Dorian Gray*)

GWENDOLEN, LADY: Lord Henry Wotton's married sister. One
of the many people ruined by their association with Dorian
Gray. *'When you met Lady Gwendolen, not a breath of scandal had
ever touched her. Is there a single decent woman in London now who
would drive with her in the Park? Why, even her children are not
allowed to live with her.'* (Basil Hallward, *Picture of Dorian Gray*)

HALLWARD, BASIL: A fashionable London artist through whom
Lord Henry Wotton meets Dorian Gray. It is he who paints
the portrait of Dorian Gray, who subsequently murders him.
*'I did not want any external influence in my life. You know yourself,
Harry, how independent I am by nature. I have always been my own
master; had at least always been so, till I met Dorian Gray. Then——
but I don't know how to explain it to you. Something seemed to tell me
that I was on the verge of a terrible crisis in my life. I had a strange
feeling that Fate had in store for me exquisite joys and exquisite
sorrows.'* (*Picture of Dorian Gray*)

HANS, LITTLE: The Devoted Friend of Hugh the Miller, who
sacrifices his comfort and, ultimately, his life for his incubus.
'No,' answered the Linnet, 'I don't think he was distinguished at

all, except for his kind heart, and his funny, round, good-humoured face. He lived in a tiny cottage all by himself, and every day he worked in his garden. In all the countryside there was no garden so lovely as his.' (Fairy Tales: 'The Devoted Friend')

HAPPY PRINCE, THE: The bejewelled statue of a once heedless prince, who, aided by a Swallow, makes amends and earns God's blessing. *'Why are you weeping then?' asked the Swallow; 'you have quite drenched me.' 'When I was alive and had a human heart,' answered the statue, 'I did not know what tears were, for I lived in the Palace of Sans-Souci, where sorrow is not allowed to enter. . . . Happy indeed I was, if pleasure be happiness. So I lived, and so I died. And now that I am dead they have set me up here so high that I can see all the ugliness and all the misery of my city, and though my heart is made of lead I cannot choose but weep.' (Fairy Tales:* 'The Happy Prince')

HARLEY, DUCHESS OF: A luncheon guest at Lord Henry Wotton's Aunt Agatha's. *Of those ample architectural proportions that in women who are not Duchesses are described by contemporary historians as stoutness. (Picture of Dorian Gray)*

HARROWDEN, ERNEST: A guest at Lady Narborough's dinner party. *One of those middle-aged mediocrities so common in London clubs who have no enemies, but are thoroughly disliked by their friends. (Picture of Dorian Gray)*

HAUSBERG, BARON: Wealthy patron of the artist Alan Trevor, Hughie Erskine takes pity on him, thinking him to be a beggar. *'That old beggar, as you call him, is one of the richest men in Europe. He could buy all London to-morrow without overdrawing his account. He has a house in every capital, dines off gold plate, and can prevent Russia going to war when he chooses. . . . He is a great friend of mine, buys all my pictures and that sort of thing, and gave me a commission a month ago to paint him as a beggar.'* (Trevor, 'Model Millionaire')

HEROD ANTIPAS: Tetrarch of Judaea, married to Herodias whose former husband, his own elder brother, he had had murdered; stepfather and uncle of Salomé. It is his insistence upon her dancing for him that enables Salomé to demand Jokanaan's head.

Salomé, Salomé, dance for me. I pray thee dance for me. I am sad to-night. Yes, I am passing sad to-night. When I came hither I slipped in blood, which is an evil omen; and I heard, I am sure I heard in the air a beating of wings, a beating of giant wings. I cannot tell what they mean. . . . I am sad to-night. Therefore, dance for me. Dance for me, Salomé, I beseech you. If you dance for me you may ask of me what you will, and I will give it you, even unto the half of my kingdom. (Salomé)

HERODIAS : Wife of Herod Antipas, having been the wife of his elder brother, whom he had had murdered. Mother of Salomé by her first marriage. *Where is she who hath given herself to the young men of Egypt, who are clothed in fine linen and purple, whose shields are of gold, whose helmets are of silver, whose bodies are mighty? Bid her rise up from the bed of her abominations, from the bed of her incestuousness, that she may hear the words of him who prepareth the way of the Lord, that she may repent of her iniquities. Though she will never repent, but will stick fast in her abominations.* (Jokanaan, *Salomé*)

HONORIUS : The anchorite who is corrupted by Myrrhina, but simultaneously converts her. *Myrrhina, the scales have fallen from my eyes and I see now clearly what I did not see before. Take me to Alexandria and let me taste of the seven sins. (Sainte Courtisane)*

HOPPER, MR : Young Australian suitor of Lady Agatha Carlisle. *His father made a great fortune by selling some kind of food in circular tins – most palatable, I believe – I fancy it is the thing the servants always refuse to eat.* (Duchess of Berwick, *Lady Windermere's Fan*)

HUBBARD, MR : A Mayfair frame-maker summoned by Dorian Gray to remove his portrait to its hiding-place. *A florid, red-whiskered little man, whose admiration for art was considerably tempered by the inveterate impecuniosity of most of the artists who dealt with him. (Picture of Dorian Gray)*

HUGH THE MILLER : The ingenuous Little Hans's incubus. '*So devoted was the rich Miller to little Hans, that he would never go by his garden without leaning over the wall and plucking a large nosegay, or a handful of sweet herbs, or filling his pockets with plums and*

*cherries if it was the fruit season. "Real friends should have every-
thing in common," the Miller used to say, and little Hans nodded and
smiled, and felt very proud of having a friend with such noble ideas.'
(Fairy Tales:* 'The Devoted Friend')

HUGO: Headsman of Padua.

> HUGO: *Why, God love you, sir,
> I'll do you your last service on this earth.*
>
> (*Duchess of Padua*)

HUNSTANTON, JANE, LADY: Owner of Hunstanton Chase, the
scene of much of the play. *You couldn't come to a more charming
place than this, Miss Worsley, though the house is excessively damp,
quite unpardonably damp, and dear Lady Hunstanton is sometimes a
little lax about the people she asks down here.* (Lady Caroline
Pontefract, *Woman of No Importance*)

ILLINGWORTH, LORD: A politician, formerly George Harford,
who wishes to employ as his secretary Gerald Arbuthnot, his
unwitting natural son by Mrs Rachel Arbuthnot.

> GERALD: *Lord Illingworth is a successful man. He is a fashionable
> man. He is a man who lives in the world and for it. Well, I would
> give anything to be just like Lord Illingworth.*
>
> MRS ARBUTHNOT: *I would sooner see you dead.*
>
> (*Woman of No Importance*)

INFANTA, THE: The King of Spain's daughter, just turned 12.
*Although she was a real Princess and the Infanta of Spain, she had
only one birthday every year, just like the children of quite poor
people, so it was naturally a matter of great importance to the whole
country that she should have a really fine day for the occasion.*
(*Fairy Tales:* 'The Birthday of the Infanta')

ISAACS: The Jewish proprietor of the seedy theatrical company
in which Dorian Gray discovers Sybil Vane. '*When he saw me
he made me a low bow, and assured me that I was a munificent patron
of art. He was a most offensive brute, though he had an extraordinary
passion for Shakespeare. He told me once, with an air of pride, that his
five bankruptcies were entirely due to "The Bard", as he insisted on
calling him. He seemed to think it a distinction.'* (Dorian Gray,
Picture of Dorian Gray)

IVAN, CZAR: Emperor of the Russias; father of Alexis. He is assassinated by Michael Stroganoff. *A father whose name shall not be hallowed, whose kingdom shall change to a republic, whose trespasses shall not be forgiven him, because he has robbed us of our daily bread; with whom is neither might, nor right, nor glory, now or for ever.* (Vera, *Vera*)

IVANACIEVITCH, IVAN: See ALEXIS, CZAREVICH. (*Vera*)

JEDBURGH, MARCHIONESS OF: A witness, at Gladys Lady Windermere's, of the reading of Lord Arthur's palm by Mr Podgers. ('Lord Arthur Savile's Crime')
A Lady Jedburgh is a guest at Margaret, Lady Windermere's, coming-of-age party. (*Lady Windermere's Fan*)

JOKANAAN: John the Baptist, the prophet, imprisoned for denouncing the union of Herod Antipas and Herodias. He is beheaded at Salomé's whim, after rejecting her sensual advances. *How wasted he is! He is like a thin ivory statue. He is like an image of silver. I am sure he is chaste as the moon is. He is like a moonbeam, like a shaft of silver. His flesh must be cool like ivory. I would look closer at him.* (Salomé, *Salomé*)

KELVIL, MR: A Member of Parliament, guest at Lady Hunstanton's house party. *He must be quite respectable. One has never heard his name before in the whole course of one's life, which speaks volumes for a man, nowadays.* (Lady Caroline Pontefract, *Woman of No Importance*)

KING OF SPAIN: Father of the Infanta. *He thought of the young Queen, her mother, who but a short time before – so it seemed to him – had come from the gay country of France, and had withered away in the solemn splendour of the Spanish court, dying just six months after the birth of her child.* (Fairy Tales: 'The Birthday of the Infanta')

KING, THE YOUNG: A luxury-loving monarch who learns humility through three dreams. *The child of the old King's only daughter by a secret marriage with one much beneath her in station – a stranger, some said, who, by the wonderful magic of his lute-playing, had made the young Princess love him; while others spoke of an artist from Rimini, to whom the Princess had shown much, perhaps*

*too much honour, and who had suddenly disappeared from the city,
leaving his work in the Cathedral unfinished – he had been, when but
a week old, stolen away from his mother's side as she slept, and given
into the charge of a common peasant and his wife, who were without
children of their own, and lived in a remote part of the forest.* (Fairy
Tales: 'The Young King')

KOTEMKIN, COLONEL (later General): The officer in charge of
the batch of prisoners which includes Dmitri; later chief of
police in Moscow. *Nihilists in Moscow, General! With you as
head of the police! Impossible!* (Alexis, *Vera*)

LANE: Algernon Moncrieff's manservant.

    ALGERNON: *Why is it that at a bachelor's establishment the servants
    invariably drink the champagne? I ask merely for information.*

    LANE: *I attribute it to the superior quality of the wine, sir. I have
    often observed that in married households the champagne is rarely
    of a first-rate brand.*

    ALGERNON: *Good heavens! Is marriage so demoralising as that?*

    LANE: *I believe it is a very pleasant state, sir. I have had very little
    experience of it myself up to the present. I have only been married
    once. That was in consequence of a misunderstanding between
    myself and a young person.*

    ALGERNON: *I don't know that I am much interested in your
    family life, Lane.*

    LANE: *No, sir; it is not a very interesting subject. I never think of it
    myself.*   (Importance of Being Earnest)

LEAF, MRS: Dorian Gray's housekeeper in London. *In her black
silk dress, with old-fashioned thread mittens on her wrinkled hands.*
(Picture of Dorian Gray)

LORTON, LORD AUGUSTUS ('TUPPY'): Brother of the Duchess
of Berwick, he proposes successfully to Mrs Erlynne.

    CECIL GRAHAM: *By the way, Tuppy, which is it? Have you been
    twice married and once divorced, or twice divorced and once married?
    I say you've been twice divorced and once married. It seems so
    much more probable.*

    LORD AUGUSTUS: *I have a very bad memory. I really don't
    remember which.*   (Lady Windermere's Fan)

LUCY, MISTRESS: One of Beatrice's waiting-women. *O well-a day! O miserable day! O day! O misery! why, it is just nineteen years last June, at Michaelmas, since I was married to my husband, and it is August now, and here is the Duke murdered; there is a coincidence for you!* (*Duchess of Padua*)

MAGICIAN, THE: An 'old and evil-visaged man' who buys the Star-Child as his slave and sends him on errands, in the course of which the youth learns the compassion he had lacked. *The subtlest of the magicians of Libya and had learned his art from one who dwelt in the tombs of the Nile.* (*Fairy Tales:* 'The Star-Child')

MARALOFFSKI, PRINCE PAUL: Prime Minister of Russia until deposed by the new Czar Alexis, when he joins the Nihilists. *You mismanage my father's business. . . . Evil genius of his life that you are! Before you came there was some love left in him. It is you who have embittered his nature, poured into his ear the poison of treacherous council, made him hated by the whole people, made him what he is – a tyrant!* (Alexis, *Vera*)

MARCHMONT, MRS MARGARET: See BASILDON, OLIVIA, COUNTESS OF. (*Ideal Husband*)

MARFA, PROFESSOR: One of the Nihilist plotters.
PROF. MARFA: *My forte is more in writing pamphlets than in taking shots. Still a regicide has always a place in history.*
MICHAEL: *If your pistol is as harmless as your pen, this young tyrant will have a long life.* (*Vera*)

MARKBY, LADY: A friend of Gertrude Chiltern. *A pleasant, kindly, popular woman, with grey hair à la marquise and good lace.* (Stage direction in *Ideal Husband*)

MARVEL, SIR THOMAS AND LADY: Guests at Lady Windermere's. He allows Mr Podgers to read his palm, but his wife will not show hers. '*A strong Conservative, very punctual, and with a passion for collecting curiosities. Had a severe illness between the ages of sixteen and eighteen. Was left a fortune when about thirty. Great aversion to cats and Radicals.*' '*Extraordinary!*' exclaimed Sir Thomas; '*you must really tell my wife's hand, too.*' '*Your second wife's,*' said Mr Podgers quietly. ('Lord Arthur Savile's Crime')

MASON: Sir Robert Chiltern's butler. (*Ideal Husband*)

MERMAID, THE: The love from the sea, for whom the Young Fisherman banishes his Soul. *Her hair was as a wet fleece of gold, and each separate hair as a thread of fine gold in a cup of glass. Her body was as white ivory, and her tail was of silver and pearl. Silver and pearl was her tail, and the green weeds of the sea coiled round it; and like sea-shells were her ears, and her lips were like sea-coral. The cold waves dashed over her cold breasts, and the salt glistened upon her eyelids.* (*Fairy Tales*: 'The Fisherman and his Soul')

MERRIMAN: John Worthing's butler. (*Importance of Being Earnest*)

MERTON, HETTY: A village girl about to run away with Dorian Gray, whom he suddenly decides to 'spare' in a belated effort to reform his ways. '*My dear Dorian, you have the most curiously boyish moods. Do you think this girl will ever be really contented now with anyone of her own rank? I suppose she will be married some day to a rough carter or a grinning ploughman. Well, the fact of having met you, and loved you, will teach her to despise her husband, and she will be wretched. From a moral point of view, I cannot say that I think much of your great renunciation.*' (Lord Henry, *Picture of Dorian Gray*)

MERTON, LAURA: A retired Colonel's daughter, sweetheart of Hughie Erskine. His ingenuous act of generosity to Baron Hausberg results in their acquiring the necessary money for marriage. *Laura adored him, and he was ready to kiss her shoe-strings. They were the handsomest couple in London, and had not a penny-piece between them.* ('Model Millionaire')

MERTON, SYBIL: Daughter of Mr and Lady Julia Merton. Fiancée, and subsequently wife, of Lord Arthur Savile. *All the tender purity of girlhood looked out in wonder from the dreaming eyes. With her soft, clinging dress of crêpe-de-chine, and her large leaf-shaped fan, she looked like one of those delicate little figures men find in the olive-woods near Tanagra; and there was a touch of Greek grace in her pose and attitude. Yet she was not petite. She was simply perfectly proportioned – a rare thing in an age when so many women are either over life-size or insignificant.* ('Lord Arthur Savile's Crime')

MONCRIEFF, ALGERNON: Nephew of Lady Bracknell and first cousin of Gwendolen Fairfax. Friend of John Worthing, whose brother he turns out to be. While posing as John's fictitious brother Ernest, he contrives to meet, and falls in love with, Cecily Cardew.

> JACK: *It pains me very much to have to speak frankly to you, Lady Bracknell, about your nephew, but the fact is that I do not approve at all of his moral character. I suspect him of being untruthful.*
>
> LADY BRACKNELL: *Untruthful! My nephew Algernon? Impossible! He is an Oxonian.*   (*Importance of Being Earnest*)

MONMOUTH, DUKE AND DUCHESS OF: Guests of Dorian Gray at his country home, Selby Royal. '*How fond you are of saying dangerous things, Harry! In the present instance you are quite astray. I like the Duchess very much, but I don't love her.*' '*And the Duchess loves you very much, but she likes you less, so you are excellently matched.*' '*You are talking scandal, Harry, and there is never any basis for scandal.*' '*The basis for every scandal is an immoral certainty,*' *said Lord Henry, lighting a cigarette.* (*Picture of Dorian Gray*)

MONTFORD, MR: One of Sir Robert Chiltern's secretaries. *A perfectly groomed young dandy.* (Stage direction in *Ideal Husband*)

MORANZONE, COUNT: Sole survivor of Guido Ferranti's father's suite, he reappears to tell Guido his identity and urge him to his fatal destiny.

> MORANZONE: *I am known here as the Count Moranzone,*
> > *Lord of a barren castle on a rock,*
> > *With a few acres of unkindly land*
> > *And six not thrifty servants. But I was one*
> > *Of Parma's noblest princes; more than that,*
> > *I was your father's friend.*   (*Duchess of Padua*)

MURCHISON, LORD GERALD: A young man who falls in love with Lady Alroy, but repudiates her because of her mysterious habits. *He was so handsome, so high-spirited, and so honourable. We used to say of him that he would be the best of fellows, if he did not always speak the truth, but I think we really admired him all the more for his frankness.* ('The Sphinx Without a Secret')

MYRRHINA: The courtesan who corrupts an anchorite, Honorius, and is simultaneously converted by him. *She has birds' wings upon her sandals, and her tunic is the colour of green corn. It is like young corn troubled by the shadows of hawks when she moves.* (Second Man, *Sainte Courtisane*)

NAAMAN: Executioner at Herod's court. He had carried out the strangling of Herod's elder brother, Herodias' first husband.
THE CAPPADOCIAN: *It is a terrible thing to strangle a king.*
FIRST SOLDIER: *Why? Kings have but one neck, like other folk.* (*Salomé*)

NANJAC, VICOMTE DE: Attaché at the French Embassy in London. *Known for his neckties and his Anglomania.* (Stage direction in *Ideal Husband*)

NARBOROUGH, LADY: A Society hostess whose party Dorian Gray attends immediately after the disposal of Alan Campbell's remains. *A very clever woman, with what Lord Henry used to describe as the remains of really remarkable ugliness.* (*Picture of Dorian Gray*)

NARRABOTH (The Young Syrian): Captain of Herod's guard. He kills himself in anguish at witnessing Salomé's approaches to Jokanaan. *In the evening we used to walk by the river, among the almond trees, and he would tell me of the things of his country. He spake ever very low. The sound of his voice was like the sound of the flute, of a flute player. Also he much loved to gaze at himself in the river. I used to reproach him for that.* (Page of Herodias, *Salomé*)

NIGHTINGALE, THE: A bird who sacrifices her life to stain a white rose red with her blood for a student lover's sake. *And when the moon shone in the Heavens the Nightingale flew to the Rose-tree, and set her breast against the thorn. All night long she sang, with her breast against the thorn, and the cold crystal Moon leaned down and listened. All night long she sang, and the thorn went deeper and deeper into her breast, and her life-blood ebbed away from her.* (*Fairy Tales:* 'The Nightingale and the Rose')

OTIS, HIRAM B.: American Minister to Great Britain and purchaser of the haunted Canterville Chase, near Ascot. *I am also informed by Mrs Otis, who, I may say, is no mean authority upon Art – having had the privilege of spending several winters in Boston when she was a girl – that these gems are of great monetary worth, and if offered for sale would fetch a tall price. Under these circumstances, Lord Canterville, I feel sure that you will recognise how impossible it would be for me to allow them to remain in the possession of any member of my family; and, indeed, all such vain gauds and toys, however suitable or necessary to the dignity of the British aristocracy, would be completely out of place among those who have been brought up on the severe and I believe immortal principles of republican simplicity.* ('Canterville Ghost')

OTIS, MRS HIRAM B.: Formerly Miss Lucretia R. Tappan. Wife of the American Minister to Great Britain. *Had been a celebrated New York belle . . . now a very handsome, middle-aged woman, with fine eyes and a superb profile.* ('Canterville Ghost')

OTIS, VIRGINIA E.: Fifteen-year-old daughter of Mr and Mrs Hiram B. Otis and sister of Washington and 'The Stars and Stripes'. Through her compassion the Canterville Ghost achieves rest. She subsequently marries the Duke of Cheshire. *Lithe and lovely as a fawn, and with a fine freedom in her large blue eyes. She was a wonderful amazon, and had once raced old Lord Bilton on her pony twice round the park, winning by a length and a half, just in front of the Achilles statue.* ('Canterville Ghost')

OTIS, WASHINGTON: Son of Mr and Mrs Hiram B. Otis and brother of Virginia and 'The Stars and Stripes'. *A fair-haired, rather good-looking young man, who had qualified himself for American diplomacy by leading the German at the Newport Casino for three successive seasons, and even in London was well known as an excellent dancer.* ('Canterville Ghost')

PADUA, DUKE AND DUCHESS OF: See GESSO, SIMONE, and BEATRICE. (*Duchess of Padua*)

PAGE OF HERODIAS, THE: Close companion of the suicide, Narraboth. *I knew that the moon was seeking a dead thing, but I knew not that it was he whom she sought. Ah! why did I not hide him from the moon? If I had hidden him in a cavern she would not have seen him.* (*Salomé*)

PAISLEY, DUCHESS OF: One of Lady Windermere's guests whose palm is read by Mr Podgers. *'Economy is not the least of your Grace's virtues,' continued Mr Podgers, and Lady Windermere went off into fits of laughter. 'Economy is a very good thing,' remarked the Duchess complacently; 'when I married Paisley he had eleven castles, and not a single house fit to live in.' 'And now he has twelve houses, and not a single castle,' cried Lady Windermere.* ('Lord Arthur Savile's Crime')

PARKER: Basil Hallward's butler. (*Picture of Dorian Gray*)

PARKER: Lord and Lady Windermere's butler. (*Lady Windermere's Fan*)

PERCY, JANE: Daughter of the Dean of Chichester and cousin of Lord Arthur Savile. It is from a letter of hers that Lord Arthur learns of the failure of his attempt to murder her father. *'We have had great fun over a clock that an unknown admirer sent papa last Thursday. . . . We were all sitting there on Friday morning when just as the clock struck twelve we heard a whirring noise, a little puff of smoke came from the pedestal of the figure, and the goddess of Liberty fell off, and broke her nose on the fender! . . . Papa said it must not remain in the library as it made a noise, so Reggie carried it away to the schoolroom, and does nothing but have small explosions all day long. Do you think Arthur would like one for a wedding present?'* ('Lord Arthur Savile's Crime')

PETOUCHOF, COUNT: The Czar Ivan's new Ambassador to Berlin.

PRINCE PAUL: *He is come to kiss hands on his appointment.*

CZAR: *To kiss my hand? There is some plot in it. He wants to poison me. There, kiss my son's hand; it will do quite as well.*

(*Vera*)

PETROVITCH, PRINCE: A member of the Czar Ivan's Cabinet, he is banished by Czar Alexis.

PRINCE PAUL: *What has happened to you, my dear Petrovitch? You seem quite out of sorts. You haven't quarrelled with your cook, I hope? What a tragedy that would be for you; you would lose all your friends.*

PETROVITCH: *I fear I wouldn't be so fortunate as that.* (*Vera*)

PETRUCCI, MAFFIO: See BARDI, TADDEO. (*Duchess of Padua*)

PHIPPS: Lord Goring's manservant. (*He has been termed by enthusiasts the Ideal Butler. The Sphinx is not so incommunicable. He is a mask with a manner. Of his intellectual or emotional life, history knows nothing. He represents the dominance of form.* (Stage direction in *Ideal Husband*)

PLYMDALE, LADY LAURA: A guest at Lady Windermere's coming-of-age party. *Those straw-coloured women have dreadful tempers.* (Mrs Erlynne, *Lady Windermere's Fan*)

PODGERS, SEPTIMUS R.: Professional cheiromanist of 1030 West Moon Street who reads Lord Arthur Savile's palm, with fatal results to himself. '*He is not a bit like a cheiromantist. I mean he is not mysterious, or esoteric, or romantic-looking. He is a little, stout man, with a funny, bald head, and great gold-rimmed spectacles; something between a family doctor and a country attorney.*' (Lady Windermere, 'Lord Arthur Savile's Crime')

POIVRARD, MARQUIS DE: A member of the Czar Ivan's Cabinet, appointed Governor of Archangel. The appointment is cancelled, and he is banished by Czar Alexis. *What is the use of the people except for us to get money out of?* (*Vera*)

POLLAJULO, ANDREAS: Cardinal of Padua.
    DUKE: *The Cardinal!*
        Men follow my creed, and they gabble his.
        I do not think much of the Cardinal. (*Duchess of Padua*)

PONTEFRACT, SIR JOHN AND LADY CAROLINE: House guests at Lady Hunstanton's.
    LADY CAROLINE: *John, the grass is too damp for you. You had better go and put on your overshoes at once.*
    SIR JOHN: *I am quite comfortable, Caroline, I assure you.*
    LADY CAROLINE: *You must allow me to be the best judge of that, John. Pray do as I tell you.*
    LADY HUNSTANTON: *You spoil him, Caroline, you do indeed!*
                    (*Woman of No Importance*)

PRISM, LAETITIA: Cecily Cardew's governess, responsible, many years before, for losing the baby Algernon Moncrieff when she was his nursemaid.

LADY BRACKNELL: *Is this Miss Prism a female of repellent aspect, remotely connected with education?*

CANON CHASUBLE: *She is the most cultivated of ladies, and the very picture of respectability.*

LADY BRACKNELL: *It is obviously the same person.*

(Importance of Being Earnest)

RADLEY, LORD: Dorian Gray's guardian. (*Picture of Dorian Gray*)

RAFF, BARON: A member of the Czar Ivan's Cabinet, he is banished by Czar Alexis.

BARON RAFF: *What a mistake it is to be sincere.*

PRINCE PETROVITCH: *The only folly you never committed, Baron.* (*Vera*)

ROCKET, THE REMARKABLE: A self-important firework whose boasting brings about his unremarkable comedown. '*I am a very remarkable Rocket, and come of remarkable parents. My mother was the most celebrated Catherine Wheel of her day, and was renowned for her graceful dancing. When she made her great public appearance she spun round nineteen times before she went out, and each time that she did so she threw into the air seven pink stars. She was three feet and a half in diameter, and made of the very best gunpowder. My father was a Rocket like myself, and of French extraction. He flew so high that the people were afraid that he would never come down again. He did, though, for he was of a kindly disposition, and he made a most brilliant descent in a shower of golden rain. The newspapers wrote about his performance in very flattering terms.*' (*Fairy Tales*: 'The Remarkable Rocket')

ROSALIE: Lady Windermere's maid. (*Lady Windermere's Fan*)

ROUVALOFF, COUNT: A Russian friend of Lord Arthur Savile, whom the latter consults in scheming to blow up the Dean of Chichester. *Count Rouvaloff was supposed to be writing a life of Peter the Great, and to have come over to England for the purpose of studying the documents relating to that Tsar's residence in this country as a ship-carpenter; but it was generally suspected that he was a Nihilist agent, and there was no doubt that the Russian Embassy did not look with any favour upon his presence in London.* ('Lord Arthur Savile's Crime')

A Count Rouvaloff is a member of the Czar Ivan's Cabinet, banished by the Czar Alexis. (*Vera*)

RUFFORD, LORD ALFRED: A house guest at Lady Hunstanton's. *One must have some occupation nowadays. If I hadn't my debts I shouldn't have anything to think about.* (*Woman of No Importance*)

RUXTON, LADY: A guest at Lady Narborough's dinner party. *An overdressed woman of forty-seven, with a hooked nose, who was always trying to get herself compromised, but was so peculiarly plain that to her great disappointment no one would ever believe anything against her.* (*Picture of Dorian Gray*)

SABOUROFF, DMITRI: Son of Peter and brother of Vera. A student, he is sent to Siberia for Nihilism, but is released by the new Czar. *There's Dmitri! Could have stayed here and kept the inn; many a young lad would have jumped at the offer in these hard times; but the scatterbrained featherhead of a boy must needs go off to Moscow to study the law! What does he want knowing about the law! Let a man do his duty, say I, and no one will trouble him.* (Peter Sabouroff, *Vera*)

SABOUROFF, PETER: An innkeeper, father of Vera and Dmitri. *I don't think much of ideas myself; I've got on well enough in life without 'em; why shouldn't my children?* (*Vera*)

SABOUROFF, VERA: Daughter of Peter and sister of Dmitri. Becoming a prominent Nihilist, she loves Alexis, who proves to be the Czarevitch, undertakes to kill him as a traitor to their cause, but sacrifices herself to save him when she hears his enlightened views of sovereignty. *To strangle whatever nature is in me, neither to love nor to be loved, neither to pity nor to be pitied. Ay! it is an oath, an oath. Methinks the spirit of Charlotte Corday has entered my soul now. I shall carve my name on the world, and be ranked among the great heroines. Ay! the spirit of Charlotte Corday beats in each petty vein, and nerves my woman's heart to hate.* (*Vera*)

SALOMÉ: Daughter of Herodias by her first marriage. Stepdaughter and niece of Herod Antipas. She demands the head of Jokanaan as her reward for performing the dance of the seven veils, after Jokanaan has rejected her advances.
SALOMÉ: *Let me kiss thy mouth.*

JOKANAAN: *Never, daughter of Babylon! Daughter of Sodom! Never.*

SALOMÉ: *I will kiss thy mouth, Jokanaan. I will kiss thy mouth.*

THE YOUNG SYRIAN: *Princess, Princess, thou who art like a garden of myrrh, thou who art the dove of all doves, look not at this man, look not at him! Do not speak such words to him. I cannot suffer them. . . . Princess, Princess, do not speak these things.*

SALOMÉ: *I will kiss thy mouth, Jokanaan.* (*Salomé*)

SAVILE, LORD ARTHUR: Brother of Lord Surbiton; engaged, and subsequently married, to Sybil Merton. He insists, with a fatal outcome, on having his palm read by Septimus R. Podgers. *Suddenly Mr Podgers dropped Lord Arthur's right hand, and seized hold of his left, bending down so low to examine it that the gold rims of his spectacles seemed almost to touch the palm. For a moment his face became a white mask of horror, but he soon recovered his* sang-froid, *and looking up at Lady Windermere, said with a forced smile, 'It is the hand of a charming young man.'* ('Lord Arthur Savile's Crime')

SIMONE: Merchant husband of Bianca who perceives her affection for Guido Bardi, challenges, and kills him.

BIANCA: *I pray you pardon my good husband here,*
His soul stands ever in the market-place,
And his heart beats but at the price of wool.

(*Florentine Tragedy*)

SINGLETON, ADRIAN: One of the victims of Dorian Gray's decadent influence, later encountered by him in a London dockland opium den. *A young man with smooth yellow hair, who was bending over a lamp, lighting a long thin pipe.* (*Picture of Dorian Gray*)

STAR-CHILD, THE: A child found by woodcutters looking for a fallen star, and brought up by one of them. He grows up beautiful and vain and only has his princehood revealed to him after he has learned compassion. *Every year he became more beautiful to look at, so that all those who dwelt in the village were filled with wonder, for, while they were swarthy and black-haired, he was white and delicate as sawn ivory, and his curls were like the rings of the daffodil, and his eyes were like violets by a river of pure water, and his body like the narcissus of a field where the mower comes not.* (*Fairy Tales:* 'The Star-Child')

STAR-CHILD'S MOTHER, THE: Rejected by her son in his vanity, she is at length revealed as a queen, whose husband is the leper on whom the Star-Child has had compassion, and he is forgiven. '*The robbers stole thee from me, and left thee to die,*' she murmured, '*but I recognised thee when I saw thee, and the signs also have I recognised, the cloak of golden tissue and the amber chain, Therefore, I pray thee come with me, for over the whole world have I wandered in search of thee. Come with me, my son, for I have need of thy love.*' *But the Star-Child stirred not from his place, but shut the doors of his heart against her.* (*Fairy Tales:* 'The Star-Child')

'STARS AND STRIPES, THE': Twin younger sons of Mr and Mrs Hiram B. Otis; brothers of Washington and Virginia. *Usually called 'The Stars and Stripes', as they were always getting swished. They were delightful boys, and with the exception of the worthy Minister the only true republicans of the family.* ('Canterville Ghost')

STROGANOFF, MICHAEL: One of Prince Maraloffski's game-keepers, he becomes a member of the Nihilist plot and assassinates the Czar Ivan. *You're young, and wouldn't be ill-favoured either, had God or thy mother given thee another face.* (Peter Stroubanoff, *Vera*

STUDENT, THE: The lover of the Professor's daughter, who will only dance with him if he brings her a red rose, which the Nightingale sacrifices herself to supply. '*Here at last is a true lover,*' said the Nightingale. '*Night after night have I sung of him, though I knew him not: night after night have I told his story to the stars and now I see him. His hair is dark as the hyacinth-blossom, and his lips are red as the rose of his desire; but passion has made his face pale like ivory, and sorrow has set her seal upon his brow.*' (Fairy Tales: 'The Nightingale and the Rose'

STUTFIELD, LADY: A house guest at Lady Hunstanton's.

MRS ALLONBY: *Is she such a mystery?*

LORD ILLINGWORTH: *She is more than a mystery – she is a mood.*

MRS ALLONBY: *Moods don't last.*

LORD ILLINGWORTH: *It is their chief charm.*

(*Woman of No Importance*)
A Lady Stutfield is also among the guests at Lady Windermere's coming-of-age party in *Lady Windermere's Fan.*

SURBITON, LORD: Lord Arthur Savile's brother. They holiday together in Italy while Lord Arthur is awaiting news of his murder attempt upon Lady Clementina Beauchamp. ('Lord Arthur Savile's Crime')

SWALLOW, THE: A bird who shelters under the Happy Prince's statue, helps him to ease his conscience and dies of the effort, earning God's blessing on them both. *The Swallow flew over the great city, and saw the rich making merry in their beautiful houses, while the beggars were sitting at the gates. He flew into dark lanes, and saw the white faces of starving children looking out listlessly at the black streets. Under the archway of a bridge two little boys were lying in one another's arms to try and keep themselves warm. 'How hungry we are!' they said. 'You must not lie here,' shouted the watchman, and they wandered out into the rain. Then he flew back and told the Prince what he had seen. 'I am covered with fine gold,' said the Prince, 'you must take it off, leaf by leaf, and give it to the poor.'* (*Fairy Tales:* 'The Happy Prince')

TCHERNAVITCH, PETER: President of the Nihilists. *I know more about the inside of prisons than of palaces.* (*Vera*)

THORNTON: Dorian Gray's gamekeeper at Selby Royal. (*Picture of Dorian Gray*)

TIERRA-NUEVA, COUNT OF: One of the Infanta of Spain's birthday guests. *A wonderfully handsome lad of about fourteen years of age, uncovering his head with all the grace of a born hidalgo and grandee of Spain.* (*Fairy Tales:* 'The Birthday of the Infanta')

TIGELLINUS: A young Roman at the court of Herod. (*Salomé*)

TRAFFORD, TOMMY: One of Sir Robert Chiltern's secretaries with whom Mabel Chiltern flirts for Lord Goring's benefit. He does not appear in the play. (*Ideal Husband*)

TREVOR, ALAN: Artist friend of Hughie Erskine, patronized by the wealthy Baron Hausberg. *Trevor was a painter. Indeed, few people escape that nowadays. But he was also an artist and artists are rather rare. Personally he was a strange rough fellow, with a freckled face and a red ragged beard.* ('Model Millionaire')

TUPPY: See LORTON, LORD AUGUSTUS. (*Lady Windermere's Fan*)

UMNEY, MRS: Housekeeper to the Otis family. *An old woman, neatly dressed in black silk, with a white cap and apron . . . made them each a low curtsey as they alighted, and said in a quaint, old-fashioned manner, 'I bid you welcome to Canterville Chase.'* ('Canterville Ghost')

VANDALEUR, MRS: A luncheon guest at Lord Henry Wotton's Aunt Agatha's. *A perfect saint amongst women, but so dreadfully dowdy that she reminded one of a badly bound hymn-book.* (*Picture of Dorian Gray*)

VANE, JAMES: Seaman brother of Sybil Vane, for whose death he attempts vengeance upon Dorian Gray. He is accidentally killed in a game shoot. *A young lad with rough brown hair came into the room. He was thick-set of figure, and his hands and feet were large, and somewhat clumsy in movement. He was not so finely bred as his sister. One would hardly have guessed the close relationship that existed between them.* (*Picture of Dorian Gray*)

VANE, MRS: Mother of Sybil and James. A member of Isaacs's seedy theatrical company in which Sybil plays. *'A faded tired woman who played Lady Capulet in a sort of magenta dressing-wrapper on the first night, and looks as if she had seen better days.'* (Dorian Gray, *Picture of Dorian Gray*)

VANE, SYBIL: Sister of James Vane. A pretty actress in a third-rate Shakespearian company who kills herself when Dorian Gray renounces her for unwittingly destroying his illusion of her. *She has played her last part. But you must think of that lonely death in the tawdry dressing-room simply as a strange lurid fragment from some Jacobean tragedy, as a wonderful scene from Webster, or Ford, or Cyril Tourneur. The girl never really lived, and so she has never really died. To you at least, she was always a dream, a phantom that flitted through Shakespeare's plays and left them lovelier for its*

*presence, a reed through which Shakespeare's music sounded richer
and more full of joy. The moment she touched actual life, she marred
it, and it marred her, and so she passed away. Mourn for Ophelia, if
you like. Put ashes on your head because Cordelia was strangled. Cry
out against Heaven because the daughter of Brabantio died. But don't
waste your tears over Sybil Vane. She was less real than they are.'*
(Lord Henry, *Picture of Dorian Gray*)

VERA: See SABOUROFF, VERA. (*Vera*)

VICTOR: Dorian Gray's French manservant for some years. '*I
believe he married Lady Radley's maid, and has established her in
Paris as an English dressmaker.* Anglomanie *is very fashionable
over there now, I hear. It seems silly of the French, doesn't it?'*
(Dorian Gray, *Picture of Dorian Gray*)

VITELLOZZO, JEPPO: See BARDI, TADDEO. (*Duchess of Padua*)

WINCKELKOPF, HERR: Creator of explosive devices, living in
Soho, recommended to Lord Arthur Savile by Count Rouvaloff. The time bomb he provides for the murder of the Dean
of Chichester is a failure. *Herr Winckelkopf himself acknowledged
that everything is so adulterated nowadays that even dynamite can
hardly be got in a pure condition. The little German, however,
while admitting that something must have gone wrong with the
machinery, was not without hope that the clock might still go off, and
instanced the case of a barometer that he had once sent to the Military
Governor at Odessa, which, though timed to explode in ten days,
had not done so for something like three months.* ('Lord Arthur
Savile's Crime')

WINDERMERE, GLADYS, LADY: London Society hostess who
invites Septimus R. Podgers to read her guests' palms, with
fatal results. *She was a curious psychological study. Early in life
she had discovered the important truth that nothing looks so like
innocence as an indiscretion; and by a series of reckless escapades,
half of them quite harmless, she had acquired all the privileges of a
personality. She had more than once changed her husband; indeed,
Debrett credits her with three marriages; but as she had never changed
her lover the world had long ago ceased to talk scandal about her. She
was now forty years of age, childless, and with that inordinate passion*

for pleasure which is the secret of remaining young. (Lord Arthur Savile's Crime')

WINDERMERE, LORD: Husband of Margaret, Lady Windermere, suspected by her of being romantically involved with Mrs Erlynne. *London is full of women who trust their husbands. One can always recognise them. They look so thoroughly unhappy. I am not going to be one of them.* (Lady Windermere, *Lady Windermere's Fan*)

WINDERMERE, MARGARET, LADY: Lord Windermere's wife and (unknown to herself) Mrs Erlynne's daughter. She is just turned twenty-one. *I have something of the Puritan in me. I was brought up like that. I am glad of it. My mother died when I was a mere child. I lived always with Lady Julia, my father's elder sister, you know. She was stern to me, but she taught me what the world is forgetting, the difference that there is between what is right and what is wrong. She allowed of no compromise. I allow of none.* (*Lady Windermere's Fan*)

WITCH, THE: The sorceress consulted by the Young Fisherman wishing to get rid of his Soul. *She brushed her hair back from her forehead, and smiling strangely she said to him, 'What men call the shadow of the body is not the shadow of the body, but is the body of the Soul. Stand on the seashore with thy back to the moon, and cut away from around thy feet thy Shadow, which is the Soul's body, and bid thy soul leave thee, and it will do so.'* (*Fairy Tales:* 'The Fisherman and his Soul')

WORSLEY, HESTER: Orphaned daughter of an American millionaire, assaulted at Lady Hunstanton's by Lord Illingworth, the natural father of the young man she loves, Gerald Arbuthnot. *I don't mind plain women being Puritans. It is the only excuse they have for being plain. But she is decidedly pretty. I admire her immensely.* (Lord Illingworth, *Woman of No Importance*)

WORTHING, JOHN, J. P. (JACK): Supposedly an orphan, he had been brought up by an adoptive father, Thomas Cardew, who had subsequntly made him guardian of his granddaughter Cecily Cardew. Worthing is in love with Gwendolen Fairfax, whose cousin, Algernon Moncrieff, turns out to be his brother. To excuse his visits to town to see Gwendolen he has passed himself off there as his own fictitious brother, the profligate Ernest Worthing.

ALGERNON: *Your name isn't Jack at all; it is Ernest.*

JACK: *It isn't Ernest; it's Jack.*

ALGERNON: *You have always told me it was Ernest. I have introduced you to every one as Ernest. You answer to the name of Ernest. You are the most earnest-looking person I ever saw in my life.*   (*Importance of Being Earnest*)

WOTTON, LORD HENRY: The cynical epigrammatist who corrupts Dorian Gray into the conviction that he is above the moral and ethical standards by which most men allow themselves to be governed. He is the nephew of Lord Fermor and brother of Lady Gwendolen, whose reputation Gray ruins. Lord Henry's wife, Victoria, leaves him for another man, and they are divorced. *Dorian Gray frowned and turned his head away. He could not help liking the tall, graceful young man who was standing by him. His romantic olive-coloured face and worn expression interested him. There was something in his low, languid voice that was absolutely fascinating. His cool, white, flower-like hands, even, had a curious charm. They moved, as he spoke, like music, and seemed to have a language of their own. But he felt afraid of him, and ashamed of being afraid. Why had it been left for a stranger to reveal him to himself?* (*Picture of Dorian Gray*)

WOTTON, LADY VICTORIA: Lord Henry Wotton's wife. She leaves him for another man, and they are divorced. *She was a curious woman, whose dresses always looked as if they had been designed in a rage and put on in a tempest. She was usually in love with somebody, and, as her passion was never returned, she had kept all her illusions. She tried to look picturesque, but only succeeded in being untidy. Her name was Victoria, and she had a perfect mania for going to church.* (*Picture of Dorian Gray*)

YOUNG SYRIAN, THE: See NARRABOTH. (*Salomé*)

Poetry

THROUGHOUT his university career Oscar Wilde was an omni-
vorous reader of poetry. His highly retentive memory hung on to
almost everything he fed to it, and he knew much of the work of
the English and classic poets by heart. While still a student he
began to write verse himself and got some of it published in Irish
periodicals. Then, in 1878, he achieved the notable feat of winning
the Newdigate Prize for poetry at Oxford. Established in 1805 in
memory of the university's benefactor Sir Roger Newdigate,
who died in the following year, the prize is awarded annually by
competition amongst undergraduates writing on a set theme. In
Wilde's year the subject was the ancient Italian city of Ravenna;
and it so happened that he had been there only the previous year
and had soaked up its timeless atmosphere.

So, on 26 June, he read his poem *Ravenna* to an audience of
dons and fellow students. His musical voice evidently did full
justice to his smoothly-flowing lines, for he was warmly con-
gratulated. The Newdigate Prize itself was (and still is) insub-
stantial in material terms – twenty-one guineas, plus, on this
occasion, the bonus of a marble bust of the young Augustus,
bequeathed by a former Fellow of Magdalen, a Dr Daubeny, for
award to the first undergraduate from his college to win the
prize. In terms of prestige its value was considerable – Dean
Stanley, Ruskin, Matthew Arnold and J. A. Symonds had been
among the winners before Wilde. He was highly elated. 'It is
too delightful altogether this display of fireworks at the end
of my career', he wrote to a friend: his First in Greats had been
announced only a few days earlier. Printed in pamphlet form by
an Oxford firm to coincide with his reading, *Ravenna* was the
first of Oscar Wilde's works to achieve publication outside the
pages of periodicals.

His next volume of poetry, published three years later, was to be very differently received in Oxford. *Poems*, a gathering together of pieces he had published in journals at sporadic intervals, appeared in June or July 1881, printed by a London publisher, David Bogue, at Wilde's expense. He lost no time in sending a copy to the Oxford Union. Normally, such presentations were received as a matter of course. On this occasion, for the first time in that distinguished debating society's history, the gift was rejected, owing to the objection of a member, Oliver Elton, who had this to say of it:

It is not that these poems are thin–and they *are* thin: it is not that they are immoral–and they *are* immoral: it is not that they are this and that–and they *are* all this and all that: it is that they are for the most part not by their putative father at all, but by a number of better-known and more deservedly reputed authors. They are in fact by William Shakespeare, by Philip Sidney, by John Donne, by Lord Byron, by William Morris, by Algernon Swinburne, and by sixty more, whose works have furnished the list of passages which I hold in my hand at this moment. The Union Library already contains better and fuller editions of all these poets.

Wilde's reaction is unknown. He would have been justified in being rather aggrieved: the poems were heavily derivative, as most reviewers easily saw; they are thin, and in some of them there are traces of decadence. But compared with some of the ponderous offerings accepted by the Oxford Union, they at least had many qualities of colour, of light and of youthful aspiration. 'Poetry should be like a crystal, it should make life more beautiful and less real', Wilde wrote some years later; and if this view is acceptable, then much of his poetry reflects it faithfully, even if he did hew his crystal to some extent to the models of others. 'Artificial and insincere', epithets which would be applied sooner or later to almost everything Oscar Wilde wrote, were used about his poems; but there is a good deal in his poetry that rings sincerely enough, and artificiality was a confessed part of his artistic credo. Most reviewers conceded some 'cleverness' and technical ability, but found it misapplied.

Work of this nature has no element of endurance, and Mr Wilde's poems, in spite of some grace and beauty, as we have said, will, when their temporary notoriety is exhausted, find a place on the shelves of those only who hunt after the curious in literature. (*Athenaeum*)

The author possesses cleverness, astonishing fluency, a rich and full vocabulary, and nothing to say. (*Saturday Review*)

Mr Oscar Wilde is no poet, but a cleverish man who has an infinite contempt for his readers, and thinks he can take them in with a little mouthing verse. Perhaps he is right for the moment; but this we can say with some confidence, that the book is the trash of a man of a certain amount of mimetic ability, and trash the trashiness of which the author is much too cultivated not to recognise quite clearly. (*Spectator*)

> Aesthete of Aesthetes!
> What's in a name?
> The poet is Wilde,
> But his poetry's tame. (*Punch*)

Some reviews, especially in America, were more favourable; and even the hostile ones aroused public curiosity through their references to the immoral tone of some of the poems. It was all publicity, and the volume went through the best part of five editions in a year. The editions were of only 250 copies each, but a sale of over a thousand copies of a book of verse was very good. Presentation copies of the handsomely bound volume served later as a valuable visiting card for Wilde to use to gain introductions to notable men of letters in America and France. The American edition was produced by Roberts Brothers, of Boston.

A further English edition appeared in May 1892, published by Elkin Mathews & John Lane, and these and other poems by Wilde were included in the Collected Edition of his works in 1908. He appears to have written little poetry after the publication of that first volume. The two most notable exceptions were the long poems *The Sphinx*, published by Elkin Mathews & John Lane in June 1894, and *The Ballad of Reading Gaol*, published by Leonard Smithers in February 1898.

The Sphinx was begun while Wilde was still at Oxford, largely composed in Paris in 1883, but touched up at intervals until its publication eleven years later. It is a trance-like impression of the Sphinx's long career as symbol, prophet, lover, object of worship and much more, couched in luxuriant language employing many unfamiliar and strange-sounding words, some of which Wilde employed because he liked strange-sounding words, others because, having used one, he had often to find a rhyme for it, and only succeeded in doing so after long searching through a rhyming dictionary and the minds of friends, the result almost inevitably being an even stranger word. The metre, as reviewers were not slow to note, is that of Tennyson's *In Memoriam*, the opening is almost a parody of Edgar Allan Poe in *The Raven*, and there are the usual echoes of other poets. The notices were, on the whole, unfavourable, picking out artificiality, sensation for sensation's sake, grotesqueness of imaginary and contrivance of rhyme for criticism, but again, occasionally conceding technical skill.

The Ballad of Reading Gaol stands in a class of its own amongst Oscar Wilde's poetry, and its more extravagant champions have claimed it to be one of the greatest works in the ballad form ever composed. For once he had something to say, something urgent and deeply felt to communicate. It expresses the mounting horror of the fellow prisoners of a soldier, condemned to death for murder, as they watch him during his last days and share the terror of his last night. Instead of playing with coloured words and languorous images, Wilde used direct, colloquial English. 'It aims at eternity', he told Ross while writing it, but except in one or two purple patches that ambitious aim is not chased in the self-conscious extravagance of Wilde's customary poetic style. He wrote most of it at Berneval-sur-Mer, in the summer of 1897, within weeks of his release from prison, and completed it, after much struggling, in October. Leonard Smithers agreed to publish it in England, and it underwent further alterations and some additions during the printing stages. There was much discussion about the choice of illustrator, but it was finally decided to publish it unillustrated.

During the production period, long for those days, efforts were being made through an agent to sell *The Ballad* in America for serialization in a periodical, the means by which it might make the most money. Wilde agreed that his name might be used or not, in the interests of securing the best possible deal. To his chagrin, there was no spirited competition for the work, and his agent at length reported that the only offer was a take-it-or-leave-it one hundred dollars. The serialization did not eventuate, and *The Ballad* made its first American appearance in book form in 1899, published by Benjamin R. Tucker of New York.

It had come out in England in February 1898. Afraid that the notoriety of his name would kill it, Wilde used the pseudonym 'C.3.3', the number he had borne in Reading Gaol (Block C, third cell on the third floor). That he was the author must have become widely known, but the contempt in which he was held in England certainly did nothing to hinder the widespread recognition of the work's sincerity and strength. Reviewers on the whole were, perhaps inhibitedly, reserved, but some were generous to the point of enthusiasm. The first edition of eight hundred copies sold out in a matter of days. Edition after edition followed, until thousands of copies had been sold. The seventh edition used, for the first time, Wilde's name in brackets after 'C.3.3'. Since his death *The Ballad of Reading Gaol* has become one of the most widely-known works of English verse in the world. Its success was too late to help its author, socially or financially, but the work has undoubtedly been one of the foundation stones of Wilde's posthumous reputation.

Ravenna

A year ago I breathed the Italian air, –
And yet, methinks this northern Spring is fair, –
These fields made golden with the flower of March,
The throstle singing on the feathered larch,
The cawing rooks, the wood-doves fluttering by,
The little clouds that race across the sky;
And fair the violet's gentle drooping head,

The primrose, pale for love uncomforted,
The rose that burgeons on the climbing brier,
The crocus-bed (that seems a moon of fire
Round-girdled with a purple marriage-ring);
And all the flowers of our English Spring,
Fond snowdrops, and the bright-starred daffodil.
Up starts the lark beside the murmuring mill,
And breaks the gossamer-threads of early dew;
And down the river, like a flame of blue,
Keen as an arrow flies the water-king,
While the brown linnets in the greenwood sing.
A year ago! – it seems a little time
Since last I saw that lordly southern clime,
Where flower and fruit to purple radiance blow,
And like bright lamps the fabled apples glow.
Full Spring it was – and by rich flowering vines,
Dark olive-groves and noble forest-pines,
I rode at will; the moist glad air was sweet,
The white road rang beneath my horse's feet,
And musing on Ravenna's ancient name,
I watched the day till, marked with wounds of flame,
The turquoise sky to burnished gold was turned . . .

Hélas!

To drift with every passion till my soul
Is a stringed lute on which all winds can play,
Is it for this that I have given away
Mine ancient wisdom, and austere control?
Methinks my life is a twice-written scroll
Scrawled over on some boyish holiday
With idle songs for pipe and virelay,
Which do but mar the secret of the whole.
Surely there was a time I might have trod
The sunlit heights, and from life's dissonance
Struck one clear chord to reach the ears of God;
Is that time dead? lo! with a little rod
I did but touch the honey of romance –
And must I lose a soul's inheritance?

Requiescat

Tread lightly, she is near
    Under the snow,
Speak gently, she can hear
    The daisies grow.

All her bright golden hair
    Tarnished with rust,
She that was young and fair
    Fallen to dust.

Lily-like, white as snow,
    She hardly knew
She was a woman, so
    Sweetly she grew.

Coffin-board, heavy stone,
    Lie on her breast,
I vex my heart alone,
    She is at rest.

Peace, peace, she cannot hear
    Lyre or sonnet,
All my life's buried here
    Heap earth upon it.

E Tenebris

Come down, O Christ, and help me! reach Thy hand,
    For I am drowning in a stormier sea
Than Simon on Thy lake of Galilee:
    The wine of life is spilt upon the sand,
My heart is as some famine-murdered land
    Whence all good things have perished utterly,
And well I know my soul in Hell must lie
    If I this night before God's throne should stand.
"He sleeps perchance, or rideth to the chase,
    Like Baal, when his prophets howled that name
From morn to noon on Carmel's smitten height."
    Nay, peace, I shall behold, before the night,
The feet of brass, the robe more white than flame,
    The wounded hands, the weary human face.

My Voice

Within this restless, hurried, modern world
    We took our hearts' full pleasure – You and I,
And now the white sails of our ship are furled,
    And spent the lading of our argosy.

Wherefore my cheeks before their time are wan,
    For very weeping is my gladness fled,
Sorrow has paled my young mouth's vermilion,
    And Ruin draws the curtains of my bed.

But all this crowded life has been to thee
    No more than lyre, or lute, or subtle spell
Of viols, or the music, of the sea
    That sleeps, a mimic echo, in the shell.

Humanitad

It is full winter now: the trees are bare,
    Save where the cattle huddle from the cold
Beneath the pine, for it doth never wear
    The Autumn's gaudy livery whose gold
Her jealous brother pilfers, but is true
To the green doublet; bitter is the wind, as though it blew

From Saturn's cave; a few thin wisps of hay
    Lie on the sharp black hedges, where the wain
Dragged the sweet pillage of a summer's day
    From the low meadows up the narrow lane;
Upon the half-thawed snow the bleating sheep
Press close against the hurdles, and the shivering house-dogs
    creep

From the shut stable to the frozen stream
    And back again disconsolate, and miss
The bawling shepherds and the noisy team;
    And overhead in circling listlessness
The cawing rooks whirl round the frosted stack,
Or crowd the dripping boughs; and in the fen the icepools
    crack

Where the gaunt bittern stalks among the reeds
  And flaps his wings, and stretches back his neck,
And hoots to see the moon; across the meads
  Limps the poor frightened hare, a little speck;
And a stray seamew with its fretful cry
Flits like a sudden drift of snow against the dull grey sky.

Full winter; and the lusty goodman brings
  His load of faggots from the chilly byre,
And stamps his feet upon the hearth, and flings
  The sappy billets on the waning fire,
And laughs to see the sudden lightening scare
His children at their play; and yet, – the Spring is in the air . . .

Ah! It was easy when the world was young
  To keep one's life free and inviolate,
From our sad lips another song is rung,
  By our hands our heads are desecrate,
Wanderers in drear exile, and dispossessed
Of what should be our own, we can but feed on wild unrest.

Somehow, the grace, the bloom of things has flown,
  And of all men we are most wretched who
Must live each other's lives and not our own
  For very pity's sake and then undo
All that we lived for – it was otherwise
When soul and body seemed to blend in mystic symphonies.

But we have left those gentle haunts to pass
  With weary feet to the new Calvary,
Where we behold, as one who in a glass
  Sees his own face, self-slain Humanity,
And in the dumb reproach of that sad gaze
Learn what an awful phantom the red hand of man can raise.

O smitten mouth! O forehead crowned with thorn!
  O chalice of all common miseries!
Thou for our sakes that loved thee not hast borne
  An agony of endless centuries,

And we were vain and ignorant nor knew
That when we stabbed thy heart it was our own real hearts we
    slew.

Being ourselves the sowers and the seeds
    The night that covers and the lights that fade,
The spear that pierces and the side that bleeds,
    The lips betraying and the life betrayed;
The deep hath calm: the moon hath rest; but we
Lords of the natural world are yet our own dread enemy.

Wasted Days

(From a Picture Painted by Miss V. T.)

A fair slim boy not made for this world's pain,
    With hair of gold thick clustering round his ears,
    And longing eyes half veiled by foolish tears
Like bluest water seen through mists of rain;
Pale cheeks whereon no kiss hath left its stain,
    Red under-lip drawn in for fear of Love,
    And white throat whiter than the breast of dove –
Alas! alas! if all should be in vain.

Corn-fields behind, and reapers all a-row
In weariest labour toiling wearily,
To no sweet sound of laughter or of lute.

And careless of the crimson sunset glow,
The boy still dreams; nor knows that night is night,
And in the night-time no man gathers fruit.

The Harlot's House

We caught the tread of dancing feet,
We loitered down the moonlit street,
And stopped beneath the harlot's house.

Inside, above the din and fray,
We heard the loud musicians play
The "Treues Liebes Herz" of Strauss.

Like strange mechanical grotesques,
Making fantastic arabesques,
The shadows raced across the blind.

We watched the ghostly dancers spin
To sound of horn and violin,
Like black leaves wheeling in the wind.

Like wire-pulled automatons,
Slim silhouetted skeletons
Went sidling through the slow quadrille

They took each other by the hand,
And danced a stately saraband;
Their laughter echoed thin and shrill.

Sometimes a clockwork puppet pressed
A phantom lover to her breast,
Sometimes they seemed to try to sing.

Sometimes a horrible marionette
Came out, and smoked its cigarette
Upon the steps like a live thing.

Then, turning to my love, I said,
"The dead are dancing with the dead,
The dust is whirling with the dust."

But she – she heard the violin,
And left my side, and entered in:
Love passed into the house of lust.

Then suddenly the tune went false,
The dancers wearied of the waltz,
The shadows ceased to wheel and whirl

And down the long and silent street,
The dawn, with silver-sandalled feet,
Crept like a frightened girl.

Symphony in Yellow

An omnibus across the bridge
  Crawls like a yellow butterfly,
  And, here and there, a passer-by
Shows like a little restless midge.

Big barges full of yellow hay
  Are moved against the shadowy wharf,
  And, like a yellow silken scarf,
The thick fog hangs along the quay.

The yellow leaves begin to fade
  And flutter from the Temple elms,
  And at my feet the pale green Thames
Lies like a rod of rippled jade.

To My Wife

with a copy of my poems

I can write no stately poem
  As a prelude to my lay;
From a poet to a poem
  I would dare to say.

For if of these fallen petals
  One to you seem fair,
Love will waft it till it settles
  On your hair.

And when wind and winter harden
  All the loveless land,
It will whisper of the garden,
  You will understand.

The Sphinx

In a dim corner of my room for longer than my fancy thinks
A beautiful and silent Sphinx has watched me through the
shifting gloom.
Inviolate and immobile she does not rise she does not stir
For silver moons are naught to her and naught to her the
suns that reel . . .

Come forth, my lovely seneschal! so somnolent, so statuesque!
Come forth you exquisite grotesque! half woman and half
animal!
Come forth my lovely languorous Sphinx! and put your head
upon my knee!
And let me stroke your throat and see your body spotted like
the Lynx!
And let me touch those curving claws of yellow ivory and
grasp
The tail that like a monstrous Asp coils round your heavy
velvet paws!
A thousand weary centuries are thine while I have hardly seen
Some twenty summers cast their green for Autumn's gaudy
liveries.
But you can read the Hieroglyphs on the great sand-stone
obelisks,
And you have talked with Basilisks, and you have looked on
Hippogriffs . . .

Your lovers are not dead, I know. They will rise up and hear
your voice
And clash their cymbals and rejoice and run to kiss your
mouth! And so,
Set wings upon your argosies! Set horses to your ebon car!
Back to your Nile! Or if you are grown sick of dead divinities
Follow some roving lion's spoor across the copper-coloured
plain,
Reach out and hale him by the mane and bid him be your
paramour!
Couch by his side upon the grass and set your white teeth in
his throat

And when you hear his dying note lash your long flanks of
polished brass
And take a tiger for your mate, whose amber sides are flecked
with black,
And ride upon his gilded back in triumph through the Theban
gate,
And toy with him in amorous jests, and when he turns, and
snarls, and gnaws,
O smite him with your jasper claws! and bruise him with your
agate breasts!
Why are you tarrying? Get hence! I weary of your sullen
ways,
I weary of your steadfast gaze, your somnolent magnificence.
Your horrible and heavy breath makes the light flicker in the
lamp,
And on my brow I feel the damp and dreadful dews of night
and death.
Your eyes are like fantastic moons that shiver in some stagnant
lake,
Your tongue is like a scarlet snake that dances to fantastic
tunes,
Your pulse makes poisonous melodies, and your black throat
is like the hole
Left by some torch or burning coal on Saracenic tapestries . . .

Get hence, you loathsome mystery! Hideous animal, get hence!
You wake in me each bestial sense, you make me what I would
not be.
You make my creed a barren sham, you wake foul dreams of
sensual life,
And Atys with his blood-stained knife were better than the
thing I am.
False Sphinx! False Sphinx! By reedy Styx old Charon
leaning on his oar,
Waits for my coin. Go thou before, and leave me to my
crucifix,
Whose pallid burden, sick with pain, watches the world with
wearied eyes,
And weeps for every soul that dies, and weeps for ever soul
in vain.

The Ballad of Reading Gaol

He did not wear his scarlet coat,
  For blood and wine are red,
And blood and wine were on his hands
  When they found him with the dead,
The poor dead woman whom he loved,
  And murdered in her bed.

He walked amongst the Trial Men
  In a suit of shabby grey;
A cricket cap was on his head,
  And his step seemed light and gay;
But I never saw a man who looked
  So wistfully at the day.

I never saw a man who looked
  With such a wistful eye
Upon that little tent of blue
  Which prisoners call the sky,
And at every drifting cloud that went
  With sails of silver by.

I walked, with other souls in pain,
  Within another ring,
And was wondering if the man had done
  A great or little thing,
When a voice behind me whispered low,
  'That fellow's got to swing.'

Dear Christ! The very prison walls
  Suddenly seemed to reel,
And the sky above my head became
  Like a casque of scorching steel;
And, though I was a soul in pain,
  My pain I could not feel.

I only knew what hunted thought
  Quickened his step, and why
He looked upon the garish day
  With such a wistful eye;

The man had killed the thing he loved,
    And so he had to die.

Yet each man kills the thing he loves,
    By each let this be heard,
Some do it with a bitter look,
    Some with a flattering word,
The coward does it with a kiss,
    The brave man with a sword! . . .

For oak and elm have pleasant leaves
    That in the spring-time shoot;
But grim to see is the gallows-tree,
    With its adder-bitten root,
And, green or dry, a man must die
    Before it bears its fruit!

The loftiest place is that seat of grace
    For which all worldlings try;
But who would stand in hempen band
    Upon a scaffold high,
And through a murderer's collar take
    His last look at the sky?

It is sweet to dance to violins
    When Love and Life are fair:
To dance to flutes, to dance to lutes
    Is delicate and rare:
But it is not sweet with nimble feet
    To dance upon the air! . . .

The Governor was strong upon
    The Regulation Act:
The Doctor said that Death was but
    A scientific fact:
And twice a day the Chaplain called,
    And left a little tract . . .

We tore the tarry rope to shreds
    With blunt and bleeding nails;

We rubbed the doors, and scrubbed the floors,
  And cleaned the shining rails:
And, rank by rank, we soaped the plank,
  And clattered with the pails.

We sewed the sacks, we broke the stones,
  We turned the dusty drill:
We banged the tins, and bawled the hymns,
  And sweated on the mill:
But in the heart of every man
  Terror was lying still . . .

At six o'clock we cleaned our cells,
  At seven all was still,
But the sough and swing of a mighty wing
  The prison seemed to fill,
For the Lord of Death with icy breath
  Had entered in to kill.

He did not pass in purple pomp,
  Nor ride a moon-white steed,
Three yards of cord and a sliding board
  Are all the gallows' need;
So with rope of shame the Herald came
  To do the secret deed . . .

With sudden shock the prison-clock
  Smote on the shivering air,
And from all the gaol rose up a wail
  Of impotent despair,
Like the sound that frightened marches hear
  From some leper in his lair.

And as one sees most fearful things
  In the crystal of a dream,
We saw the greasy hempen rope
  Hooked to the blackened beam,
And heard the prayer the hangman's snare
  Strangled into a scream.

And all the woe that moved him so
  That he gave that bitter cry,
And the wild regrets, and the bloody sweats,
  None knew so well as I:
For he who lives more lives than one
  More deaths than one must die . . .

Like ape or clown, in monstrous garb
  With crooked arrows starred,
Silently we went round and round
  The slippery asphalte yard;
Silently we went round and round,
  And no man spoke a word.

Silently we went round and round,
  And through each hollow mind
The Memory of dreadful things
  Rushed like a dreadful wind,
And Horror stalked before each man,
  And Terror crept behind.

The warders strutted up and down,
  And watched their herd of brutes,
Their uniforms were spick and span,
  And they wore their Sunday suits,
But we knew the work they had been at,
  By the quicklime on their boots.

For where a grave had opened wide,
  There was no grave at all:
Only a stretch of mud and sand
  By the hideous prison-wall,
And a little heap of burning lime,
  That the man should have his pall.

For he has a pall, this wretched man,
  Such as few men can claim:
Deep down below a prison-yard,
  Naked for greater shame,
He lies, with fetters on each foot,
  Wrapt in a sheet of flame!

And all the while the burning lime
  Eats flesh and bone away,
It eats the brittle bone by night,
  And the soft flesh by day,
It eats the flesh and bone by turns,
  But it eats the heart alway . . .

Out of his mouth a red, red rose!
  Out of his heart a white!
For who can say by what strange way,
  Christ brings His will to light,
Since the barren staff the pilgrim bore
  Bloomed in the great Pope's sight?

But neither milk-white rose nor red
  May bloom in prison-air;
The shard, the pebble, and the flint,
  Are what they give us there:
For flowers have been known to heal
  A common man's despair.

So never will wine-red rose or white,
  Petal by petal, fall
On that stretch of mud and sand that lies
  By the hideous prison-wall,
To tell the men who tramp the yard
  That God's Son died for all . . .

I know not whether Laws be right,
  Or whether Laws be wrong;
All that we know who lie in gaol
  Is that the wall is strong;
And that each day is like a year,
  A year whose days are long.

But this I know, that every Law
  That men hath made for Man,
Since first Man took his brother's life,
  And the sad world began,
But straws the wheat and saves the chaff
  With a most evil fan.

This too I know – and wise it were
　　If each could know the same –
That every prison that men build
　　Is built with bricks of shame,
And bound with bars lest Christ should see
　　How men their brothers maim.

With bars they blur the gracious moon,
　　And blind the goodly sun;
And they do well to hide their Hell,
　　For in it things are done
That Son of God nor son of Man
　　Ever should look upon!

The vilest deeds like poison weeds,
　　Bloom well in prison-air;
It is only what is good in Man
　　That wastes and withers there:
Pale Anguish keeps the heavy gate,
　　And the Warder is Despair.

For they starve the little frightened child
　　Till it weeps both night and day:
And they scourge the weak, and flog the fool,
　　And gibe the old and grey,
And some grow mad, and all grow bad,
　　And none a word may say.

Each narrow cell in which we dwell
　　Is a foul and dark latrine,
And the fetid breath of living Death
　　Chokes up each grated screen,
And all, but Lust, is turned to dust
　　In Humanity's machine.

The brackish water that we drink
　　Creeps with a loathsome slime,
And the bitter bread they weigh in scales
　　Is full of chalk and lime,
And Sleep will not lie down, but walks
　　Wild-eyed, and cries to Time . . .

In Reading gaol by Reading town
 There is a pit of shame,
And in it lies a wretched man
 Eaten by teeth of flame,
In a burning winding-sheet he lies,
 And his grave has got no name.

And there, till Christ call forth the dead,
 In silence let him lie:
No need to waste the foolish tear,
 Or heave the windy sigh:
The man had killed the thing he loved,
 And so he had to die.

And all men kill the thing they love,
 By all let this be heard,
Some do it with a bitter look,
 Some with a flattering word,
The coward does it with a kiss,
 The brave man with a sword!

Fairy Tales and Poems in Prose

OSCAR WILDE'S two volumes of fairy-tales were written between 1887 and 1890, the relatively busy period in which he was editing the magazine *Woman's World*, writing short stories, book reviews and essays, and living generally by journalism. 'Transcribed' might be a better word than 'written', for these sometimes over-embroidered paradoxes are examples of Wilde's celebrated table-talk. It is hard today to imagine a dinner guest holding a table of adults entranced by telling such stories; but Wilde did, and many invitations came his way on the strength of his story-telling. It is worth repeating that his audiences were adult: unlike many fairy-tales, these were not conceived for children (Wilde's own were only two and one in 1888 when the first volume appeared). A reviewer of the second volume who asked whether the stories were intended for children, adding that if they were they were highly unsuitable, was told by their author, 'I had about as much intention of pleasing the British child as I had of pleasing the British public.' But he had pleased a segment of the British public in private by telling these stories, which he would vary and re-decorate from time to time, and he thought them worth putting into print for a wider audience.

The first volume, *The Happy Prince and Other Tales*, was published in London by David Nutt in May 1888, and contained, besides the title story, 'The Nightingale and the Rose', 'The Selfish Giant', 'The Devoted Friend', 'The Remarkable Rocket'; and the 'Poems in Prose': 'The Artist', 'The Doer of Good', 'The Disciple', 'The Master', 'The House of Judgment', and 'The Teacher of Wisdom'. Its reviews were generally friendly. *The Athenaeum* said, 'Though with a distinct character of their own, they are not unworthy to compare with Hans Andersen, and it is not easy to give higher praise than this.' The *Saturday Review* saw much Andersen in the literary manner, but felt that 'the dominant spirit of these stories is satire – a bitter satire differing widely from that of Hans Andersen'. Wilde was especially buoyed up by a letter of unreserved praise from Walter Pater, under whom he had studied at Oxford. First publication in the United States was by Roberts Brothers, Boston, in 1888.

The House of Pomegranates, comprising four stories, 'The Young King', 'The Birthday of the Infanta', 'The Fisherman and his Soul' and 'The Star-Child', was first published by Osgood, McIlvaine & Co, London, in November 1891. It was designed and illustrated by Charles Ricketts, who designed a number of Wilde's later works. Wilde's writing was this time justifiably more criticized than praised, on the grounds of pretension and over-ornamentation, and the engravings tended to be tarred with the same brush. *The Athenaeum* concluded its notice: 'It is, perhaps, as well that the book is not meant for the "British Child"; for it would certainly make him scream, according to his disposition, with terror or amusement.' American publication in the same year was by Dodd, Mead & Co, New York. Sales in both countries were poor.

Oscar Wilde's fairy-tales have lived on in collected editions and have enjoyed a fair life of their own, especially in translation, and it is significant that some—usually from the first volume—find their way into anthologies for children. They are all that the contemporary reviewers said they were: at times amusing, moving, over-written, gaudy, clever, and, here and there, profound in their irony. Time has given them another dimension. Reading these stories in the knowledge of the disastrous life which was just around the corner for Wilde, one is aware of some quality of vanishing innocence, of departing happiness, of danger approaching an essentially nice man who could compose such charmingly compassionate fables, and one's thought is not, as later, 'silly Oscar' or 'degraded Oscar', but 'poor Oscar'.

THE HAPPY PRINCE

A SWALLOW, in love with a Reed, lingers with her after his friends have flown off to Egypt for the winter. Suddenly tiring of her, he sets off after them and gets as far as a city in the north of Europe, where he perches for the night at the foot of the city's proudest statue, that of its former prince, bejewelled and magnificent on a tall column. Although there is not a cloud in the sky the Swallow feels 'rain' falling on him. He finds that it is the tears of the 'Happy Prince', who tells him that he is weeping with pity for all the ugliness and misery in the city, of which he took no heed in his lifetime, only occupying himself with pleasure.

The Prince asks the Swallow to help him make amends by picking off the jewels on his sword-hilt and those that represent his eyes and carrying them to needy people: a seamstress with a sick child, a poor playwright, a shoeless little match-girl. The Swallow performs these errands, delaying his departure for Egypt day by day. When the Prince has become completely blind he urges the Swallow to go, but the bird says he will stay with him always. The Prince persuades him to remove, leaf by leaf, the gold with which his statue is covered and carry it to the poor. When this is done, and the statue is reduced to a dull grey, the snow and frost come. Starving and cold, the Swallow bids the Prince farewell and dies, at which the statue's leaden heart is heard to crack in two.

Early the next morning the Mayor was walking in the square below in company with the Town Councillors. As they passed the column he looked up at the statue: 'Dear me! how shabby the Happy Prince looks!' he said.

'How shabby, indeed!' cried the Town Councillors, who always agreed with the Mayor; and they went up to look at it.

'The ruby has fallen out of his sword, his eyes are gone, and he is golden no longer,' said the Mayor; 'in fact, he is little better than a beggar!'

'Little better than a beggar,' said the Town Councillors.

'And here is actually a dead bird at his feet!' continued the Mayor. 'We must really issue a proclamation that birds are not to be allowed to die here.' And the Town Clerk made a note of the suggestion.

So they pulled down the statue of the Happy Prince. 'As he is no longer beautiful he is no longer useful,' said the Art Professor at the University.

Then they melted the statue in a furnace, and the Mayor held a meeting of the Corporation to decide what was to be done with the metal. 'We must have another statue, of course,' he said, 'and it shall be a statue of myself.'

'Of myself,' said each of the Town Councillors, and they quarrelled. When I last heard of them they were quarrelling still.

'What a strange thing!' said the overseer of the workmen at the foundry. 'This broken lead heart will not melt in the furnace. We must throw it away.' So they threw it on a dust-heap where the dead Swallow was also lying.

'Bring me the two most precious things in the city,' said God to one of His Angels; and the Angel brought Him the leaden heart and the dead bird.

'You have rightly chosen,' said God, 'for in my garden of Paradise this little bird shall sing for evermore, and in my city of gold the Happy Prince shall praise me.'

THE NIGHTINGALE AND THE ROSE

A STUDENT wishes to woo the Professor's Daughter, but she refuses to dance with him at the Prince's ball unless he brings her a red rose. None is available: 'I have read all that the wise men have written, and all the secrets of philosophy are mine, yet for want of a red rose is my life made wretched,' laments the Student.

He is overheard by the Nightingale, who rejoices to have encountered a true lover at last. She flies to a rose-tree and asks it for a red bloom to take to the Student; but all the roses are yellow. She tries another, but its red buds have been nipped by the frost.

It tells her there is only one way to obtain a red rose: 'You must build it out of music by moonlight, and stain it with your own heart's-blood. You must sing to me with your breast against a thorn. All night long you must sing to me, and the thorn must pierce your heart, and your life-blood must flow into my veins, and become mine.'

Reflecting that death is a high price to pay for a rose, but that Love is more important than Life, the Nightingale obeys. When the moon rises she flies to the rose tree, presses against a thorn, and sings of the birth and growth of love between a boy and a girl. A splendid pale rose begins to blossom, deepening in colour as the night advances and the bird's song becomes more passionate. But day approaches and the bloom is not yet completed:

So the Nightingale pressed closer against the thorn, and the thorn touched her heart, and a fierce pang of pain shot through her. Bitter, bitter was the pain, and wilder and wilder grew her song, for she sang of the Love that is perfected by Death, of the Love that dies not in the tomb.

And the marvellous rose became crimson, like the rose of the eastern sky. Crimson was the girdle of petals, and crimson as a ruby was the heart.

But the Nightingale's voice grew fainter, and her little wings began to beat, and a film came over her eyes. Fainter and fainter grew her song, and she felt something choking her in her throat.

Then she gave one last burst of music. The white Moon heard it, and she forgot the dawn, and lingered on in the sky. The red rose heard it, and it trembled all over with ecstasy, and opened its petals to the cold morning air. Echo bore it to her purple cavern in the hills, and woke the sleeping shepherds from their dreams. It floated through the reeds of the river, and they carried its message to the sea.

'Look, look!' cried the Tree, 'the rose is finished now'; but the Nightingale made no answer, for she was lying dead in the long grass, with the thorn in her heart.

At noon the Student opens his window and sees the rose. Over-joyed, he plucks it and runs with it to the Professor's house to claim his promise of reward. The Professor's Daughter frowns at the rose. It would not, she says, go with the dress she is going to wear; besides, another admirer has sent her jewels, which are infinitely preferable to roses. 'What a silly thing Love is!' the Student reflects as he walks away. 'It is not half as useful as Logic, for it does not prove anything, and it is always telling one of things that are not going to happen, and making one believe things that are not true.' He returns to his room, takes up a dusty learned tome, and settles down to read.

THE SELFISH GIANT

EVERY afternoon, on their way from school, the children love to play in the Giant's beautiful garden, where flowers, trees and grass grow in profusion and birds sing sweet songs to them. One day the Giant returns from a seven-year visit to his friend the Cornish ogre, sees the little trespassers, and drives them away. 'My garden is my own garden,' he says, and builds a high wall round it and puts up a warning notice, leaving the children nowhere to play except the stony, dusty road.

When Spring comes, nothing blossoms in the Giant's garden. Snow and frost remain on the grass and the trees, and no birds come to sing. Summer passes, and Autumn returns, but it is still Winter in the Giant's garden. Then, one morning as he lies in bed, he hears some lovely music. He looks out and sees a wonderful sight:

Through a little hole in the wall the children had crept in, and they were sitting in the branches of the trees. In every tree that he could see there was a little child. And the trees were so glad to have the children back again that they had covered themselves with blossoms, and were waving their arms gently above the children's heads. The birds were flying about and twittering with delight, and the flowers were looking up through the green grass and laughing. It was a lovely scene, only in one corner it was still winter. It was the farthest corner of the garden, and in it was standing a little boy. He was so small that he could not reach up to the branches of the tree, and he was wandering all round it, crying bitterly. The poor tree was still covered with frost and snow, and the North Wind was blowing and roaring above it. 'Climb up! little boy,' said the Tree, and it bent its branches down as low as it could but the boy was too tiny.

And the Giant's heart melted as he looked out. 'How selfish I have been!' he said; 'now I know why the Spring would not come here. I will put that poor little boy on the top of the tree, and then I will knock down the wall, and my garden shall be the children's playground for ever and ever.'

The thankful Giant goes out to greet the children, but they all run away except for the small boy. The Giant picks him up and sets him gently in the tree, which at once breaks into blossom. The other children come running back, and the Giant tells them his garden is now theirs. But when they come to say goodbye to the Giant in the evening the little boy is missing. Every day when the children come the Giant looks for him, but he never returns.

Years pass and the Giant grows old and feeble. One snowy Winter's morning he looks out, and is astonished to see the tree blossoming as though it were full Summer: the missing child is standing under the fruit-laden tree.

Downstairs ran the Giant in great joy, and out into the garden. He hastened across the grass, and came near to the child. And when he came quite close his face grew red with anger, and he said, 'Who hath dared to wound thee?' For on the palms of the child's hands were the prints of two nails, and the prints of two nails were on the little feet.

'Who hath dared to wound thee?' cried the Giant; 'tell me, that I may take my big sword and slay him.'

'Nay!' answered the child: 'but these are the wounds of Love.'

'Who art thou?' said the Giant, and a strange awe fell on him, and he knelt before the little child.

And the child smiled on the Giant, and said to him, 'You let me play once in your garden, to-day you shall come with me to my garden, which is Paradise.'

And when the children ran in that afternoon, they found the Giant lying dead under the tree, all covered with white blossoms.

THE DEVOTED FRIEND

DOWN at the pond, the Linnet tells the Water-rat and the Duck a story about Little Hans, a cottager liked by everyone in his neighbourhood, and big Hugh the Miller. Hans has the most beautiful of gardens, and every time the Miller passes he stops to lean over the wall and pick blooms and fruits. The rich Miller never offers Hans anything back in exchange, but it does not occur to good-natured Hans to suggest it.

After a long, hard winter, during which the Miller has not troubled to visit Hans, he does so, and learns that his little friend has had to sell his wheelbarrow to make ends meet. Hugh becomes magnanimity itself:

'Hans,' said the Miller, 'I will give you my wheelbarrow. It is not in very good repair; indeed, one side is gone, and there is something wrong with the wheel-spokes; but in spite of that I will give it to you. I know it is very generous of me, and a great many people would think me extremely foolish for parting with it, but I am not like the rest of the world. I think that generosity is the essence of friendship, and, besides, I have got a new wheelbarrow for myself. Yes, you may set your mind at ease. I will give you my wheelbarrow.'

'Well, really, that is generous of you,' said little Hans, and his funny round face glowed all over with pleasure. 'I can easily put it in repair, as I have a plank of wood in the house.'

'A plank of wood!' said the Miller; 'why, that is just what I want for the roof of my barn. There is a very large hole in it, and the corn will all get damp if I don't stop it up. How lucky you mentioned it! It is quite remarkable how one good action always breeds another. I have given you my wheelbarrow, and now you are going to give me your plank. Of course, the wheelbarrow is worth far more than the plank, but true friendship never notices things like that.'

In the days following Hans has plenty of opportunity to see the Miller's principles of friendship in action. Hugh calls on him with one demand after another, reminding him, if he ventures to pro-test, that he has promised to give Hans his wheelbarrow, and that there is no work so delightful as the work one does for others. Little Hans runs errands for the Miller, mends his barn-roof for him, and drives his sheep to the mountain; but the wheelbarrow is never quite forthcoming.

One night, when a terrible storm is raging, the Miller calls little Hans out to fetch the doctor to his little boy, who has been injured. Hans obeys, as ever. On the way back his horse wanders from the road on to the moor, where there are many deep holes. The body of Hans is found drowned in one of them next day. At his funeral tea the Miller laments: 'Why, I had as good as given him my wheelbarrow, and now I really don't know what to do with it. It is very much in my way at home, and it is in such bad repair that I could not get anything for it if I sold it. I will certainly take care not to give anything away again. One certainly suffers from being generous.'

THE REMARKABLE ROCKET

A GRAND fireworks display is to be the climax to the King's son's wedding celebrations. The waiting fireworks are talking amongst themselves when they are interrupted by a supercilious-looking Rocket. Speaking in a slow, distinguished manner – 'as if he were dictating his memoirs' – he tells them how honoured the Prince is to be getting married just when so remarkable a Rocket as he is ready to be let off. The other fireworks, who had had the impression that they were to be let off in the Prince's honour, are astonished, and then indignant, and finally disgusted by the boastful Rocket's manner. When he accuses them of not understanding his friendship with the Prince, they point out that he does not even know the Prince, which reduces him to tears of frustration.

They are interrupted by the beginning of the celebrations. After the dancing and feasting, midnight arrives and the fireworks display begins:

It was certainly a magnificent display.

Whizz! Whizz! went the Catherine Wheel, as she spun round and round. Boom! Boom! went the Roman Candle. Then the Squibs danced all over the place, and the Bengal Lights made everything look scarlet. 'Good-bye,' cried the Fire-balloon, as he soared away, dropping tiny blue sparks. Bang! Bang! answered the Crackers, who were enjoying themselves immensely. Every one was a great success except the Remarkable Rocket. He was so damped with crying that he could not go off at all. The best thing in him was the gunpowder, and that was so wet with tears that it was of no use. All his poor relations, to whom he would never speak, except with a sneer, shot up into the sky like wonderful golden flowers with blossoms of fire. Huzza! Huzza! cried the Court; and the little Princess laughed with pleasure.

The Rocket is left lying on the ground. Next day a party of workmen come to clear up. He imagines them to be a deputation sent to honour him, but they merely throw him over a wall. He falls into a muddy ditch. Such is his nature that he is able to convince himself that it is a fashionable watering-place to which he has been considerately sent to recuperate. Various creatures are prepared to chat affably with him, but his condescending manner and boasting alienate them. At length some boys find him. Mistaking him for an old piece of stick, they put him on to a fire they have made, and lie down for a sleep while their kettle boils.

The Rocket was very damp, so he took a long time to burn. At last, however, the fire caught him.

'Now I am going off!' he cried, and he made himself very stiff and straight. 'I know I shall go much higher than the stars, much higher than the moon, much higher than the sun. In fact, I shall go so high that—.'

Fizz! Fizz! Fizz! and he went straight up into the air.

'Delightful!' he cried, 'I shall go on like this for ever. What a success I am!'

But nobody saw him.

Then he began to feel a curious tingling sensation all over him.

'Now I am going to explode,' he cried. 'I shall set the whole world on fire, and make such a noise that nobody will talk about anything else for a whole year.' And he certainly did explode. Bang! Bang! Bang! went the gunpowder. There was no doubt about it.

But nobody heard him, not even the two little boys, for they were sound asleep.

Then all that was left of him was the stick, and this fell down on the back of a Goose who was taking a walk by the side of the ditch.

'Good heavens!' cried the Goose. 'It is going to rain sticks'; and she rushed into the water.

'I knew I should create a great sensation,' gasped the Rocket, and he went out.

THE ARTIST

AN artist desires to fashion an image of *The Pleasure that abideth for a Moment*, but can find no supply of bronze. The only piece available is that which he himself had sculpted for the tomb of 'the dead thing he had most loved': 'And out of the bronze of the image of *The Sorrow that endureth for Ever* he fashioned an image of *The Pleasure that abideth for a Moment.*'

THE DOER OF GOOD

'IT was night-time and He was alone.'

He sees a city and enters it. Passing through a rich house He sees a young man, with lips red with wine, reclining on a couch. He asks him why he lives in this way, and the reply is, 'I was a leper once, and you healed me. How else should I live?'

Going into the street again He sees a luxuriantly-clad harlot, followed by a young hunter whose eyes are bright with lust. He asks the hunter why he looks at the woman in this way, and is told, 'I was blind once, and you gave me sight. At what else should I look?'

The woman turns round and recognizes Him, as He asks her, 'Is there no other way in which to walk save the way of sin?' She laughs: 'You forgave me my sins, and the way is a pleasant way.'

He leaves the city and sees a young man weeping beside the road. He asks him why. The answer is, 'I was dead once and you raised me from the dead. What else should I do but weep?'

THE DISCIPLE
(Oscar Wilde's full version)

When Narcissus died the pool of his pleasure changed from a cup of sweet waters into a cup of salt tears, and the Oreads came weeping through the woodland that they might sing to the pool and give it comfort.

And when they saw that the pool had changed from a cup of sweet waters into a cup of salt tears, they loosened the green tresses of their hair and cried to the pool and said, 'We do not wonder that you should mourn in this manner for Narcissus, so beautiful was he.'

'But was Narcissus beautiful?' said the pool.

'Who should know that better than you?' answered the Oreads. 'Us did he ever pass by, but you he sought for, and would lie on your banks and look down at you, and in the mirror of your waters he would mirror his own beauty.'

And the pool answered, 'But I loved Narcissus because, as he lay on my banks and looked down at me, in the mirror of his eyes I saw ever my own beauty mirrored.'

THE MASTER
(Oscar Wilde's full version)

Now when the darkness came over the earth Joseph of Arimathea, having lighted a torch of pinewood, passed down from the hill into the valley. For he had business in his own home.

And kneeling on the flint stones of the Valley of Desolation he saw a young man who was naked and weeping. His hair was the colour of honey, and his body was as a white flower, but he had wounded his body with thorns and on his hair had he set ashes as a crown.

And he who had great possessions said to the young man who was naked and weeping, 'I do not wonder that your sorrow is so great, for surely He was a just man.'

And the young man answered, 'It is not for Him that I am weeping, but for myself. I too have changed water into wine, and I have healed the leper and given sight to the blind. I have walked upon the waters, and from the dwellers in the tombs I have cast out devils. I have fed the hungry in the desert where there was no food, and I have raised the dead from their narrow house, and at my bidding, and before a great multitude of people, a barren fig-tree withered away. All things that this man has done I have done also. And yet they have not crucified me.'

THE HOUSE OF JUDGMENT

IN the house of Judgment, God consults Man's record in the Book of Life and rebukes him for his greed, covetousness, lust, lack of charity, and other sins, all of which Man admits. God sentences Man to Hell.

And the Man cried out, 'Thou canst not.'

And God said to the Man, 'Wherefore can I not send thee to Hell, and for what reason?'

'Because in Hell have I always lived,' answered the Man.

And there was silence in the House of Judgment.

And after a space God spake, and said to the Man, 'Seeing that I may not send thee into Hell, surely I will send thee unto Heaven. Even unto Heaven will I send thee.'

And the Man cried out, 'Thou canst not.'

And God said to the Man, 'Wherefore can I not send thee unto Heaven, and for what reason?'

'Because never, and in no place, have I been able to imagine it,' answered the Man.

And there was silence in the House of Judgment.

THE TEACHER OF WISDOM

'FROM his childhood he had been as one filled with the perfect knowledge of God, and even while he was yet but a lad many of the saints, as well as certain holy women who dwelt in the free city of his birth, had been stirred to much wonder by the grave wisdom of his answers.'

When he reaches manhood he sets forth into the world to speak the word of God. He passes through eleven cities, attracting a band of disciples as he goes out converting many pagans to the love of God. Yet he feels an increasing burden of sorrow weighing on him, and sits in solitude on a mountain to ask his Soul what it means.

And his Soul answered him and said, 'God filled thee with the perfect knowledge of Himself, and thou hast given this knowledge away to others. The pearl of great price thou hast divided, and the vesture without seam thou hast parted asunder. He who giveth away wisdom robbeth himself. He is as one who giveth his treasure to a robber. Is not God wiser than thou art? Who art thou to give away the secret that God hath told thee? I was rich once, and thou hast made me poor. Once I saw God, and now thou hast hidden Him from me.'

So he determines to keep to himself what remains exclusively of his knowledge of God. To the dismay of the multitude who have followed him into the desert and gone without food he will speak no more to them. They disperse sadly, leaving him to set his face to the moon and journey alone for seven months until he reaches a cave, where he settles down with a bed of reeds and lives as a hermit, praising God hourly.

One evening he sees a young man 'of evil and beautiful face' passing with empty hands and returning with his hands 'full of purple and pearls'. Evening after evening he watches this robber of the merchants pass in the same way, until at length the young man demands to know why the Hermit looks at him in a way which makes him uneasy. The Hermit tells him he pities the robber with pity for the ungodly. The robber threatens him with his sword unless he will reveal the knowledge of God, which he has described as 'more precious than all the purple and the pearls of the world.' The Hermit refuses to disclose it. The robber changes from threats to pleading, but the Hermit will not tell him what he knows, and the young man finally declares that he will go to the

City of the Seven Sins. He is followed all the way by the Hermit, beseeching him not to enter in there, but the robber replies that he will only desist if the Hermit will reveal what remains of his knowledge of God. When, after three days, they reach the city's scarlet gates the Hermit relents and whispers to the robber all he knows.

And when the Hermit had given away his knowledge of God, he fell upon the ground and wept, and a great darkness hid from him the city and the young Robber, so that he saw them no more.

And as he lay there weeping he was aware of One who was standing beside him; and He who was standing beside him had feet of brass and hair like fine wool. And He raised the Hermit up, and said to him: 'Before this time thou hadst the perfect knowledge of God. Now thou shalt have the perfect love of God. Wherefore art thou weeping?' And He kissed him.

THE YOUNG KING

I T is the eve of the coronation of the sixteen-year-old young King. He had been the only child of the old King's daughter, as a result of her secret marriage with some unknown young man beneath her station. When the child was a week old he had been stolen from his mother and put into the care of a peasant couple living in a remote part of the forest. The Princess had died within an hour of wakening to find him gone. At length, when the old King was on his death-bed, he had sent messengers to bring him back to the palace as his heir, and for the first time he had set eyes on the man-made objects of beauty which would quickly become his obsession:

Those who accompanied him to the suite of rooms set apart for his service, often spoke of the cry of pleasure that broke from his lips when he saw the delicate raiment and rich jewels that had been prepared for him, and of the almost fierce joy with which he flung aside his rough eathern tunic and coarse sheepskin cloak. He missed, indeed, at times the freedom of the forest life, and was always apt to chafe at the tedious

Court ceremonies that occupied so much of each day, but the wonderful palace – *Joyeuse*, as they called it – of which he now found himself lord, seemed to him to be a new world fresh-fashioned for his delight; and as soon as he could escape from the council-board or audience-chamber, he would run down the great staircase, with its lions of gilt bronze and its steps of bright porphyry, and wander from room to room, and from corridor to corridor, like one who was seeking to find in beauty an anodyne from pain, a sort of restoration from sickness.

Upon these journeys of discovery, as he would call them – and, indeed, they were to him real voyages through a marvellous land, he would sometimes be accompanied by the slim, fair-haired Court pages, with their floating mantles, and gay fluttering ribands; but more often he would be alone, feeling through a certain quick instinct, which was almost a divination, that the secrets of art are best learned in secret, and that Beauty, like Wisdom, loves the lonely worshipper.

Many curious stories were related about him at this period. It was said that a stout Burgomaster, who had come to deliver a florid oratorical address on behalf of the citizens of the town, had caught sight of him kneeling in real adoration before a great picture that had just been brought from Venice, and that seemed to herald the worship of some new Gods. On another occasion he had been missed for several hours, and after a lengthened search had been discovered in a little chamber in one of the northern turrets of the palace gazing, as one in a trance, at a Greek gem carved with the figure of Adonis. He had been seen, so the tale ran, pressing his warm lips to the marble brow of an antique statue that had been discovered in the bed of the river on the occasion of the building of the stone bridge, and was inscribed with the name of the Bithynian slave of Hadrian. He had passed a whole night in noting the effect of the moonlight on a silver image of Endymion.

He has sent merchants far and wide to secure rare jewels, carpets and garments; but his chief preoccupation now, as his coronation day approaches, is the robe of tissued gold he is to wear, and the ruby-studded crown, and the sceptre with its rows and rings of pearls. He thinks of them as he falls asleep, and he dreams three dreams.

In the first, he is in a dark attic, where haggard, half-starved weavers are at work, watched by their pale children. The King asks why they work so hard in a free land.

'In war,' answered the weaver, 'the strong make slaves of the weak, and in peace the rich make slaves of the poor. . . . The merchants grind us down, and we must needs do their bidding. The priest rides by and tells his beads, and no man has care of us. Through our sunless lanes creeps Poverty with her hungry eyes, and Sin with his sodden face follows close behind her. Misery wakes us in the morning, and Shame sits with us at night. But what are these things to thee? Thou art not one of us. They face is too happy.' And he turned away scowling, and threw the shuttle across the loom, and the young King saw that it was threaded with a thread of gold.

And a great terror seized upon him, and he said to the weaver, 'What robe is this that thou art weaving?'

'It is the robe for the coronation of the young King,' he answered.

The young King wakes, troubled by his experiences, but soon falls asleep again, and finds himself on an Arab galley manned by slaves. He sees the anchor dropped and one of the slaves sent down repeatedly into the sea, each time bringing back with him a beautiful pearl.

Then the diver came up for the last time, and the pearl that he brought with him was fairer than all the pearls of Ormuz, for it was shaped like the full moon, and whiter than the morning star. But his face was strangely pale, and as he fell upon the deck the blood gushed from his ears and nostrils. He quivered for a little, and then he was still. The negroes shrugged their shoulders, and threw the body overboard.

And the master of the galley laughed, and, reaching out, he took the pearl, and when he saw it he pressed it to his forehead and bowed. 'It shall be,' he said, 'for the sceptre of the young King.'

The young King wakes with a cry; but dawn is only approaching, and he sleeps again. He is in a tropical forest where men are digging busily in great pits. He sees Death and Avarice looking on. Death demands a third of the men, but Avarice will give none away, so Death demands one of the three grains of corn Avarice holds in her hand. She refuses. Death conjures up Ague, and a third of the men die. Avarice will still not surrender any of the corn, so Death sends Fever and then Plague, until all the men are dead and Avarice has fled shrieking through the forest:

And the young King wept, and said: 'Who were these men, and for what were they seeking?'

'For rubies for a king's crown,' answered one who stood behind him.

And the young King started, and, turning round, he saw a man habited as a pilgrim and holding in his hand a mirror of silver.

And he grew pale, and said: 'For what king?'

And the pilgrim answered: 'Look in this mirror, and thou shalt see him.'

And he looked in the mirror, and, seeing his own face, he gave a great cry and woke, and the bright sunlight was streaming into the room, and from the trees of the garden and pleasaunce the birds were singing.

When the high officers of State attend the young King with his coronation robe and regalia he astonishes them by refusing to wear them. He dismisses all his pages except one favourite and puts on a leathern tunic and a rough sheepskin coat, and takes up a shepherd's staff. Thus robed and sceptred, and with a circlet of wild briar for a crown, he rides to the cathedral, mocked at by nobles and populace. The Bishop who is to crown him tries his own form of reasoning:

'Is not He who made misery wiser than thou art? Wherefore I praise thee not for this that thou hast done, but I bid thee ride back to the Palace and make thy face glad, and put on the raiment that beseemeth a king, and with the crown of gold I will crown thee, and the sceptre of pearl will I place in thy hand. And as for thy dreams, think no more of them. The burden of this world is too great for one man to bear, and the world's sorrow too heavy for one heart to suffer.'

Nobles with drawn swords burst in, about to kill the young man as an unworthy ruler. He turns from prayer to face them.

And lo! through the painted windows came the sunlight streaming upon him, and the sunbeams wove round him a tissued robe that was fairer than the robe that had been fashioned for his pleasure. The dead staff blossomed, and bare lilies that were whiter than pearls. The dry thorn blossomed, and bare roses that were redder than rubies. Whiter than fine pearls were the lilies, and their stems were of bright silver. Redder than male rubies were the roses, and their leaves were of beaten gold.

He stood there in the raiment of a king, and the gates of the jewelled shrine flew open and from the crystal of the many-rayed monstrance shone a marvellous and mystical light. He stood there in a king's raiment, and the Glory of God filled the place, and the saints in their carven niches seemed to move. In the fair raiment of a king he stood before them, and the organ pealed out its music, and the trumpeters blew upon their trumpets, and the singing boys sang.

The people fall to their knees, the nobles sheath their swords, and the Bishop kneels before the young King, whose face 'was like the face of an angel'.

THE BIRTHDAY OF THE INFANTA

IT is the twelfth birthday of the Infanta, the daughter of the King of Spain. The melancholy King, whose beautiful young French wife had died six months after the child's birth, has allowed his little daughter to invite all the friends she wishes to share her celebration.

The finely-dressed little aristocrats watch a series of entertainments, each more delightful than the last. There is a mock bull-fight by the boys, with the French Ambassador's son disguised as the bull; a tightrope walker, puppets, a juggler and snake charmer, and then a troop of gipsies with an exciting dance and a performing bear. But the most popular of all the events proves to be the dancing of a little Dwarf:

When he stumbled into the arena, waddling on his crooked legs and wagging his huge misshapen head from side to side, the children went off into a loud shout of delight, and the Infanta herself laughed so much that the Camerera was obliged to remind her that although there were many precedents in Spain for a King's daughter weeping before her equals, there were none for a Princess of the blood royal making so merry before those who were her inferiors in birth.

The little Dwarf had been found running wild in the forest only the day before. He is entranced by the beauty of the Infanta herself, and when she throws him the rose from her hair when his dance is finished he takes it as a serious token of love. The Infanta gives orders that he is to dance again after the hour of siesta, and she and her guests retire into the palace.

The little Dwarf is so delighted to be going to dance for her once more that he runs round the garden telling his joy to the flowers, who recoil from the ugly spectacle. But the birds and the lizards like him, and try to amuse him as he lies in the grass to rest. But the little Dwarf is too restless to lie down for long. He is impatient to see the Infanta again and persuade her to go back to the forest with him, where he will show her all nature's wonders and introduce her to his wild animal friends, and make her jewels of berries and acorns that will be quite as fine as any she has now.

He finds a private door into the palace. No one is about, so, still clutching the Infanta's rose, he wanders from one vast chamber to another, awed by the sombre magnificence of everything, but determined to find the Princess. At last he enters a brighter and more beautiful room than the rest and sees another figure at the far end. As he moves towards it it moves to him. A cry of joy breaks from the little Dwarf's lips; but it is not the Infanta coming to greet him:

It was a monster, the most grotesque monster he had ever beheld. Not properly shaped as all other people were, but hunchbacked, and crooked-limbed, with huge lolling head and mane of black hair. The little Dwarf frowned, and the monster frowned also. He laughed, and it laughed with him, and held its hands to its sides, just as he himself was doing. He made it a mocking bow, and it returned him a low reverence. He went towards it, and it came to meet him, copying each step that he made, and stopping when he stopped himself. He shouted with amusement, and ran forward, and reached out his hand, and the hand of the monster touched his, and it was as cold as ice. He grew afraid, and moved his hand across, and the monster's hand followed it quickly. He tried to press on, but something smooth and hard stopped him. The face of the monster was now close to his own, and seemed full of terror. He brushed his hair off his eyes. It imitated him. He struck at it, and it returned blow for blow. He loathed it, and it made hideous faces at him. He drew back, and it retreated.

What is it? He thought for a moment, and looked round at the rest of the room. It was strange, but everything seemed to have its double in this invisible wall of clear water. Yes, picture for picture was repeated, and couch for couch. The sleeping Faun that lay in the alcove by the doorway had its twin brother that slumbered, and the silver Venus that stood in the sunlight held out her arms to a Venus as lovely as herself.

Was it Echo? He had called to her once in the valley, and she had answered him word for word. Could she mock the eye, as she mocked the voice? Could she make a mimic world just like the real world? Could the shadows of things have colour and life and movement? Could it be that . . .?

He started, and taking from his breast the beautiful white rose, he turned round, and kissed it. The monster had a rose of its own, petal for petal the same! It kissed it with like kisses, and pressed it to its heart with horrible gestures.

As the truth of the mirror dawns upon him the little Dwarf flings himself to the ground, sobbing with despair at the realization that the Infanta and her guests had been laughing, not with delight at his grace and skill, but at his grotesqueness. He tears the rose to pieces and lies writhing and beating the ground with his hands. The Infanta and her guests enter at this moment and are delighted by these new antics. She tells him it is time for him to dance for her again. He does not respond. She petulantly stamps her foot and calls the Chamberlain to order the Dwarf to do as she commands. He kneels beside the twisted form for a few moments, then rises and bows:

'*Mi bella Princesa*, your funny little Dwarf will never dance again. It is a pity, for he is so ugly that he might have made the King smile.'

'But why will he not dance again?' asked the Infanta, laughing.

'Because his heart is broken,' answered the Chamberlain.

And the Infanta frowned, and her dainty rose-leaf lips curled in pretty disdain. 'For the future let those who come to play with me have no hearts,' she cried, and she ran out into the garden.

THE FISHERMAN AND HIS SOUL

WHEN the young Fisherman draws in his net one evening it is so heavy that he can scarcely get it out of the sea: instead of the useless monster he expects, he finds he has caught a sleeping Mermaid. Her beauty spellbinds him, but as soon as he touches her she wakes and struggles to escape. He says he will only let her go if she will promise to come up and sing whenever he calls, for the fish are attracted by the song of the Sea-folk and his nets will be full. She agrees and he puts her back into the sea. Every evening after that he calls her to sing, and the fish come in abundance; but they are not the only ones to be fascinated by her song:

For she sang of the Sea-folk who drive their flocks from cave to cave, and carry the little calves on their shoulders; of the Tritons who have long green beards, and hairy breasts, and blow through twisted conchs when the King passes by; of the palace of the King which is all of amber, with a roof of clear emerald, and a pavement of bright pearl; and of the gardens of the sea where the great filigrane fans of coral wave all day long, and the fish dart about like silver birds, and the anemones cling to the rocks, and the pinks bourgeon in the ribbed yellow sand. She sang of the big whales that come down from the north seas and have sharp icicles hanging to their fins; of the Sirens who tell of such wonderful things that the merchants have to stop their ears with wax lest they should hear them, and leap into the water and be drowned; of the sunken galleys with their tall masts, and the frozen sailors clinging to the rigging, and the mackerel swimming in and out of the open portholes; of the little barnacles who are great travellers, and cling to the keels of the ships and go round and round the world; and of the cuttlefish who live in the sides of the cliffs and stretch out their long black arms, and can make night come when they will it. She sang of the nautilus who has a boat of her own that is carved out of an opal and steered with a silken sail; of the happy Mermen who play upon harps and can charm the great Kraken to sleep; of the little children who catch hold of the slippery porpoises and ride laughing upon their backs; of the Mermaids who lie in the white foam and hold out their arms to the mariners; and of the sea-lions with their curved tusks, and the sea-horses with their floating manes.

One evening the Fisherman calls to her, 'Little Mermaid, little Mermaid, I love thee. Take me for thy bridegroom.' She answers that the Sea-folk have no Souls, so that she can only marry him if he will get rid of his. Next day he goes to the Priest's to ask how this can be done. The Priest censures him and tells him that the Sea-folk are accursed and that the love of the body is vile. The Fisherman goes next to the merchants to try to sell his Soul, but they will offer him nothing for it. He is left musing, 'How strange a thing this is! The Priest telleth me that the Soul is worth all the gold in the world, and the merchants say that it is not worth a clipped piece of silver.'

He remembers a young witch who lives in a cave at the head of the bay, and takes his problem to her. She agrees to show him what to do if he will dance with her at the Witches' Sabbath. He does, and she tries to seduce him for herself, but he forces her to give up the secret, which is to stand on the seashore with his back to the moon and cut away from around his feet his shadow, which is his Soul's body, with a knife she gives him. His Soul, hearing his intention, pleads not to be sent away, but he does as the Witch instructed and orders his Soul to be gone.

'Once every year I will come to this place, and call to thee,' said the Soul. 'It may be that thou wilt have need of me.'

'What need should I have of thee?' cried the young Fisherman, 'but be it as thou wilt,' and he plunged into the water, and the Tritons blew their horns, and the little Mermaid rose up to meet him, and put her arms around his neck and kissed him on the mouth.

And the Soul stood on the lonely beach and watched them. And when they had sunk down into the sea, it went weeping away over the marshes.

Each year his Soul returns and the young Fisherman comes up from the sea to hear its tales of its wanderings in far countries, where it has been introduced to such Wisdom and Riches as may be the Fisherman's if he will go back there with his Soul. He replies each time that Love is more desirable, and returns to the sea. On the third occasion, though, his Soul tells him of a place where wine is drunk and a veiled girl dances on naked feet. The Mermaid cannot dance for him, and the Fisherman responds to the temptation to go and experience this pleasure, telling himself that he will be back with his love within a day. He leaves the water, and his Soul joyously attaches itself to him again.

The journey is longer than the young Fisherman had expected. They pass through a succession of cities, and at each one his Soul persuades him to commit some crime; stealing a silver cup, smiting a child, and striking down and robbing a merchant who has given them hospitality. The Fisherman shrinks from his own behaviour, and asks his Soul why it has provoked him to do such things. It replies that when he had sent it away from him he had given it no heart, so it has learned to love sin above all things. Once again the Fisherman draws the Witch's knife and cuts away his shadow, but his Soul will not go, telling him, 'Once in his life may a man send his Soul away, but he who receiveth back his Soul must keep it with him for ever, and this is his punishment and his reward.'

Refusing to yield to his Soul's temptings with further sinful pleasures, the young Fisherman returns to the seashore. Every morning, noon and night he calls to his love, but she does not appear. After two years his Soul desists from trying to tempt him, acknowledges the strength of love over sin, and begs to be taken back into the Fisherman's heart. Out of compassion for his Soul's remorse the Fisherman welcomes it back. At once there is a cry of mourning from the sea, and the waves bear up the dead body of the little Mermaid. The Fisherman agonizedly confesses his sins to the dead ears. As he does so, the sea rolls nearer. His Soul bids him fly to safety, but he will not and is drowned, his Soul finding entrance into his heart as he dies.

The next morning the Priest comes down to bless the sea and finds the bodies of the young Fisherman and the Mermaid clasped in one another's arms. He gives orders for them to be buried in an unmarked grave in the Field of the Fullers, and refuses to bless the sea and its folk. One holy day, three years later, the Priest prepares to deliver a sermon on the wrath of God, when he notices on the altar a profusion of strange and beautiful flowers.

The beauty of the white flowers troubled him, and their odour was sweet in his nostrils, and there came another word into his lips, and he spake not of the wrath of God, but of the God whose name is Love. And why he so spake, he knew not.

And when he had finished his word the people wept, and the Priest went back to his sacristy, and his eyes were full of tears. And the deacons came in and began to unrobe him, and took from him the alb and the girdle, the maniple and the stole. And he stood as one in a dream.

And after that they had unrobed him, he looked at them and said, 'What are the flowers that stand on the altar, and whence do they come?'

And they answered him, 'What flowers they are we cannot tell, but they come from the corner of the Fullers' Field.' And the Priest trembled, and returned to his own house and prayed.

And in the morning, while it was still dawn, he went forth with the monks and the musicians, and the candlebearers, and the swingers of censers, and a great company, and came to the shore of the sea, and blessed the sea, and all the wild things that are in it. The Fauns also he blessed, and the little things that dance in the woodland, and the bright-eyed things that peer through the leaves. All the things in God's world he blessed, and the people were filled with joy and wonder. Yet never again in the corner of the Fullers' Field grew flowers of any kind, but the field remained barren even as before. Nor came the Sea-folk into the bay as they had been wont to do, for they went to another part of the sea.

THE STAR-CHILD

Two poor woodcutters are walking homeward through a great pine-forest in winter. They are discussing the hardship of their lives when they see a star fall from heaven and slip down behind a clump of willow trees. Hurrying to the spot in the hope of discovering a crock of gold, they find a sleeping baby in a cloak of golden tissue with a chain of amber round his neck. One is for leaving it there, but the other takes it home. His wife, with many children to care for on little money, is angry at first, but relents and brings the child up fondly with their own children.

As he grows older, the Star-Child, knowing of his beauty and his heavenly origin, becomes arrogant and proud. He treats everyone as his inferiors and servants, mocks his foster-parents and the priest when they try to persuade him into good ways, and leads the village children into acts of cruelty to animals and weaklings.

One day a beggar-woman passes through the village. When the Star-Child stones her he is rebuked by the woodcutter, who reminds him of the pity he had shown him when he had found him in the snow of the forest. The woman hears this and tells the woodcutter that ten years earlier she had lost a child in the forest: he had been wearing a cloak of gold tissue and an amber necklet. The woodcutter shows her the cloak and the necklet, and she identifies them. The Star-Child furiously refuses to accept the ragged woman as his mother:

'Alas! my son,' she cried, 'wilt thou not kiss me before I go? For I have suffered much to find thee.'

'Nay,' said the Star-Child, 'but thou are too foul to look at, and rather would I kiss the adder or the toad than thee.'

So the woman rose up, and went away into the forest weeping bitterly, and when the Star-Child saw that she had gone, he was glad, and ran back to his playmates that he might play with them.

But when they beheld him coming, they mocked him and said, 'Why, thou art as foul as the toad, and as loathsome as the adder. Get thee hence, for we will not suffer thee to play with us,' and they drave him out of the garden.

And the Star-Child frowned and said to himself, 'What is this that they say to me? I will go to the well of water and look into it, and it shall tell me of my beauty.'

So he went to the well of water and looked into it, and lo! his face was as the face of a toad, and his body was scaled like an adder. And he flung himself down on the grass and wept, and said to himself, 'Surely this has come upon me by reason of my sin. For I have denied my mother, and driven her away, and been proud, and cruel to her. Wherefore I will go and seek her through the whole world, nor will I rest till I have found her.'

He runs into the forest, calling for his mother, but in vain. The animals and birds cannot help him look for her, for he has maimed them all. The children of villages through which he passes mock and stone him in the way it had once been his pleasure to do. Three years' fruitless wandering bring him at last to a city, where soldiers seize him and sell him as slave to an evil old magician, who keeps him in a dungeon and proceeds to send him out on three errands after three pieces of gold, coloured white, yellow and red, with threats of punishment if he fails to bring them to him.

With the help of a hare the Star-Child finds the pieces of gold; but on his way back to the magician's each time he encounters a leper, takes pity on him, and gives him the piece of gold. The magician beats the Star-Child on the first two occasions and promises to slay him if he fails again; but the Star-Child's compassion for the leper is too great. He gives him the third piece of gold and returns to the city to meet his fate.

To his astonishment the city guards bow down to him and the citizens hurry forward to greet him, calling him their lord. Caught in the surge of the crowd he finds himself in front of the palace. An officer holds up a mirrored shield, and the Star-Child sees that his lost beauty has returned. Amongst the crowd he recognizes his mother beside the leper. He falls at his mother's feet, and she and the leper bid him to rise:

And he rose up from his feet, and looked at them, and lo! they were a King and a Queen.

And the Queen said to him, 'This is thy father whom thou hast succoured.'

And the King said, 'This is thy mother whose feet thou hast washed with thy tears.'

And they fell on his neck and kissed him, and brought him into the palace and clothed him in fair raiment, and set the crown upon his head, and the sceptre in his hand, and over the city that stood by the river he ruled, and was its lord. Much justice and mercy did he show to all, and the evil Magician he banished, and to the Woodcutter and his wife he sent many rich gifts, and to their children he gave high honour. Nor would he suffer any to be cruel to bird or beast, but taught love and loving-kindness and charity, and to the poor he gave bread, and to the naked he gave raiment, and there was peace and plenty in the land.

Yet ruled he not long, so great had been his suffering, and so bitter the fire of his testing, for after the space of three years he died. And he who came after him ruled evilly.

Stories

OSCAR WILDE told many stories. He put some of them into print in the form of the 'Fairy Tales' and 'Poems in Prose'. A few others he published as 'stories', varying in length from the few hundred words of 'The Sphinx Without a Secret' and 'The Model Millionaire' to the novel-sized *The Picture of Dorian Gray*. These three, together with 'The Canterville Ghost' and 'Lord Arthur Savile's Crime', comprise the entirety of his surviving fictional prose.

Hesketh Pearson reports the *Punch* cartoonist Sir Bernard Partridge as having recounted a telling by Wilde of 'Lord Arthur Savile's Crime' which lasted the best part of an hour and was fascinating. To the suggestion that he publish it Wilde replied, 'I don't think so, my dear fellow: it's such a bore writing these things out.' As Pearson remarks, there were dozens of other stories of his which might have attracted the same suggestion and response. Wilde once–perhaps more than once–said, 'I have put my genius into my life – I have put only my talent into my works.' There is a good deal of evidence of this in these five printed stories: what may have been grippingly spoken often flops tamely into print. Yet, discounting the two shortest tales which are little more than anecdotes, the stories have lived to become known to many readers today, have been translated and dramatized, and possess many positive qualities, of which perhaps the chief is ingenuity. In the hands of a more disciplined writer who had developed and polished them more assiduously, they might have been amongst the masterpieces of the short story.

The first to appear was 'The Canterville Ghost', published in the London magazine *Court and Society Review* in February 1887. 'Lord Arthur Savile's Crime' appeared in the same journal in three instalments that May. Both these and the two shorter pieces, which also first appeared early in 1887, were published together in book form as *Lord Arthur Savile's Crime and Other Stories* by Osgood, McIlvaine & Co., London, in July 1891, and several hundred copies of the edition were taken for the United States by Dodd, Mead & Co., New York. The reviews seem to have been lukewarm.

The Picture of Dorian Gray, as we know it today, is longer than the original version, which appeared in the July 1890 issue of *Lippincott's Monthly Magazine* in both England and the U.S.A.: six chapters and the epigrammatic preface were added for its publication in book form in April 1891, simultaneously in England and the U.S.A., by Ward, Lock & Co., London.

Those were the days, however, when so much fiction first reached the public through magazines that it received as much attention from reviewers as work in book form. As a magazine story, *Dorian Gray* attracted something like two hundred and fifty reviews, almost all of which condemned the story's perverse immorality. Decadence was not then the selling point it is now. It did gain Wilde something extra in sales, but nothing huge, and the price it cost was a notoriety which was to intensify his contempt of philistinism to the point of recklessness and to arm his opponents a few years later with a deadly weapon.

'Not being curious in ordure, and not wishing to offend the nostrils of decent persons, we do not propose to analyse *The Picture of Dorian Gray*: that would be to advertise the developments of an esoteric prurience,' wrote the *St. James's Gazette* reviewer; he then proceeded to do so and to perpetrate the sentence which is a veritable collector's piece: 'The writer airs his cheap research among the garbage of the French *Décadents* like any drivelling pedant.' The *Daily Chronicle* also thought it recognized the compost from which the work had been cultivated: 'It is a tale spawned from the leprous literature of the French *Décadents* – a poisonous book, the atmosphere of which is heavy with the mephitic odours of moral and spiritual putrefaction – a gloating study of the mental and physical corruption of a fresh, fair and golden youth, which might be horrible and fascinating but for its effeminate frivolity, its studied insincerity, its theatrical cynicism, its tawdry mysticism, its flippant philosophisings. . . .'

Wilde replied with a mixture of dignity and pique to this and some of the other reviews, notably that of the *St. James's Gazette*, and a considerable correspondence ensued, mostly concerning the story's 'moral' or lack of one. His insistence that 'The sphere of art and the sphere of ethics are absolutely distinct and separate', which he expressed in various forms, was to be turned against him with damaging effect at the Queensberry trial by Edward Carson; and since it provides one of the earliest examples of a kind of argument that has raged often since over specific books, plays, films and the question of 'literary' censorship in general, a little space may perhaps be devoted here to some extracts:

CARSON: You are of opinion, I believe, that there is no such thing as an immoral book?

WILDE: Yes.

CARSON: Am I right in saying that you do not consider the effect in creating morality or immorality?

WILDE: Certainly I do not. . . . In writing a play or a book I am concerned entirely with literature: that is, with art. I aim not at doing good or evil, but in trying to make a thing that will have some quality or form of beauty or wit. . . .

CARSON: Then I take it that no matter how immoral a book may be, if it is well written it is, in your opinion, a good book?

WILDE: Yes; if it were well written so as to produce a sense of beauty, which is the highest sense of which a human being can be capable. If it were badly written it would produce a sense of disgust.

CARSON: Then a well-written book putting forward perverted moral views may be a good book?

WILDE: No work of art ever puts forward views. Views belong to people who are not artists.

CARSON: A perverted novel might be a good book?

WILDE: I do not know what you mean by a perverted novel.

CARSON: Then I will suggest *Dorian Gray* as open to the interpretation of being such a novel.

WILDE: That could only be to brutes and illiterates. The views of Philistines on art are incalculably stupid. . . .

CARSON: Do you think the majority of people live up to the position you are giving us?

WILDE: I am afraid they are not cultivated enough.

CARSON: Not cultivated enough to draw the distinction between a good book and a bad book?

WILDE: Certainly not.

This sort of thing has been said since, if less offensively and with more objective sincerity, in many witness-boxes. Coming from Wilde, in 1895, it was just the stuff to influence a jury against himself and to alienate contemporary public feeling. Yet much of what he said lies at the heart of the censorship issue, in particular his proposition that it is the literary quality of the work being examined that determines its right to unrestricted publication or exhibition. The question, begged by himself, is whether *The Picture of Dorian Gray* is well written. There is much in it that is excessive, in language and idea; much melodrama that should be drama; bathos that should be restrained sentiment; sickly affectation of the kind that makes one, like Chesterton's book-reviewer (*A Ballade of a Book-Reviewer*), want to 'read "Jack Redskin on the Quest", and fill my brain with better things'. But the elements which fuse into *Dorian Gray* are our essential Oscar, and, for worse or better, it remains one of his best-known works in many countries, and not only on the strength of its nastier details. It has character, atmosphere and plot; and while the purist can easily list defects in them all, the general reader, whom, ironically, Wilde affected to despise, appreciates such things more than any notions of 'art for art's sake.' On its level, *Dorian Gray* is well enough done to endure alongside, say, *Dr Jekyll and Mr Hyde*, and is certain to do so.

LORD ARTHUR SAVILE'S CRIME
A Study of Duty

LADY WINDERMERE is giving her last reception of the pre-Easter season at her London home, Bentinck House. Amongst the high-placed guests, one very ordinary-looking little man moves. He is Mr Septimus R. Podgers, a professional cheiromantist, whom Lady Windermere is in the habit of consulting twice a week. As she tells the Duchess of Paisley:

'Next year, for instance, I am in great danger both by land and sea, so I am going to live in a balloon, and draw up my dinner in a basket every evening. It is all written down on my little finger, or on the palm of my hand, I forget which.'

'But surely that is tempting Providence, Gladys.'

'My dear Duchess, surely Providence can resist temptation by this time. I think every one should have their hands told once a month, so as to know what not to do. Of course, one does it all the same, but it is so pleasant to be warned.'

Mr Podgers is introduced and proceeds to read the Duchess's palm and those of several other guests. An interested though bashful volunteer is the young Lord Arthur Savile, whose engagement to Sybil Merton, one of the most beautiful girls in London, has recently been announced. Mr Podgers obliges:

But when Mr Podgers saw Lord Arthur's hand he grew curiously pale, and said nothing. A shudder seemed to pass through him, and his great bushy eyebrows twitched convulsively, in an odd, irritating way they had when he was puzzled. Then some huge beads of perspiration broke out on his yellow forehead, like a poisonous dew, and his fat fingers grew cold and clammy.

Mr Podgers will say no more about what he sees than that Mr Podgers will say nothing more about what he sees than that Lord Arthur will go on a voyage within the next few months and will lose a relative. The young man takes the palm-reader aside afterwards and presses him for more details, offering a handsome fee. It is accepted. Mr Podgers draws a small magnifying glass from his pocket and bends over Lord Arthur's palm. Ten minutes later Lord Arthur is hurrying blindly from Bentinck House:

Murder! that is what the cheiromantist had seen there. Murder! The very night seemed to know it, and the desolate wind to howl it in his ear. The dark corners of the streets were full of it. It grinned at him from the roofs of the houses.

First he came to the Park, whose sombre woodland seemed to fascinate him. He leaned wearily up against the railings, cooling his brow against the wet metal, and listening to the tremulous silence of the trees. 'Murder! Murder!' he kept repeating, as though iteration could dim the horror of the word. The sound of his own voice made him shudder, yet he almost hoped that Echo might hear him, and wake the slumbering city from its dreams. He felt a mad desire to stop the casual passer-by, and tell him everything.

Then he wandered across Oxford Street into narrow, shameful alleys. Two women with painted faces mocked at him as he went by. From a dark courtyard came a sound of oaths and blows, followed by shrill screams, and, huddled upon a damp door-step, he saw the crook-backed forms of poverty and eld. A strange pity came over him. Were these children of sin and misery predestined to their end, as he to his? Were they, like him, merely the puppets of a monstrous show?

He roams the London streets until dawn. But not long after waking in his house in Belgrave Square at noon, Lord Arthur Savile has found it possible to come to terms with his destiny. Feeling himself unable to marry Sybil Merton with the 'doom of murder hanging over his head', yet not intending to give her up, he is left facing merely the question of whom to murder and so get that part of his fate over and done with. 'Not being a genius, he had no enemies'; and he is altruistic enough not to wish to cause any of his friends unnecessary inconvenience, nor to want to gain materially through the murder. From a list of possible candidates he selects his elderly and ailing second cousin, Lady Clementina Beauchamp. He decides upon poison and manages to obtain from a chemist a capsule of aconitine—swift, painless, but deadly— which he says he wishes to use to destroy a mastiff with incipient rabies. He buys an attractive silver *bonbonnière*, pops the capsule into it, presents it charmingly to Lady Clem, as everyone calls her, and hastily goes abroad.

In Venice Lord Arthur meets his brother, Lord Surbiton. They spend three weeks together: uneasy weeks for Lord Arthur, who scans the obituary column of *The Times* every day in vain. At last a telegram arrives with the news that Lady Clem has died suddenly. With a sense of immense relief, Lord Arthur hurries home –

to discover that the old lady had died of a heart attack and that the *bonbon* lies untouched in its little silver box.

Frustrated, he returns to his list and picks out his uncle, the Dean of Chichester. The Dean is an enthusiastic clock collector, and it occurs to Lord Arthur to send him an anonymous present of an interesting specimen loaded with dynamite. Obtaining explosive proves more complicated than getting poison, until he remembers a Russian revolutionary acquaintance in London, who is able to introduce him to an Anarchist with the pseudonym Herr Winckelkopf. The latter proves accommodating, but cautionary:

'I can supply you with an excellent article, and guarantee that you will be satisfied with the result. May I ask for whom it is intended? If it is for the police, or for any one connected with Scotland Yard, I am afraid I cannot do anything for you. The English detectives are really our best friends, and I have always found that by relying on their stupidity we can do exactly what we like. I could not spare one of them.'

'I assure you,' said Lord Arthur, 'that it has nothing to do with the police at all. In fact, the clock is intended for the Dean of Chichester.'

'Dear me! I had no idea that you felt so strongly about religion, Lord Arthur. Few young men do nowadays.'

The clock is dispatched. This time Lord Arthur remains in London to await events, but they take several days to materialize: his mother receives a letter from the Dean's daughter telling her how a new addition to her father's collection, a mantelpiece clock, had suddenly emitted a whirring noise and a small puff of smoke, and has been banished to the children's schoolroom, where the succession of harmless little explosions it makes will not disturb her papa.

Sickened with failure, and beginning to see no alternative to breaking off his engagement, Lord Arthur dines at his club. But he is in no mood for the flippancy of his clubmates, and he wanders off alone to the Thames Embankment, where he sits for hours, vacantly watching the river and brooding. It is not until Big Ben strikes 2.0 a.m. that he rises and begins to stroll towards Black-friars. Approaching Cleopatra's Needle, he suddenly stops at the sight of a man leaning over the parapet, his face illuminated by the gas-light:

It was Mr Podgers, the cheiromantist! No one could mistake the fat, flabby face, the gold-rimmed spectacles, the sickly feeble smile, the sensual mouth.

Lord Arthur stopped. A brilliant idea flashed across him, and he stole softly up behind. In a moment he had seized Mr Podgers by the legs, and flung him into the Thames. There was a coarse oath, a heavy splash, and all was still. Lord Arthur looked anxiously over, but could see nothing of the cheiromantist but a tall hat, pirouetting in an eddy of moonlit water. After a time it also sank, and no trace of Mr Podgers was visible. Once he thought that he caught sight of the bulky misshapen figure striking out for the staircase by the bridge, and a horrible feeling of failure came over him, but it turned out to be merely a reflection, and when the moon shone out from behind a cloud it passed away. At last he seemed to have realised the decree of Destiny. He heaved a deep sigh of relief, and Sybil's name came to his lips.

'Have you dropped anything, sir?' said a voice behind him suddenly. He turned round, and saw a policeman with a bull's-eye lantern.

'Nothing of importance, sergeant,' he answered, smiling, and hailing a passing hansom he jumped in and told the man to drive to Belgrave Square.

The Coroner's verdict is suicide. Lord Arthur Savile and Sybil Merton are married with all speed. They live happily ever after, and are blessed with beautiful children. But for all his return to his lighthearted self, there is one subject about which Lord Arthur will allow no one to jest: it is cheiromancy.

THE CANTERVILLE GHOST
A Hylo-Idealistic Romance

His Excellency Hiram B. Otis, United States Minister to Great Britain, has bought Lord Canterville's home, Canterville Chase, seven miles from Ascot. With his wife and their four children, Washington, Virginia, and twin boys known as 'The Stars and

Stripes', they arrive one lovely July evening to be welcomed by the old housekeeper Mrs Umney. One of the first things to catch Mrs Otis's eye is a red stain on the library floor. Mrs Umney tells them it is the irremovable bloodstain left at the murder in 1575 of Lady Eleanore de Canterville by her husband, Sir Simon de Canterville. Sir Simon had disappeared nine years later and his body had never been found, though his spirit still haunts the Chase.

'That is all nonsense,' cried Washington Otis; 'Pinkerton's Champion Stain Remover and Paragon Detergent will clean it up in no time,' and before the terrified housekeeper could interfere he had fallen upon his knees, and was rapidly scouring the floor with a small stick of what looked like a black cosmetic. In a few moments no trace of the blood-stain could be seen.

'I knew Pinkerton would do it,' he exclaimed triumphantly, as he looked round at his admiring family; but no sooner had he said these words than a terrible flash of lightning lit up the sombre room, a fearful peal of thunder made them all start to their feet, and Mrs Umney fainted.

The storm rages all night, and next morning the stain has reappeared. It is expunged twice more, and twice again returns. On the third night Mr Otis is awakened by the approaching clank of metal in the corridor outside his room. He dons his slippers and goes outside, to encounter 'an old man of terrible aspect. His eyes were as red as burning coals; long grey hair fell over his shoulders in matted coils; his garments, which were of antique cut, were soiled and ragged, and from his wrists and ankles hung heavy manacles and rusty gyves.' The American Minister addresses him:

'My dear sir,' said Mr Otis, 'I really must insist on your oiling those chains, and have brought you for that purpose a small bottle of the Tammany Rising Sun Lubricator. It is said to be completely efficacious upon one application, and there are several testimonials to that effect on the wrapper from some of our most eminent native divines. I shall leave it here for you by the bedroom candles, and will be happy to supply you with more should you require it.' With these words the United States Minister laid the bottle down on a marble table, and, closing the door, retired to rest.

For a moment the Canterville ghost stood quite motionless in natural indignation; then, dashing the bottle violently upon the polished floor, he fled down the corridor, uttering hollow groans, and emitting a ghastly green light. Just, however, as he reached the top of the great oak staircase, a door was flung open, two little white-robed figures appeared, and a large pillow whizzed past his head! There was evidently no time to be lost, so, hastily adopting the Fourth Dimension of Space as means of escape, he vanished through the wainscoting, and the house became quite quiet.

It takes the Ghost several days to get over the shock and indignity of such treatment. His next effort, on the following Sunday night, is no more successful. He is brought down by the peashooters of 'The Stars and Stripes' and has to make another hasty retreat:

On reaching the top of the staircase he recovered himself, and determined to give his celebrated peal of demoniac laughter. This he had on more than one occasion found extremely useful. It was said to have turned Lord Raker's wig grey in a single night, and had certainly made three of Lady Canterville's French governesses give warning before their month was up. He accordingly laughed his most horrible laugh, till the old vaulted roof rang and rang again, but hardly had the fearful echo died away when a door opened, and Mrs Otis came out in a light blue dressing-gown. 'I am afraid you are far from well,' she said, 'and have brought you a bottle of Dr Dobell's tincture. If it is indigestion, you will find it a most excellent remedy.' The ghost glared at her in fury, and began at once to make preparations for turning himself into a large black dog, an accomplishment for which he was justly renowned, and to which the family doctor always attributed the permanent idiocy of Lord Canterville's uncle, the Hon. Thomas Horton. The sound of approaching footsteps, however, made him hesitate in his fell purpose, so he contented himself with becoming faintly phosphorescent, and vanished with a deep churchyard groan.

The Ghost keeps up his attempted hauntings for days, but it is always he who emerges the persecuted. Effects which have stood him in good stead for centuries make no impression on the Americans. He has, in fact, changed roles from haunter to victim, ambushed, petrified and assaulted at every turn by the terrible twins. He takes to creeping about the passages, carrying a small arquebuse in case of attack by them, and is seen no more of nights. Mrs Otis gives a lavish clambake, which astonishes the county; the boys settle down to lacrosse, euchre, poker, 'and other American national games', and the curly-haired young Duke of Cheshire comes to spend the last week of his holidays from Eton riding the lanes with Virginia Otis. The Ghost dares not interfere by so much as a hollow groan.

While riding one day, Virginia tears her habit badly negotiating a hedge and decides to enter the house unobserved by a back staircase. The door of the Tapestry Chamber chances to be open, and there she sees, seated dejectedly, the Canterville Ghost. She lectures him firmly on the nuisance he has caused and scolds him for stealing the paints from her box in order to keep refurbishing the bloodstain: he can only answer that real blood is a difficult thing to obtain in these modern times. Relenting a little, she offers to ask her father to get him a free passage to America, where he will have great curiosity value. He declines, but begs her not to leave him to his loneliness and weariness: he has not slept for three hundred years.

The child is genuinely moved and listens to him describe the distant Garden of Death, where rest awaits him if he can only get there. She can help him to do so. He reminds her of an old prophecy inscribed on the library window:

> When a golden girl can win
> Prayer from out the lips of sin,
> When the barren almond bears,
> And a little child gives away its tears,
> Then shall all the house be still
> And peace come to Canterville.

'They mean,' he said sadly, 'that you must weep for me for my sins, because I have no tears, and pray with me for my soul, because I have no faith, and then, if you have always been sweet, and good, and gentle, the Angel of Death will have mercy on me. You will see fearful shapes in darkness, and wicked voices will whisper in your ear, but they will not harm you, for against the purity of a little child the powers of Hell cannot prevail.'

Virginia made no answer, and the ghost wrung his hands in wild despair as he looked down at her bowed golden head. Suddenly she stood up, very pale, and with a strange light in her eyes. 'I am not afraid,' she said firmly, 'and I will ask the Angel to have mercy on you.'

Virginia is missing at tea-time and the house is searched in vain. Mr Otis telegraphs to the police throughout the county and he and the Duke of Cheshire scour the neighbourhood on horseback. By midnight Virginia has still not returned. Mr Otis ordains that it will be best for everyone to go to bed and leave the matter to the police, but they are forestalled by a succession of violent noises and a strain of unearthly music, after which a panel at the head of the staircase flies back to reveal a pale Virginia, clutching a small casket which proves to be crammed with jewels of great beauty. She leads them back through the panelling, down a narrow corridor, and into a low, vaulted room, where they see a chained skeleton whose outstretched hands reach just short of a water-jug and a plate bearing the remains of what must have been food. One of the twins happens to glance through the one tiny grated window and sees in the moonlight that the withered old almond-tree is in blossom.

Four nights later the Ghost's earthly remains are given formal burial in the local churchyard. Next day, Mr Otis offers the box of jewels back to Lord Canterville, who had come to attend his ancestor's funeral, but they are refused, on the grounds that they constitute part of what the American had bought when he acquired Canterville Chase. So they pass to Virginia, who is duly married to the Duke of Cheshire. After the honeymoon, the young couple visit the Ghost's grave and place roses on it. Then they stroll into the ruined chancel of the old abbey. The young Duke takes his wife's hand and gently reminds her that she has never told him what happened to her while she was locked away with the Ghost:

'I have never told any one, Cecil,' said Virginia gravely.
'I know that, but you might tell me.'

'Please don't ask me, Cecil, I cannot tell you. Poor Sir Simon! I owe him a great deal. Yes, don't laugh, Cecil, I really do. He made me see what Life is, and what Death signifies, and why Love is stronger than both.'

The Duke rose and kissed his wife lovingly.

'You can have your secret as long as I have your heart,' he murmured.

'You have always had that, Cecil.'

'And you will tell our children some day, won't you?'

Virginia blushed.

THE SPHINX WITHOUT A SECRET
An Etching

ONE afternoon the Narrator is sitting outside the Café de la Paix in Paris when he is hailed by a former Oxford friend, Lord Murchison. He finds him a good deal changed:

He looked anxious and puzzled, and seemed to be in doubt about something. I felt it could not be modern scepticism, for Murchison was the stoutest of Tories, and believed in the Pentateuch as firmly as he believed in the House of Peers; so I concluded that it was a woman, and asked him if he was married yet.

'I don't understand women well enough,' he answered.

'My dear Gerald,' I said, 'women are meant to be loved, not to be understood.'

'I cannot love where I cannot trust,' he replied.

'I believe you have a mystery in your life, Gerald,' I exclaimed; 'tell me about it.'

Lord Murchison produces a little photograph case containing the picture of a strangely attractive woman. The two friends go on to a restaurant to dine, and afterwards Murchison tells how he had first seen the woman in a carriage in Bond Street and had been fascinated by her. Some days later he had chanced to meet her at a dinner-party and had taken the opportunity to ask if he might call on her. After hesitating she had consented; but when he had arrived at her Park Lane address next afternoon the butler had told him that Lady Alroy had gone out. Aggrieved, Murchison had written to ask if he might try again. Several days later a reply had come, agreeing, but asking him in future to write to an accommodation address.

Lord Murchison had continued to meet this fascinating and enigmatic widow, as he had discovered her to be, throughout the season, but had never succeeded in getting the measure of her personality, even to the extent of wondering whether she might be under the power of some other man. However, he had at length determined to ask her to marry him, and had written to arrange a further meeting. Going to lunch with his uncle earlier in the day it was to take place, he had taken a short cut through some back streets and had been astonished to see Lady Alroy walking quickly ahead of him. She had hurried up the steps of the last house in the street, opened the door with a key of her own, and gone in. As he stared at the shabby house, Murchison had seen her handkerchief lying on the steps and picked it up before walking away much distressed.

When he kept his appointment with Lady Alroy that evening he had at once produced the handkerchief and accused her of having gone to the house to meet someone. She had angrily refused to be interrogated, but had denied having met anyone at all at the house. Murchison had lost control, abused her hysterically, run from her house, and immediately gone abroad. On returning home a month later he had read of Lady Alroy's death as a result of a chill.

Tortured by doubt, he had gone to the back-street house of mystery and interviewed the landlady. She proved to be a respectable-looking woman, who told him that the lady whose photograph he showed her had been her best tenant, paying her three guineas a week merely to come and sit in her drawing-rooms from time to time, always quite alone, reading books and drinking tea.

His story at an end, Lord Murchison asks the Narrator whether he believes the landlady had told him the truth:

'I do.'

'Then why did Lady Alroy go there?'

'My dear Gerald,' I answered, 'Lady Alroy was simply a woman with a mania for mystery. She took these rooms for the pleasure of going there with her veil down and imagining she was a heroine. She had a passion for secrecy, but she herself was merely a Sphinx without a secret.'

'Do you really think so?'

'I am sure of it,' I replied.

He took out the morocco case, opened it, and looked at the photograph. 'I wonder,' he said at last.

THE MODEL MILLIONAIRE

A Note of Admiration

Unless one is wealthy there is no use in being a charming fellow. Romance is the privilege of the rich, not the profession of the unemployed. The poor should be practical and prosaic. It is better to have a permanent income than to be fascinating. These are the great truths of modern life.

HUGHIE ERSKINE is charming but impecunious. He is in love with Laura Merton, whose father, a retired colonel, will not hear of a marriage until Hughie can come to him with ten thousand pounds to his name.

On his way to visit Laura one morning, Hughie calls at the home of an artist friend, Alan Trevor. He finds him in his studio, at work on the portrait of a wizened old beggar-man clad in tattered clothes and holding out a battered hat for alms. The good-natured Hughie is moved by the model's wretched condition and almost indignant to learn that his modelling fee is a shilling an hour, for a picture which will bring the artist two thousand guineas:

'I think the model should have a percentage,' cried Hughie, laughing; 'they work quite as hard as you do.'

'Nonsense, nonsense! Why, look at the trouble of laying on the paint alone, and standing all day long at one's easel! It's all very well, Hughie, for you to talk, but I assure you that there are moments when Art almost attains to the dignity of manual labour.'

Alan Trevor is called out of his studio for a few moments. Hughie takes the opportunity to slip the few coins he has into the beggar's hat, for which he is politely thanked. That evening he meets the artist again at their club and is both surprised to learn that the beggar has been asking for his private address and annoyed to know that he has been told by Alan Trevor all about the obstacle to Hughie's and Laura's marriage. A greater surprise awaits him, though: Trevor reveals that the 'beggar' was his great friend Baron Hausberg, one of the richest men in Europe, whose whim it had been to commission a portrait of himself in rags. Deeply embarrassed at the thought of having made such a fool of himself as to tip a millionaire, Hughie goes home despondently.

Next morning he receives a visitor, a representative of Baron Hausberg. With a smile the man hands him a sealed envelope:

On the outside was written, 'A wedding present to Hugh Erskine and Laura Merton, from an old beggar,' and inside was a cheque for £10,000.

When they were married Alan Trevor was the best man, and the Baron made a speech at the wedding breakfast.

'Millionaire models,' remarked Alan, 'are rare enough; but, by Jove, model millionaires are rarer still!'

THE PICTURE OF DORIAN GRAY

THE rich, indolent and cynical Lord Henry Wotton is paying a visit to the studio of his friend from Oxford days, Basil Hallward, a fashionable portrait painter:

The studio was filled with the rich odour of roses, and when the light summer wind stirred amidst the trees of the garden, there came through the open door the heavy scent of the lilac, or the more delicate perfume of the pink-flowering thorn.

From the corner of the divan of Persian saddle-bags on which he was lying, smoking, as was his custom, innumerable cigarettes, Lord Henry Wotton could just catch the gleam of the honey-sweet and honey-coloured blossoms of a laburnum, whose tremulous branches seemed hardly able to bear the burden of a beauty so flame-like as theirs; and now and then the fantastic shadows of birds in flight flitted across the long tussore-silk curtains that were stretched in front of the huge window, producing a kind of momentary Japanese effect, and making him think of those pallid jade-faced painters of Tokio who, through the medium of an art that is necessarily immobile, seek to convey the sense of swiftness and motion. The sullen murmur of the bees shouldering their way through the long unmown grass, or circling with monotonous insistence round the dusty gilt horns of the straggling woodbine, seemed to make the stillness more oppressive. The dim roar of London was like the bourdon note of a distant organ.

Hallward is putting some last touches to the full-length picture of a young man of extraordinary beauty. Pressed by his friend, he reveals how he had met this twenty-year-old youth, Dorian Gray, at a society function, had been fascinated by him, and had persuaded him to sit for him. He has no intention of exhibiting the picture: Dorian Gray has become more to him than any other subject.

Lord Henry's curiosity is intensely aroused, to Hallward's alarm, for he has no intention of risking his new friend's being influenced by Lord Henry's corruptive theories. But there is no opportunity to resist: the manservant announces that Dorian Gray has arrived. Hallward can only plead with Lord Henry not to take away from him the one person upon whom his life 'as an artist' depends, before reluctantly performing the introduction. He tries to persuade Lord Henry to go while Dorian Gray sits for the last details, but a spark has instantly been kindled between the two men who have just shaken hands for the first time. Although Lord Henry takes up his hat and gloves, Dorian Gray presses him to stay. He does so, and from the first his words impress the young man profoundly:

'I believe that if one man were to live out his life fully and completely, were to give form to every feeling, expression to every thought, reality to every dream – I believe that the world would gain such a fresh impulse of joy that we would forget all the maladies of mediaevalism, and return to the Hellenic ideal – to something finer, richer, than the Hellenic ideal, it may be. But the bravest man amongst us is afraid of himself. The mutilation of the savage has its tragic survival in the self-denial that mars our lives. We are punished for our refusals. Every impulse that we strive to strangle broods in the mind, and poisons us. The body sins once, and has done with its sin, for action is a mode of purification. Nothing remains then but the recollection of a pleasure, or the luxury of a regret. The only way to get rid of a temptation is to yield to it. Resist it, and your soul grows sick with longing for the things it has forbidden to itself, with desire for what its monstrous laws have made monstrous and unlawful. It has been said that the great events of the world take place in the brain. It is in the brain, and the brain only, that the great sins of the world take place also. You, Mr Gray, you yourself, with your rose-red youth and your rose-white boyhood, you have had passions that have made you afraid, thoughts that have filled you with terror, day-dreams and sleeping dreams whose mere memory might stain your cheek with shame—'

'Stop!' faltered Dorian Gray, 'stop! you bewilder me. I don't know what to say. There is some answer to you, but I cannot find it. Don't speak. Let me think. Or, rather, let me try not to think.'

For nearly ten minutes he stood there, motionless, with parted lips, and eyes strangely bright. He was dimly conscious that entirely fresh influences were at work within him. Yet they seemed to him to have come really from himself. The few words that Basil's friend had said to him – words spoken by chance, no doubt, and with wilful paradox in them – had touched some secret chord that had never been touched before, but that he felt was now vibrating and throbbing to curious pulses.

Dorian Gray is lost to Basil Hallward from this moment. He and Lord Henry stroll in the garden for a time while Hallward finishes the picture, and Dorian finds himself virtually mesmerized by the older man's panegyric on youth and his insistence that its pleasures must be drained to the last drop before jealous Time achieves its inevitable triumph. He pictures himself as he has never done before: grown old and feeble, his beauty, of which he is only too aware, destroyed. Hallward calls them in to view the completed portrait:

'How sad it is!' murmured Dorian Gray, with his eyes still fixed upon his own portrait. 'How sad it is! I shall grow old, and horrible, and dreadful. But this picture will remain always young. It will never be older than this particular day of June. . . . If it were only the other way! If it were I who was to be always young, and the picture that was to grow old! For that – for that – I would give everything! Yes, there is nothing in the whole world I would not give! I would give my soul for that!'

Hallward accuses Lord Henry of having precipitated this reckless oath and threatens to destroy the portrait. He seizes a palette-knife, but Dorian Gray restrains him. In any case, the picture is his property: Hallward had promised it to him before it was begun. The painter can only promise to have it varnished and framed and delivered to Dorian's home.

During the next weeks Dorian Gray is a frequent visitor to Lord Henry's house. About a month after their first meeting he tells his friend of a bizarre experience he has had. Strolling in some of the more sinful neighbourhoods of the West End of London, indulging his new realization of the delight of danger, he had been persuaded to enter a seedy little theatre. The play was, surprisingly, *Romeo and Juliet*. The scenery was tawdry and the players grotesquely bad – with one exception:

'But Juliet! Harry, imagine a girl, hardly seventeen years of age, with a little flower-like face, a small Greek head with plaited coils of dark-brown hair, eyes that were violet wells of passion, lips that were like the petals of a rose. She was the loveliest thing I had ever seen in my life. You said to me once that pathos left you unmoved, but that beauty, mere beauty, could fill your eyes with tears. I tell you, Harry, I could hardly see this girl for the mist of tears that came across me.'

Her name, he had discovered, is Sybil Vane, and after returning to the theatre on the two nights following he had contrived to go to her dressing-room. He had not given his name, but the girl had at once dubbed the handsome visitor 'Prince Charming', and they had let it go at that. Her mother, with whom she lives, is also a member of the company, and an unprepossessing person; but this cannot detract from Dorian's enchantment with his Sybil. He now wishes to take his best friends, Lord Henry and Basil Hallward, to the theatre to see her play Juliet again. Lord Henry agrees with some amusement. The young man's infatuation with a girl is, for him, not a matter for jealousy, but an interesting development in his study and manipulation of his protégé:

Human life – that appeared to him [Lord Henry] the one thing worth investigating. Compared to it there was nothing else of any value. It was true that as one watched life in its curious crucible of pain and pleasure, one could not wear over one's face a mask of glass, nor keep the sulphurous fumes from troubling the brain, and making the imagination turbid with monstrous fancies and misshapen dreams. There were poisons so subtle that to know their properties one had to sicken of them. There were maladies so strange that one had to pass through them if one sought to understand their nature. And, yet, what a great reward one received! How wonderful the whole world became to one! To note the curious hard logic of passion, and the emotional coloured life of the intellect – to observe where they met, and where they separated, at what point they were in unison, and at what point they were at discord – there was a delight in that! What matter what the cost was? One could never pay too high a price for any sensation.

Sybil Vane, too, is exulting in the experience of love. Her mother's chief concern is for the money advanced them by the theatre proprietor, Isaacs, that they would have to pay back if Sybil were to marry and give up acting; but a different prospect is troubling Sybil's brother James, a merchant seaman about to leave for a long voyage. He fears that Sybil's 'Prince Charming' will simply seduce her and then cast her aside. Taking a farewell walk together, he and Sybil see Dorian Gray pass by in an open carriage with two ladies. James Vane warns his sister that if 'Prince Charming' ever does her any wrong he will kill him.

The three gentlemen duly arrive at the theatre. The heat is oppressive and the noise raucous. Lord Henry and Basil Hallward wait tolerantly for Dorian Gray's 'divinity' to appear; and when she does, to a torrent of applause, they appreciate her charms. Yet, when Sybil Vane begins to speak, something is wrong. Her voice is exquisite, but her delivery is stilted, her acting absurdly artificial. By the time the second act is over the audience is talking loudly and whistling. Murmuring sympathetic words to their friend, Lord Henry and Hallward leave. Dorian Gray sees the whole fiasco through, then goes round as usual to Sybil Vane's dressing-room. She greets him as rapturously as though she had just achieved the greatest performance of her career:

'Dorian, Dorian,' she cried, 'before I knew you, acting was the one reality of my life. It was only in the theatre that I lived. I thought that it was all true. I was Rosalind one night, and Portia the other. The joy of Beatrice was my joy, and the sorrows of Cordelia were mine also. I believed in everything. The common people who acted with me seemed to me to be godlike. The painted scenes were my world. I knew nothing but shadows, and I thought them real. You came – oh, my beautiful love! – and you freed my soul from prison. You taught me what reality really is. To-night, for the first time in my life, I saw through the hollowness, the sham, the silliness of the empty pageant in which I had always played. To-night, for the first time, I became conscious that the Romeo was hideous, and old, and painted, that the moonlight in the orchard was false, that the scenery was vulgar, and that the words I had to speak were unreal, were not my words, were not what I wanted to say. You had brought me something higher, something of which all art is but a reflection. You had made me understand what love really is. My love! my love! Prince Charming!'

Dorian Gray draws away from her attempted embrace, and goes to the door, telling her: 'You have killed my love. You used to stir my imagination. Now you don't even stir my curiosity. You simply produce no effect. I loved you because you were marvellous, because you had genius and intellect, because you realized the dreams of great poets and gave shape and substance to the shadows of art. You have thrown it all away.'

Heedless of her tears and entreaties, Dorian Gray leaves the theatre and tramps the streets of London until dawn, when he finds himself in Covent Garden market, hails a hansom cab, and is driven home. As he passes through the library towards his bedroom, his eye falls on Basil Hallward's portrait of him:

He started back as if in surprise. Then he went on into his own room, looking somewhat puzzled. After he had taken the buttonhole out of his coat, he seemed to hesitate. Finally he came back, went over to the picture, and examined it. In the dim arrested light that struggled through the cream-coloured silk blinds, the face appeared to him to be a little changed. The expression looked different. One would have said that there was a touch of cruelty in the mouth. It was certainly strange.

There is no mistaking the slight change that has come across its features. He flings himself down into a chair and considers the events of the day. At least he can come to terms with himself over his treatment of Sybil Vane; but the picture . . .

It was watching him, with its beautiful marred face and its cruel smile. Its bright hair gleamed in the early sunlight. Its blue eyes met his own. A sense of infinite pity, not for himself, but for the painted image of himself, came over him. It had altered already, and would alter more. Its gold would wither into grey. Its red and white roses would die. For every sin that he committed, a stain would fleck and wreck its fairness. But he would not sin. The picture, changed or unchanged, would be to him the visible emblem of conscience. He would resist temptation. He would not see Lord Henry any more – would not, at any rate, listen to those subtle poisonous theories that in Basil Hallward's garden had first stirred within him the passion for impossible things. He would go back to Sybil Vane, make her amends, marry her, try to love her again. Yes, it was his duty to do so. She must have suffered more than he had. Poor child! He had been selfish and cruel to her. The fascination that she had exercised over him would return. They would be happy together. His life with her would be beautiful and pure.

Dorian Gray draws a large screen in front of his portrait and retires to bed, thinking happily of Sybil. It is long past noon of the next day when he awakes and makes his leisurely toilet. The sight of the screen across his portrait comes as a disturbing reminder of the previous evening. Dreading, yet knowing, what he will see, he locks the door and draws the screen from in front of the portrait: there is no doubt about the change that the face has undergone.

He sits for a long time, wondering what course to pursue. At length he writes a passionately loving letter to Sybil, and the act seems to purge his soul. Before he can dispatch it Lord Henry insists upon being admitted. He has come to commiserate with Dorian about Sybil Vane. Dorian tells him what had occurred between them after the performance, and admits his cruelty to the girl, but says he is about to make amends by marrying her. Amazed, Lord Henry reveals the real cause of his visit of sympathy, which he had not realized Dorian Gray did not know: the morning newspapers have reported Sybil's death by self-poisoning.

Dorian Gray is briefly shattered by the news; but with the subtle encouragement of Lord Henry he persuades himself that in pursuing Sybil he has been chasing an artistic illusion, not an individual woman. His burden of remorse lifts at once, and he joins Lord Henry and his sister, Lady Gwendolen, at the opera that evening.

Next day Basil Hallward calls to offer his condolences and is shocked to find Dorian apparently unaffected by the tragedy. He asks, while he is there, for a look at his portrait, and is surprised to be refused. He blurts out a confession of the extent of his feeling for Dorian, who in return is courteous but faintly patronizing. As soon as he has managed to get rid of Hallward, he has the painting transferred to his old schoolroom, disused and permanently locked, at the top of the house. He pockets the key and goes downstairs to his library for some tea.

His eye fell on the yellow book that Lord Henry had sent him. What was it, he wondered. He went towards the little pearl-coloured octagonal stand, that had always looked to him like the work of some strange Egyptian bees that wrought in silver, and taking up the volume, flung himself into an arm-chair, and began to turn over the leaves. After a few minutes he became absorbed. It was the strangest book that he had ever read. It seemed to him that in exquisite raiment, and to the delicate sound of flutes, the sins of the world were passing in dumb show before him. Things that he had dimly dreamed of were suddenly made real to him. Things of which he had never dreamed were gradually revealed.

It was a novel without a plot, and with only one character, being, indeed, simply a psychological study of a certain young Parisian, who spent his life trying to realise in the nineteenth century all the passions and modes of thought that belonged to every century except his own, and to sum up, as it were, in himself the various moods through which the world-spirit had ever passed, loving for their mere artificiality those renunciations that men have unwisely called virtue, as much as those natural rebellions that wise men still call sin. The style in which it was written was that curious jewelled style, vivid and obscure at once, full of argot and of archaisms, of technical expressions and of elaborate paraphrases, that characterises the work of some of the finest artists of the French school of *Symbolistes*. There were in it metaphors as monstrous as orchids, and as subtle in colour. The life of the senses was described in the terms of mystical philosophy. One hardly knew at times whether one was reading the spiritual ecstasies of some mediaeval saint or the morbid confessions of a modern sinner. It was a poisonous book. They heavy odour of incense seemed to cling about its pages and to trouble the brain. The mere cadence of the sentences, the subtle monotony of their music, so full as it was of complex refrains and movements elaborately repeated, produced in the mind of the lad, as he passed from chapter to chapter, a form of reverie, a malady of dreaming, that made him unconscious of the falling day and creeping shadows.

Cloudless, and pierced by one solitary star, a copper-green sky gleamed through the windows. He read on by its wan light till he could read no more. Then, after his valet had reminded him several times of the lateness of the hour he got up, and, going into the next room, placed the book on the little Florentine table that always stood at his bedside, and began to dress for dinner.

It was almost nine o'clock before he reached the club, where he found Lord Henry sitting alone, in the morning-room, looking very much bored.

'I am so sorry, Harry,' he cried, 'but really it is entirely your fault. That book you sent me so fascinated me that I forgot how the time was going.'

'Yes: I thought you would like it,' replied his host, rising from his chair.

'I didn't say I liked it, Harry. I said it fascinated me. There is a great difference.'

'Ah, you have discovered that?' murmured Lord Henry. And they passed into the dining-room.

Henceforward, Dorian Gray is utterly under the influence of that book, emulating its young hero's pursuit of every possible sensation and experience. But unlike the Parisian, the passing years breed in Dorian Gray no fear of mirrors or polished surfaces in which he may see the reflection of his face; for although the name Dorian Gray comes to be associated in London society with one addicted to strange, secret vices, his face belies the rumours, never losing the slightest touch of its youthful beauty. Yet whenever he pays one of his compulsive visits to the locked room, he finds his portrait further changed:

The very sharpness of the contrast used to quicken his sense of pleasure. He grew more and more enamoured of his own beauty, more and more interested in the corruption of his own soul. He would examine with minute care, and sometimes with a monstrous and terrible delight, the hideous lines that seared the wrinkling forehead, or crawled around the heavy sensual mouth, wondering sometimes which were the more horrible, the signs of sin or the signs of age. He would place his white hands beside the coarse bloated hands of the picture, and smile. He mocked the misshapen body and the failing limbs.

His sensuous preoccupations include Roman Catholic ritual, music, perfumes, jewellery, materials, ecclesiastical vestments, embroideries, and many other costly and exotic items which he toys with for whole days upon end in his home. At the other extreme, his interests take him to the lowest dockside taverns and opium dens, and into the company of men and women of the most degraded kind.

Eighteen years pass in this way. On the ninth of November, the eve of his thirty-eighth birthday, Dorian Gray is making his way home on foot from Sir Henry's through a cold London fog when he encounters Basil Hallward, who tells him he is about to leave for Paris but had hoped for a word with Dorian first. They return to Dorian's house, where Hallward had called earlier and had waited for some time before telling the manservant he must leave to catch his train. Hallward's purpose is to make a last plea that Dorian should mend his ways while there is still time. He is talked about everywhere in connection with his mysterious loose-living, in addition to which numerous society scandals are attributed to him and several men and women of high family are said to have lost their reputations through him. Hallward asks Dorian to assure him that the worst of these stories are untrue, to cast off his dubious associates, and use his influence for good. Suddenly seizing a lamp from the table, Dorian rises and motions Hallward to follow him: 'You have chattered enough about corruption. Now you shall look on it face to face.'

He leads him to the locked schoolroom, holds up the lamp in front of the shrouded portrait and tears its covers away. As the artist recoils from the foul portrait, then moves closer to examine the signature and verify that it is in truth the transformation of the one he himself had painted, Dorian Gray watches him steadily, without emotion. But when Hallward begins to upbraid and lecture him, and to moralize, Dorian Gray suddenly experiences an uncontrollable feeling of hatred, picks up a knife lying nearby, and plunges it again and again into the back of his former friend's head. He feels no emotion. Returning to the library, he hides Hallward's coat and travelling bag. The artist had been shown out of the house earlier by Dorian's valet on his way to the station. No one had seen the two men return. For all anyone knows, Hallward is by now on the way to Paris and will not be missed for months.

After an excellent night's sleep Dorian Gray sends his servant with a letter to a Mr Alan Campbell, a scientist friend of his of five years earlier. Campbell comes at his summons, though with no friendship for the man who had caused his downfall. Dorian Gray politely requests him to dispose chemically of a dead body in the house. Campbell refuses, but it takes only the slightest reminder by Dorian of what he could do to the remains of Campbell's career to make him capitulate. He fetches his equipment from his house and locks himself away with the body. Several hours later he comes down again and Dorian Gray sees him to the door:

As soon as Campbell had left, he went upstairs. There was a horrible smell of nitric acid in the room. But the thing that had been sitting at the table was gone.

That same evening Dorian Gray attends a fashionable dinner-party and then goes to one of his dockside haunts, where he encounters one of his opium-addicted victims, a young man of good birth named Adrian Singleton. They are accosted by two women, one of whom addresses Dorian by the nickname 'Prince Charming'. The name reaches the ears of a sailor who is sprawled drowsily at one of the tables. He leaps to his feet, but Dorian has left the place. The sailor hurries after him through the drizzling rain and catches up with him, thrusting him back against a wall and raising a revolver to his face. He tells him he is James Vane, and that he has been searching for Dorian for years, with no clue to go on, in order to avenge his sister's death. After a moment of panic Dorian asks the man how long it is since his sister had died. The answer is eighteen years. Dorian invites the sailor to look at his face in the light of a near-by lamp: it is the face of a youth of twenty. James Vane lets him go; but one of the women from the bar-room had been watching. She swears to Vane that he had had at his mercy the same 'Prince Charming' who had ruined her, too, eighteen years earlier. Vane rushes after Dorian, but he has vanished.

A week later Dorian Gray is entertaining a shooting party at his country home, Selby Royal, when he sees a face watching him from outside a window: it is James Vane. He is afraid to leave the house for several days. During the shoot one of the guests, Sir Geoffrey Clouston, discharges both barrels of his gun and hears a cry of human pain. The dead body of a supposedly careless beater is found. When details of the man are brought to Dorian Gray he hurries to view the body. To his relief, it is James Vane's.

The experience of having so narrowly escaped retribution for his first great wrong, however, has shaken Dorian's composure, and he determines to reclaim himself before it is altogether too late. Alan Campbell has recently committed suicide, and there has been speculation about Basil Hallward's disappearance. Dorian's first attempt at reformation is clumsy. He had planned to take a village girl named Hetty away with him, but he now tells her that he has changed his mind. As Lord Henry laughingly points out when told of this, Dorian will merely have succeeded in breaking her heart. Nevertheless, Dorian insists that he has taken the first step on the road to redemption. Back at his London house, he goes anxiously to the schoolroom, hoping to find some slight softening in the putrefying features of his portrait. The only change he sees is a new look of cunning in the eyes, and a hypocritical curl to the lips.

Had it been merely vanity that had made him do his one good deed? Or the desire for a new sensation, as Lord Henry had hinted, with his mocking laugh? Or that passion to act a part that sometimes makes us do things finer than we are ourselves? Or, perhaps, all these? And why was the red stain larger than it had been? It seemed to have crept like a horrible disease over the wrinkled fingers. There was blood on the painted feet, as though the thing had dripped – blood even on the hand that had not held the knife. Confess? Did it mean that he was to confess? To give himself up, and be put to death? He laughed. He felt that the idea was monstrous. Besides, even if he did confess, who would believe him? There was no trace of the murdered man anywhere. Everything belonging to him had been destroyed. He himself had burned what had been below-stairs. The world would simply say that he was mad. They would shut him up if he persisted in his story. . . . Yet it was his duty to confess, to suffer public shame, and to make public atonement. There was a God who called upon men to tell their sins to earth as well as to heaven. Nothing that he could do would cleanse him till he had told his own sin. His sin? He shrugged his shoulders. The death of Basil Hallward seemed very little to him. He was thinking of Hetty Merton. For it was an unjust mirror, this mirror of his soul that he was looking at. Vanity? Curiosity? Hypocrisy? Had there been nothing more in his renunciation than that? There had been something more. At least he thought so. But who could tell? . . . No. There had been nothing more. Through vanity he had spared her. In hypocrisy he had worn the mask of goodness. For curiosity's sake he had tried the denial of self. He recognised that now.

Looking round, he sees the knife he had used to stab Basil Hallward. Picking it up, Dorian Gray stabs his portrait through.

Elsewhere in the house, and out in the street, people are startled by a terrible cry. A policeman rings the bell several times but there is no answer. Shortly after, three male servants creep upstairs from where the cry and a loud crash had come. They call at the school-room door: there is no answer. They try to force it: it will not yield. Eventually, they gain entry by way of the roof and a balcony window.

When they entered they found, hanging upon the wall, a splendid portrait of their master as they had last seen him, in all the wonder of his exquisite youth and beauty. Lying on the floor was a dead man, in evening dress, with a knife in his heart. He was withered, wrinkled, and loathsome of visage. It was not till they had examined the rings that they recognised who it was.

Essays

OSCAR WILDE's total achievement as an essayist numbers only a handful of pieces, though they add up to many thousands of words. To many people in his own time and since, these works, compounded from keen intellectual perception, characteristic paradox and epigram, impudent and original challenge to established canons of social and artistic belief and practice, and much sincerity of purpose, contain more to admire than do his 'entertainments'. 'The fact of a man being a poisoner is nothing against his prose,' he wrote in one of them ('Pen, Pencil and Poison'); but the fact of a man's being a *poseur* had, in his own case, proved very much to his prejudice in the eyes of many critics and members of the public, who believed him in consequence to be capable of nothing of worth. Many of these revised this opinion through the influence of one or more of the essays. An example is Arthur Symons, later one of Wilde's biographers, who declared in a contemporary review of the volume which contains several of the essays, *Intentions:* 'While he insists on producing his paradox, sometimes for no other reason than that it is a paradox, and would rather say something that is clever than something that is merely true, it is surprising how often he contrives to illustrate a mathematical figure by an intellectual somersault, and how often he succeeds in combining truth and cleverness. After achieving a reputation by doing nothing, he is in a fair way to beat his own record by real achievements.'

The essays have been particularly admired in countries where the arts are regarded more earnestly than they are in Great Britain, and it is very much owing to them that Wilde enjoys so high a reputation on the Continent. I am not going to quote from them. An essay is a developing argument, starting from a proposition, from which it strays repeatedly into intriguing byways, returning again and again to the original theme: at least, this is the kind of essay Oscar Wilde wrote, and wrote at quite considerable length. Nothing would be gained by fragmenting what he had to say; to lift a few epigrams from each would in no way reflect the whole. Suffice it to say that, like so many of his works, the essays are highly revelatory of Wilde's own attitude and conversation. I have included *De Profundis* amongst them, on the grounds that, although written as a letter, it is in essence an essay.

The volume *Intentions* was published in July 1891 in London by Osgood, McIlvaine & Co, with simultaneous distribution of part of the edition in the U.S.A. by Dodd, Mead & Co. The consensus of critical opinion on both sides of the Atlantic was of surprised favour, and sales were good. All the essays in it had previously appeared in periodicals, details of which accompany the brief summaries below.

'The Truth of Masks: A Note on Illusion' (originally entitled 'Shakespeare and Stage Costume', published in the *Nineteenth Century*, May 1885). An attack upon those theatre critics who had denounced the vogue for staging Shakespeare's plays with elaborate and correct detail of costuming and setting. Wilde argues that Shakespeare deliberately used costume to heighten his dramatic effects and to emphasize the personal traits and circumstances of his characters.

'The Decay of Lying: An Observation' (*Nineteenth Century*, January 1889). In 'The Truth of Masks' Wilde had remarked, 'Truth is independent of facts always, inventing or selecting them at pleasure.' Now he expands this notion, criticizing the passion for fact in preference to imagination, as Dickens had in his novel *Hard Times* (1854). The essay is presented in the form of a duologue between two men, Cyril and Vivian, discoursing lazily in the library of a country house. Vivian was recognizable to his contemporaries as pure Wilde.

'Pen, Pencil and Poison: A Study in Green' (*Fortnightly Review*, January 1889) is a biographical sketch of Thomas Griffiths Wainewright (1794–1852), essayist, artist and poisoner, a man of varied but mediocre talents who was the friend of many of the leading literary figures of his time, poisoned an unknown number of people, but in the event could be convicted of no more than forgery. He was transported to Tasmania, where he resumed his career as both artist and poisoner. Charles Dickens, who knew him, based the character of Slinkton in the story 'Hunted Down' (1859) on him. Several facets of Wainewright clearly appealed to Wilde and are discernible in 'Lord Arthur Savile's Crime' and *The Picture of Dorian Gray*.

'The Critic as Artist': Part One, 'With some remarks upon the importance of doing nothing'; Part Two, 'With some remarks upon the importance of discussing everything' (*Nineteenth Century*, July & September 1890). Wilde advances the view that criticism is an art in itself, and that the critic is wholly justified in using his notice as a vehicle for autobiography and general comment and opinion not necessarily related to the subject he is ostensibly reviewing. He dilates upon the role of criticism as the catalyst responsible for the emergence of Culture from Art and Life. This long, two-part essay is in the form of a duologue between 'Gilbert' (Wilde) and a younger man, 'Ernest', as they smoke cigarettes one night in the library of a London house.

Intentions was the only volume of collected essays Wilde published. It might have included two more. 'The Portrait of Mr. W. H.' had appeared in *Blackwood's Magazine* in July 1889, but Wilde, wishing to expand the theme, re-wrote the piece to something like twice its original length, enough to make a small book. It was accepted in this form by Elkin Mathews & John Lane, London, and advertised, but the publishing partnership broke up before it could be produced. Wilde was writing aggrieved letters about it in the autumn of 1894; by the following spring he was in prison, with the work still unpublished. The manuscript disappeared, not to be found again until long after Wilde's death, and its first publication in its entirety was by Mitchell Kennerley, New York, in 1921, in a limited edition, a few copies of which were distributed in England by Duckworth & Co. The first properly commercial edition was published by Methuen, London, in 1958, edited by Wilde's then surviving son, Vyvyan Holland.

'The Portrait of Mr. W. H.' is a circumstantially argued suggestion that the 'onlie begetter' of Shakespeare's Sonnets, 'Mr W. H.', whose identity has been the subject of so much conjecture, had in fact been a beautiful boy actor, Willie Hughes, for whom Shakespeare had entertained a deep passion and had created his leading female roles. Wilde couches his theory in the form of a short story, which conveniently enables him to leave his reader either to accept or dismiss it, or to assume that it was never intended for anything more than an ingenious piece of academic by-play. The last is the general opinion.

The other essay Wilde excluded from *Intentions* was 'The Soul of Man under Socialism', which had appeared in the *Fortnightly Review* in February 1891. It was eventually produced as a small volume, in a limited edition, by Arthur L. Humphreys, London, in 1895. If it is surprising to find the luxury-loving Wilde, social climber and eager mover in fashionable London society, propounding the ideal of a socialist Utopia, it has to be remembered, on the one hand, that he delighted in astonishing his friends and confounding his enemies, and on the other, that his heart seems to have been capable of feeling genuine compassion for the poor and the put-upon, as he showed particularly in some of his fairy tales. 'The Soul of Man under Socialism' cannot have endeared him afresh to the rich people who loved to entertain him in order to be entertained by him, and it is doubtful whether many poor people ever read it. It thrusts, sometimes almost savagely, at those who exploit the poor, are indifferent to them, or produce the wrong effects by well-meant efforts to help them. It approves agitation and protest and many other features which, in our own time, have become familiar as youthful forms of rebellion against established conventions. But once more it is the supreme importance of art and culture in life that provides the dominant theme in what Wilde is saying.

The publication in 1905, five years after his death, of *De Profundis* began the rehabilitation of Oscar Wilde's personal and literary reputation, and gave powerful impetus to the cult of him as the great homosexual martyr to English philistinism. Published by Methuen, London, and Putnam in America, it went through no fewer than twenty-eight and sixteen substantial editions respectively before the outbreak of the First World War. It was widely translated into the languages of Europe, where it was hailed as a masterpiece and is still regarded as one of the great works of English literature.

But this work, so loudly acclaimed, was, in point of fact, less than half the original: the full version did not appear until 1962, when the present Sir Rupert Hart-Davis printed it in its proper chronological place in *The Letters of Oscar Wilde* (Hart-Davis, London), appending a note about its interesting history. Wilde had written it in Reading Gaol, during the months January–March 1897, as a letter to Lord Alfred Douglas. It was many thousands of words long and bore the title *Epistola: In Carcere et Vinculis*. An application to the Prison Commissioners to allow it to be posted was turned down and it was retained by the prison governor and handed to Wilde on his release on 19 May that year. When Wilde reached Dieppe the following morning he gave the letter to the waiting Robert Ross, who had already been instructed to have a number of typewritten copies made for distribution to various people who 'will be interested to know something of what is happening to my soul—not in the theological sense, but merely in the sense of the spiritual consciousness that is separate from the actual occupations of the body', after which the original was to be sent to Douglas. What actually happened seems to be that Ross made a heavily edited version, of which he had two copies typed: he kept one himself and sent the other to Douglas (who, Rupert Hart-Davis notes, always denied having received it). This was the version published in 1905 under the title Ross had given it, *De Profundis*.

Four years after this publication, Ross gave the manuscript to the British Museum, on condition that no one be allowed to see it for fifty years. When Rupert Hart-Davis was eventually able to examine it he found that even the slightly fuller version which had been included in the 1908 Collected Edition of Wilde's works still represented only a portion of the original, and was replete with alterations and errors. The first complete and accurate version to have appeared, then, is that in Hart-Davis's own book in 1962.

In a letter referring to the 1905 version of *De Profundis*, George Bernard Shaw, who had met Wilde several times but found it only possible to chat with him on a jocular, superficial level, showed that he had discerned enough of his fellow Irishman's character to know that *De Profundis* was, in essence, a hypocritical work, and went so far as to find in it 'no real tragedy, all comedy'. This is characteristic Shavian exaggeration about a work which has moved and impressed many other people, eminent and ordinary. But Shaw was at least partly correct. *De Profundis* contains some fine writing, but a great deal of self-pity, jealous spite and maudlin theatricality. It is Wilde's account of his humiliation as a prisoner and a victim of society; it is a bitter attack on Alfred Douglas as the incubus (or succubus!) whose demands had ruined him financially, prevented him from working, and brought about his downfall; and it is a rambling exposition of the nobility of suffering, in which Wilde identifies himself, too closely for comfort, with Christ. He defiantly asserts that his fidelity to his principles will not let him change his ways, once he is out of prison.

There is no doubt that Oscar Wilde did undergo dreadful mental suffering in prison – what man of his intelligence and background would not? – and some of the more hysterical-sounding passages of the work may be ascribed to this and to genuinely-felt grievances against Douglas, Queensberry and society in general. But there is also the impression of an actor playing the hysterical martyr to art and 'the Love that dare not speak its name'. At times he is carried away by his melodrama, and acts like a demon, oblivious to everything else. Mostly, he is himself, demonstrating what he is and always will be, a wilful youth, incapable of growing up and never wishing to do so.

Plays

VERA

or

The Nihilists

(Prologue and Four Acts)

NIHILISM, as the growing revolutionary movement in imperialist Russia was first known, was much in the news in the 1870–80s; so, for very different reasons, was Oscar Wilde. In the autumn of 1880 these two elements fused into the form of a play, *Vera: or, The Nihilists*, which Wilde had written that year. He published a handful of copies privately and distributed most of them amongst actresses of note, including Ellen Terry, in the hope that they would recognize a role worthy of them. When, in March the following year, the Czar Alexander II was assassinated – the fate suffered by the Czar Ivan in the play – everything must have seemed set for an exciting theatrical event of great topicality, through which Wilde might strike back at his detractors with a major dramatic work upon a serious theme. He needed money badly, and no doubt saw this as his chance to get it in plenty.

London production was arranged for December 1881 at the Adelphi Theatre, with the up and coming Mrs Bernard Beere as Vera. It has been said that Wilde complained about some of the casting and withdrew the piece when the management opposed him. It is not easy to imagine a hard-up, first-time young dramatist with an assured West End production of a topical piece doing any such thing. The generally accepted story is that he withdrew it, perhaps at the request of his friend the Prince of Wales, because he did not wish to hurt the feelings of the British royal family – Queen Alexandra was sister-in-law to the new Czar's wife. Whatever the reason, the London presentation was cancelled.

In 1882, when he was in touch with the American actress Mary Anderson about his commission from her to write *The Duchess of Padua*, Wilde sent her a copy of *Vera*. She wrote back to say that she had found it charming and mournful, and thought she would like to play the part; but it was another American, Marie Prescott, who presented it and played *Vera* for the first time at the Union Square Theatre, New York, on 20 August 1883.

A timely theme, even when complemented by some notoriety in the dramatist, does not make a bad play a good one; and *Vera* was a bad play. It was no hostility to Wilde personally, no suspicion of his sincerity, no rejection of the socialistic sympathies of the piece that drove it off the stage for ever: the first-night audience packed the house, despite a midsummer heat which made the theatre almost intolerably uncomfortable, and gave Wilde an ovation after the second act. What killed *Vera* was its lack of dramatic technique, the implausibility of the characters, the stilted dialogue – and what the newspaper critics said of it: 'unreal, longwinded, and wearisome' (*New York Times*); 'clumsily constructed' (*New York Tribune*); 'long-drawn dramatic rot' (*New York Herald*).

Marie Prescott seems to have had some preliminary misgivings, at least to the extent of asking Wilde to cut out the comedy lines. He refused, and lectured her about the art of heightening dramatic effect by contrasting it with lighter scenes. Nevertheless, she wrote indignantly to the *New York Times*, claiming that 'prominent citizens' were protesting against the undeserved press criticisms. But the reviewers had not been wholly unkind: their general tone conveyed more regret than contempt. The *New York Mirror* went so far as to assail those members of the audience who had become rowdy during the later stages of the play for their inability to appreciate 'the nobility of character that prompted him to devote his remarkable talents to the development of a taste for all that is beautiful on earth', and termed *Vera* 'the noblest contribution to literature the stage has received in many years'.

Even so, the run of the play lasted only one week. It is said that, hoping to salvage something, Marie Prescott offered to tour the piece if Wilde would take the part of the cynical Prince Paul Maraloffski, the character who most reflects himself and utters the few epigrams which provide a thin leavening of humour and give a slight hint of the type of dramatist Wilde would become. But nothing came of her offer, and Wilde returned home without the much-needed fortune.

. . . .

Prologue

At his inn in Russia, Peter Sabouroff laments to a young peasant, Michael Stroganoff, that his son Dmitri has not written home for four months from Moscow, where he is studying law. A party of political prisoners on their way to Siberia is brought in by an escort of soldiers commanded by Colonel Kotemkin, who demands bread and water for the prisoners and good food and drink for himself. While the Colonel is out of the room having his meal, Sabouroff's daughter Vera asks the chained prisoners what crime they have committed and is answered by one who is trying to hide his face that they have spoken up for freedom from the oppression of the Czar. She recognizes the man as Dmitri and swears to avenge him.

First Act

Five years later, at No. 99 Tchernavaya, Moscow, the masked Nihilist conspirators are assembling. Presided over by Peter Tchernavitch, they recite a revolutionary oath and then unmask. One of them is seen to be Michael Stroganoff, who discloses that Vera, now notorious as a leader of their movement, is attending a masked ball at the Palace, in order to see the Czar 'and all his cursed brood' face to face. She arrives with the news that martial law, allowing citizens to be arrested and punished without trial, is to be proclaimed next day. The conspirators have twelve hours in which to attempt to forestall it.

VERA : O God, how easy it is for a king to kill his people by thousands, but we cannot rid ourselves of one crowned man in Europe! What

is there of awful majesty in these men which makes the hand un-
steady, the dagger treacherous, the pistol-shot harmless? Are they
not men of like passions with ourselves, vulnerable to the same
diseases, of flesh and blood not different from our own? What made
Olgiati tremble at the supreme crisis of that Roman life, and Guido's
nerve fail him when he should have been of iron and steel? A plague,
I say, on these fools of Naples, Berlin, and Spain! Methinks that if I
stood face to face with one of the crowned men my eye would see
more clearly, my aim be more sure, my whole body gain a strength
and power that was not my own! Oh, to think what stands between
us and freedom in Europe! a few old men, wrinkled, feeble, tot-
tering dotards whom a boy could strangle for a ducat, or a woman
stab in a night-time. These are the things that keep us from liberty.
But now methinks the brood of men is dead and the dull earth grown
sick of childbearing, else would no crowned dog pollute God's air
by living.

While the President and some of the others are conferring, Vera
catches sight of the young medical student Alexis Ivanacievitch,
who has shown himself one of their most dedicated members. He
declares that he will personally plead with the Czar for the repeal of
the decree of martial law. A few moments later he is denounced by
Michael Stroganoff as a spy in their midst. Michael has had his
suspicions for some time and had followed Alexis after their last
meeting. He had seen him take a roundabout route to the Palace
itself and enter with a private key. He had watched all night, but
Alexis had not reappeared.

The conspirators draw their knives. Vera begs Alexis to repudi-
ate what Michael has said. Instead, he confirms it, though denying
that he is a spy. The conspirators press forward, but Vera shields
Alexis with her body and tells them they will have to kill her first.
As they hesitate, a voice outside commands them to open the
door. Clapping on their masks, they admit a party of soldiers, led
by Kotemkin, now a General. It is illegal for more than five people
to meet privately, and the uproar following Michael's accusations
had attracted attention. Vera protests that they are a party of
innocent strolling players in mid-rehearsal for a new tragedy.
Missing the honest irony, Kotemkin orders her to unmask.

Alexis tells him to stand back and removes his own mask. Kotemkin recoils in recognition: His Imperial Highness the Czarevitch!

The conspirators are convinced all is over, when to their astonishment they hear Alexis supporting Vera's story by saying that it is a whim of his to wander incognito about the city in search of romantic adventure, and this is how he had come to fall in with these honest actors. He even risks some banter with the General about the notorious Vera Sabouroff; Kotemkin claims that once he nearly caught her, and with a last, now jocular, effort to get a look at Vera's face, he takes his soldiers away.

VERA: Saved! and by you!
ALEXIS: Brothers, you trust me now?

Second Act

In the palace next day the Czarevitch and members of the Cabinet are awaiting the arrival of the Czar for their meeting to begin. They indulge in spiteful bickering, in which the Prime Minister, Prince Paul Maraloffski, whose wit has a keener edge than the others', generally proves superior.

PRINCE PAUL: When you are as old as I am, Prince, you will understand that there are few things easier than to live badly and to die well.
CZAREVITCH: Easy to die well! A lesson experience cannot have taught you, much as you know of a bad life.
PRINCE PAUL: Experience, the name men give to their mistakes. I never commit any.

The Czarevitch accuses him of having poisoned the Czar's mind against his people and made him the tyrant he has become: Prince Paul admits his enjoyment of being the most hated man in Russia. The Czar enters, closely guarded and suspicious that everyone except Prince Paul is a secret enemy. It is his own son who protests vehemently at the harshness and injustice of the laws and, as he promised Vera, begs for mercy on the people.

CZAR: The people! the people! A tiger which I have let loose on myself; but I will fight with it to the death. I am done with half measures. I shall crush these Nihilists at a blow. There shall not be a man of

them, no, nor a woman either, left alive in Russia. Am I Emperor for
nothing, that a woman should hold me at bay? Vera Sabouroff shall
be in my power, I swear it, before a week is ended, though I burn my
whole city to find her. She shall be flogged by the knot, stifled in
the fortress, strangled in the square!

Prince Paul undertakes to crush every Nihilist in Russia if the
Czar will sign the proclamation of martial law. This spurs the
Czarevitch to even more impassioned denunciations and pleas,
culminating in his admission that he is a Nihilist himself. The
Czar orders his arrest and declares himself henceforward at war
with his people. He strides to the balcony and flings the window
open. A shot rings out from below, and the Czar staggers back,
mortally wounded.

Third Act

Three days later the Nihilists receive an unexpected visitor –
Prince Paul. The Czarevitch, now become Czar Alexis, has lost no
time in stripping his father's evil genius of his office and estates and
ordering his banishment to Paris. Prince Paul hopes to regain
power by supporting the revolution, although he does not say as
much: 'As I cannot be a Prime Minister, I must be a Nihilist.
There is no alternative.'

Michael Stroganoff enters and is hailed as the hero who killed
the Czar. The conspirators sit down to hold their council, but one
of them is missing: Alexis, now the Czar. Vera has been watching
anxiously for him to arrive, certain that he will not let them down.
But in any case, Article 7 of the Code of Revolution declares that
'Between the Nihilists and all men who wear crowns above their
fellows, there is war to the death'. Alexis is sentenced to die that
very night. Vera alone pleads for the Czar, asking them to give
him time to prove himself the enlightened ruler he has promised
to be. It is Michael who reminds her of her brother Dmitri in
chains, and of her vow of vengeance which had brought her to
Moscow, leaving her old father to die alone and broken-hearted.
He tells her that love for Alexis as a man is undermining her
resolution; Alexis, as the son of his father, would merely have

seduced her and then cast her off. Vera needs no further urging. The lots for assassin are cast and she eagerly hopes that she will draw the fatal one. She does so.

Vera is given a plan of the palace and a key to a private door, thoughtfully brought by Prince Paul. She is given the choice of a dagger or a vial of poison and she chooses the former. The plan is that the rest of the conspirators are to wait outside the palace, and as midnight strikes she will throw down to them the blood-stained dagger as proof of her success. If she does not, they will know she has been seized and will burst in, rescue her and kill the Czar. Vera, thoroughly roused, adds the last touches to her self-conviction.

VERA: To-night this new-fledged Czar shall post with bloody feet to hell, and greet his father there! This Czar! O traitor, liar, false to his oath, false to me! To play the patriot among us, and now to wear a crown; to sell us, like Judas, for thirty silver pieces, to betray us with a kiss! O Liberty, O mighty mother of eternal time, thy robe is purple with the blood of those who have died for thee! Thy throne is the Calvary of the people, thy crown the crown of thorns. O crucified mother, the despot has driven a nail through thy right hand, and the tyrant through thy left! Thy feet are pierced with their iron. When thou wert athirst thou calledst on the priests for water, and they gave thee bitter drink. They thrust a sword into thy side. They mocked thee in thine agony of age on age. Here, on thy altar, O Liberty, do I dedicate myself to thy service; do with me as thou wilt! The end has come now, and by thy sacred wounds, O crucified mother, O Liberty, I swear that Russia shall be saved!

Fourth Act

That night the Czar's ministers are bewailing their master's liberalism which is cutting sharply into their own purses and privileges. The Czar enters in time to overhear an insulting reference to himself and orders them to leave the country instantly. Left alone, he has a little time to think about his dilemma in having to wear an unwanted crown. The Colonel of the Guard comes in for orders: the Czar tells him he has no need of the customary cordon round the palace. His Page, too, tells Alexis that his father had never dared to sleep unattended, and begs him to let him remain in the room as usual, for he has a presentiment of danger. The Czar dismisses him. He has made up his mind to sneak out to see Vera.

It proves unnecessary, for as soon as the Page has gone and the Czar has lain down and fallen asleep, Vera enters, cloaked and daggered. She is just raising the knife to strike when the Czar awakes and, not seeing the weapon, fervently tells her of his good intentions towards the people, and how he has ordered her brother's release, and that he wants to make her his Empress, and other reassuring particulars. Vera tries to quell her true feelings, but cannot:

VERA : To strangle whatever nature is in me, neither to love nor to be loved, neither to pity nor – Oh, I am a woman! God help me, I am a woman! O Alexis! I too have broken my oath; I am a traitor. I love. Oh, do not speak, do not speak – (*kisses his lips*) – the first, the last time.

He holds her in his arms. Midnight strikes and Vera hears her comrades' voices from the street. Breaking away from Alexis, she stabs herself. He disarms her and would die with her, but she begs him to live for his country's sake, seizes back the knife and throws it out of the window to mislead the conspirators into believing that her mission is accomplished.

CZAR : What have you done?
VERA : I have saved Russia! (*Dies.*)

THE DUCHESS OF PADUA
(Five Acts)

DURING his American lecture tour in 1882 Oscar Wilde met the beautiful actress Mary Anderson, who some years later distinguished herself at Stratford-on-Avon and settled in England. He told her in detail of his idea for a tragedy in blank verse, set in 16th-century Italy, *The Duchess of Padua*. Although he averred later in life that he had never written anything with a specific player in mind, he told Mary Anderson, 'I want you to rank with the great actresses of the earth. I desire your triumph to be for all time and not for the day merely, and having in you a faith which is as flawless as it is fervent I doubt not for a moment that I can and will write for you a play which, created for you, and inspired by you, shall give you the glory of a Rachel, and may yield me the fame of a Hugo.'

Recognizing the dramatic and poetic possibilities of the theme and the role he was offering her, Mary Anderson commissioned him to write the piece, with a payment of one thousand dollars down and the promise of a further four thousand 'on acceptance'. This spurred him on, and by March the following year, back in London and much in need of money again, he was able to post off the completed piece. He waited only a few days before following it with a long, self-enthusiastic description of its elements and characters, adding that he had made drawings for both scenery and costume. Before going into such detail, though, he would await her telegraphed decision.

The answer, when it came, was not the one he sought. 'This is rather tedious, Robert,' is the comment recorded by Robert Ross, who was with him when the rejection arrived. It was more than tedious: it was a considerable blow to Wilde's finances and morale. Hesketh Pearson expresses the view that Mary Anderson should in any case have sent Wilde the balance of his money; but this possibility had been firmly excluded by her manager and stepfather, Hamilton Griffin, when terms were being agreed, and she was under no moral obligation to be philanthropic.

Another transatlantic possibility remained. While the piece was being written, the American actor-manager Lawrence Barrett had also bid for it, with what Wilde had told Mary Anderson was 'a very large offer', and he now sent it to him. Barrett accepted it, though it is doubtful whether the terms were overly generous. He did not present the play until 26 January 1891, at the Broadway Theatre, New York, with himself playing Guido and Minna K. Gale as Beatrice. Its title had been changed by Barrett to *Guido Ferranti* and the author's name was not shown. This was at Wilde's wish, because he was 'anxious to have the play judged entirely on its own merits'. It was generally known, however, who the author was; and no doubt the truth is that in the eight years since Wilde had completed the play he had come to have doubts about its quality, and preferred to watch in semi-anonymity and gauge the critical and commercial verdict before stepping forward for acclaim or beating a retreat.

Hearing from Barrett by telegram that he had achieved a big success, he let his name be publicized. But the play received only a few performances, mostly to poor houses, despite what the *New York Daily Tribune* termed the 'deep interest' of the first-night audience, who rewarded it with 'earnest applause' at 'certain telling points'. The reviewer acknowledged that the play was 'deftly constructed in five short acts, and is written in a strain of blank verse that is always melodious, often eloquent, and sometimes freighted with fanciful figures of rare beauty.' But he added that it was less tragedy than melodrama: 'The radical defect of the work is insincerity. No one in it is natural.'

For the *New York Times* critic, however, the most praiseworthy quality of the play was the dramatist's evident sincerity of purpose: 'There are a number of well-imagined and skilfully-wrought scenes in his play, and many passages that must have been written in a glow of excitement. If this poet was not inspired, he at least tried very hard to be, and certainly thought he was.' Like his colleague, the reviewer admired the melody of the verse and defended the plot in advance against the inevitable charge of improbability.

This was indeed faint praise. The piece enjoyed a further brief life in America later that year, when Minna K. Gale, the original Duchess, took it out with her touring company, opening in Philadelphia on 31 August. But it was only one of several pieces in her repertoire, and the least frequently played. In the last years of his life, when it was suggested that he might publish the play in the hope of raising a little sorely-needed cash, Wilde replied, 'The *Duchess* is unfit for publication – the only one of my works that comes under that category.' He had published a very few copies privately in 1883.

During the first American run, Wilde had written to Henry Irving, who had read the script, suggesting that he present it in London, if only for one performance, so as to gauge public response. Nothing came of this. *The Duchess of Padua* was given one performance at the St. James's Theatre on 18 March 1907, some seven years after Wilde's death, in order to establish copyright. A German version by Max Meyerfeld had been tried in Hamburg and Berlin some years after Wilde's death, but the enthusiasm for Oscar Wilde's work which has always been evident in Germany was not extended to this play.

· · · ·

First Act

It is noon in the market place of Padua in the early 16th century. The bell of the Santa Croce Cathedral is ringing and people are entering for service. Into the square come two weary young men, Guido Ferranti and Ascanio Cristofano, strangers from Perugia. Guido has been summoned to Padua by a letter from someone signing himself merely 'Your Father's Friend' who promises to reveal the secret of Guido's birth: he had been brought up by a supposed uncle after his unknown father's disappearance. There is no sign of this stranger, who has said he will be recognizable by his violet cloak with a silver falcon embroidered on the shoulder, and Ascanio is impatient to find the nearest tavern, for he is 'as hungry as a widow is for a husband, as tired as a young maid is of good advice, and as dry as a monk's sermon'. But just as Guido is about to go with him he is approached by Count Moranzone, an old man dressed as described in the letter, who detains Guido but sends Ascanio away. (It is with Moranzone's entrance that the dialogue changes from prose to blank verse.)

Moranzone astounds Guido by telling him that his father had been the great Duke Lorenzo, Prince of Parma, a valiant soldier who had been captured and ignominiously executed by Giovanni Malatesta, Lord of Rimini. His capture had been brought about by the treachery of a close friend, who had been enriched as his reward. He still lives; and as the only one of Lorenzo's followers still surviving, Moranzone, at length, has felt it his duty to inform Guido of the facts and steer him towards vengeance. Guido must send away his dear friend Ascanio and must enter the service of the man he is to kill. When he has suitably ingratiated himself with his victim he will receive from Moranzone his father's own dagger with which to do the deed. Guido is all for taking his revenge forthwith, but Moranzone convinces him that a measure of betrayal is necessary to achieve exact retribution, and he must curb his impatience. Guido asks the name of the man he is to befriend and then kill. Moranzone indicates a group of approaching men – the Duke of Padua and gentlemen of his court – and tells Guido that the one to whom he kneels in greeting is the marked man. He kneels to the Duke.

Moranzone introduces Guido as his nephew from Mantua who is anxious to serve the Duke. The Duke seems to see something familiar in Guido's eyes, but he takes him on readily enough and offers him some cynical advice about the way to get on in the world, based on his own experience:

DUKE: Be not honest: eccentricity
      Is not a thing should ever be encouraged,
      Although, in this dull stupid age of ours,
      The most eccentric thing a man can do
      Is to have brains, then the mob mocks at him;

> And for the mob, despise it as I do,
> I hold its bubble praise and windy favours
> In such account, that popularity
> Is the one insult I have never suffered.

He gives Guido his hand to kiss, and after hesitating with repugnance the young man does so. The Duke and his party move on, and Ascanio returns, to find Guido unaccountably sending him away from him for ever, with the words 'My whole past was but a schoolboy's dream, To-day my life begins.' Satisfied, Moranzone goes, too. Guido soliloquizes to his Maker:

GUIDO: Listen, thou terrible God!
> Thou God that punishest all broken oaths,
> And bid some angel write this oath in fire,
> That from this hour, till my dear father's murder
> In blood I have revenged, I do forswear
> The noble ties of honourable friendship,
> The noble joys of dear companionship,
> Affection's bonds, and loyal gratitude,
> Ay, more, from this same hour I do forswear
> All love of women, and the barren thing
> Which men call beauty. . .

His resolution lasts little more than a minute. The Cathedral organ peals and four pages in scarlet come down the steps, bearing a canopy under which walks an entrancing, richly-clad woman. Her eyes and Guido's meet, and as she leaves the market place he sees her glance back at him. 'Oh! who is that?' he cries. A passer-by answers: 'The Duchess of Padua!'

Second Act

Time has passed, and Guido has become the Duke's favourite. That the Duke himself is no one's favourite is attested by the cries for his blood audible from the luxuriously-decorated State Room in his palace, where one of his courtiers tells him there is a crowd of two thousand angry people in the square below. The Duke casually gives orders for their dispersal:

DUKE: I fear
      They have become a little out of tune,
      So I must tell my men to fire on them,
      I cannot bear bad music!

To his annoyance, his Duchess, Beatrice, whom he has long despised for her goodness, is seen preventing the soldiers from shooting. She enters the room at the head of a group of ragged supplicants and proceeds to plead their case for better food and water and less taxation:

DUCHESS: They say the bread, the very bread they eat,
               Is made of sorry chaff.
FIRST CITIZEN: Ay! so it is,
               Nothing but chaff.
DUKE: And very good food too,
               I give it to my horses.
DUCHESS: They say the water,
               Set in the public cisterns for their use,
               Has, through the breaking of the aqueduct,
               To stagnant pools and muddy puddles turned.
DUKE: They should drink wine; water is quite
               unwholesome.
SECOND CITIZEN: Alack, Your Grace, the taxes which the customs
               Take at the city gate are grown so high
               We cannot buy wine.
DUKE: Then you should bless the taxes
               Which make you temperate.

Declaring himself the foe of common men, the Duke gets rid of the unwelcome deputation and upbraids Beatrice with anger and scorn. He goes out on Guido's arm, leaving the Duchess to muse upon the anomaly of one so seemingly good-natured as the young courtier being the inseparable friend of her loathsome husband. A few moments later Guido re-enters and cuts short her sarcastic greeting with an avowal of lifelong service to her, and then, more startlingly, a declaration of love, which she soon returns with matching fervour. As they are embracing, Beatrice catches sight of Moranzone watching from the doorway. He disappears before Guido can see him, but a little later a servant interrupts them with a small silk-wrapped package for Guido. Beatrice snatches it girlishly from him, pretending that it is a present from some other woman. She opens it and finds a dagger, decorated with two leopards. Handing it to Guido, she runs off gaily to try to see the livery of the messenger who must have brought it to the palace. Guido stares at the dagger, Moranzone's signal that the time for revenge has come; and when Beatrice returns she finds her lover a changed man, telling her that a barrier has arisen between them that can never be surmounted. She reasons and pleads with him, but he is immovable.

GUIDO: I pray you speak no more, for I must go
           Forth from your life and love, and make a way
           On which you cannot follow.
DUCHESS: I have heard
           That sailors dying of thirst upon a raft,
           Poor castaways upon a lonely sea,
           Dream of green fields and pleasant water-courses,
           And then wake up with red thirst in their throats,
           And die more miserably because sleep
           Has cheated them: so they die cursing sleep
           For having sent them dreams; I will not curse you
           Though I am cast away upon the sea
           Which men call Desolation.

He leaves her and she resolves to kill herself that night. She sees Moranzone, accuses him of having separated Guido from her, and begs that he will give him back. He replies coldly that Guido does not love her and that she will never see him again. Her last hope is gone.

DUCHESS: 'Tis true men hate thee, Death, and yet I think
           Thou wilt be kinder to me than my lover,
           And so dispatch the messengers at once,
           Hurry the lazy steeds of lingering day,
           And let the night, thy sister, come instead,
           And drape the world in mourning; let the owl,
           Who is thy minister, scream from his tower

And wake the toad with hooting, and the bat,
That is the slave of dim Persephone,
Wheel through the sombre air on wandering wing!
Tear up the shrieking mandrakes from the earth
And bid them make us music, and tell the mole
To dig deep down thy cold and narrow bed,
For I shall lie within thine arms to-night.

Third Act

That night a storm is rising as Guido enters one of the palace corridors by the window, having reached it by rope ladder. He finds Moranzone sitting masked at the foot of a curtained staircase leading to the Duke's chamber. The Count tells him he has horses ready to carry them both to Parma as soon as the deed is done. The citizens there have been prepared to support their former prince's son in overthrowing the forces of Padua, so that Guido may assume his rightful place as ruler. To Moranzone's astonishment Guido tells him that he has changed his mind: he is not going to kill the Duke, but proposes to lay the dagger on his breast as he sleeps, together with a piece of paper, from which the Duke will read when he awakes who it was had him at his mercy, and spared him. If Moranzone had let him kill the Duke when he first set eyes on him and his blood was hot from what he had just been told, Guido says, he would have done it gladly; to murder in cold blood is a different matter. Moranzone sees a different reason for this softening of the heart:

MORANZONE: You have sworn an oath,
　　　　　　　See that you keep that oath.
　　　　　　　Boy, do you think I do not know your secret,
　　　　　　　Your traffic with the Duchess?
GUIDO:　　　　Silence, liar!
　　　　　　　The very moon in heaven is not more chaste,
　　　　　　　Nor the white stars so pure.
MORANZONE: And yet, you love her;
　　　　　　　Weak fool, to let love in upon your life,
　　　　　　　Save as a plaything.

A groan is heard from the Duke's room, and then another. They put them down to imagination. Moranzone makes a last appeal to Guido to take his revenge, is refused, and leaves the window by the ladder. Guido kneels to ask his father's spirit to manifest itself and confirm that he has acted rightly; but it does not. He gets out his dagger and the letter and is about to draw the stair-curtain, when Beatrice comes through, dressed all in white. To her joy, she hears him telling her that the barrier between them is gone and that he loves her with a love that will never again be swayed. He asks her to wait a moment while he carries out his errand in the Duke's chamber, so that when he wakes . . .

DUCHESS: When who wakes?
GUIDO: Why, the Duke.
DUCHESS: He will not wake again.
GUIDO: What, is he dead?
DUCHESS: Ay! he is dead.
GUIDO: O God! how wonderful
         Are all Thy secret ways! Who would have said
         That on this very night, when I had yielded
         Into Thy hands the vengeance that is Thine,
         Thou with Thy finger should have touched the man,
         And bade him come before Thy judgment seat.
DUCHESS: I have just killed him.

She tells her horrified lover how, intending to kill herself, she had suddenly seen the sleeping Duke as the barrier of which Guido had spoken, and had stabbed him to death. She shows Guido the bloodstained knife, and reaches out one of her bloody hands to touch him. He recoils. She replies, reasonably enough, that she did it for him; but he is by now picturing a new barrier between them: a barrier of blood, murder and sin. They could now never live together with Heaven's blessing. She pleads, reasons, and finally tells him that, if he had done murder, even without love for its motive, she would have helped him to bear his burden of guilt.

GUIDO: There is no love where there is any guilt.
DUCHESS: No love where there is any guilt! O God,
         How differently do we love from men!

Guido will not relent. He orders her away; but no sooner has she gone sadly through the curtain than he is calling her back to change his mind. It is too late. There is a clamour of men's voices, and Beatrice is heard crying, 'This way went he, the man who slew my lord.' Soldiers bearing torches rush down the staircase and seize Guido. Beatrice's blood-stained dagger, still in his hand, is seized and shown to the Captain of the Guard.

Fourth Act

Next day, in the Court of Justice, a group of citizens wait for Guido's trial to begin. Moranzone arrives hurriedly and asks them the accused's name. He is surprised to hear it, having last left Guido determined not to commit the murder, and when he hears that the killing has been done with a dagger belonging to the Duchess, who then gave Guido away to the guards, he becomes deeply suspicious. The Lord Justice and other Judges enter, followed by Guido, the Headsman, the Duchess, the Cardinal and gentlemen of the court. Guido is charged and refuses to plead. The Lord Justice prepares to pass sentence of death on him, but is interrupted by Moranzone, who tries to persuade Guido to tell the truth. When he refuses, Moranzone threatens to indict the Duchess himself, so Guido agrees to speak. But he has barely begun before the Duchess protests that he has no right to do so. The Lord Justice assures her that he has legal right, but she waves the statute book aside:

DUCHESS: This is no common murderer, Lord Justice,
           But a great outlaw, and a most vile traitor,
           Taken in open arms against the state.
           For he who slays the man who rules a state
           Slays the state also, widows every wife,
           And makes each child an orphan, and no less
           Is to be held a public enemy,
           Than if he came with mighty ordonnance,
           And all the spears of Venice at his back,
           To beat and batter at our city gates.

The implication of treachery gives the Judges second thoughts about Guido's rights. They retire to confer. Guido appeals to the Cardinal to intercede for him, but the Cardinal says he has no power. The Judges return to announce their decision that Guido has no right to speak; but as the Duchess is thanking them with relief, they add that the accused, not being a Paduan by birth, must be heard, as a courtesy due to an alien. The Duchess angrily rips the relevant page out of the statute book and calls for a horse to carry her to Venice. The Lord Justice politely tells her that she may not leave the court until the trial is ended. When she attempts to defy him the court doors are closed, and the Lord Justice takes up a time-glass and tells Guido that he may speak until the sand has all run through. Guido reveals his identity and tells of his mission of revenge against the late Duke, of how he had entered the castle the previous night, and had seen . . .

GUIDO:	. . . The man I hated, cursing in his sleep,
	And thinking of a most dear father murdered,
	Sold to the scaffold, bartered to the block,
	I smote the treacherous villian to the heart
	With this same dagger, which by chance I found
	Within the chamber.
DUCHESS:	Oh!
GUIDO:	I killed the Duke.
	Now, my Lord Justice, if I may crave a boon,
	Suffer me not to see another sun
	Light up the misery of this loathsome world.
LORD JUSTICE:	Thy boon is granted, thou shalt die to-night.
	Lead him away: Come, Madam.
(STAGE DIRECTION):	*Guido is led off: as he goes the Duchess stretches out her arms and rushes down the stage.*
DUCHESS:	Guido! Guido! (*Faints*)

Fifth Act

That night Guido lies asleep on a pallet in his cell, while the five soldiers guarding him play at dice and discuss the Duchess's unsuccessful attempt to gain a pardon for him. They doubt, however, that he will go to the headsman's block. Being of gentle birth, he has the choice of drinking poison instead, and a goblet of it stands on a table near him. There is knocking at the door. The Duchess, disguised in mask and cloak, is admitted. She shows a ring to the soldier in charge, who bows and takes his men out of the cell. She removes her mask and goes to look at the sleeping Guido.

DUCHESS: I have been guilty, therefore I must die.
    He loves me not, and therefore I must die:
    I would die happier if he would kiss me,
    But he will not do that. I did not know him,
    I thought he meant to sell me to the judge;
    That is not strange; we women never know
    Our lovers till they leave us.

 As the execution bell begins to toll Beatrice drinks the poison. Guido wakes. She quickly outlines her plan: he must put on her cloak and mask and leave in her place, using her signet ring to get him past any guards. Horses are waiting near the prison to take him to safety in Venice. He calmly refuses:

GUIDO: What! am I fallen so low
    That I may not have leave to die for you?
DUCHESS: Die for me? – no, my life is a vile thing,
    Thrown to the miry highways of this world;
    You shall not die for me, you shall not, Guido,
    I am a guilty woman.
GUIDO: Guilty? – let those
    Who know not what a thing temptation is,
    Let those who have not walked as we have done,
    In the red fire of passion, those whose lives
    Are dull and colourless, in a word let those,
    If any such there be, who have not loved,
    Cast stones against you. As for me.
DUCHESS: Alas!
GUIDO: You are my lady, and you are my love!
    O hair of gold, O crimson lips, O face
    Made for the luring and the love of man!
    Incarnate image of pure loveliness!

Worshipping thee I do forget the past,
Worshipping thee my soul comes close to thine,
Worshipping thee I seem to be a god,
And though they give my body to the block,
Yet is my love eternal!

They argue to and fro, but Guido will not agree to escape. Voices approach. Guido goes to drink the poison but finds the goblet empty. The poison begins to affect Beatrice. As the chanting of monks sounds outside, Guido takes her in his arms:

(STAGE DIRECTION): They kiss each other now for the first time in this Act, when suddenly the Duchess leaps up in the dreadful spasm of death, tears in agony at her dress, and finally, with face twisted and distorted with pain, falls back dead in a chair. Guido, seizing her dagger from her belt, kills himself; and, as he falls across her knees, clutches at the cloak which is on the back of the chair. There is a little pause. Then down the passage comes the tramp of Soldiers; the door is opened, and the Lord Justice, the Headsman, and the Guard enter and see this figure shrouded in black, and Guido lying dead across her. The Lord Justice rushes forward and drags the cloak off the Duchess, whose face is now the marble image of peace, the sign of God's forgiveness.

A FLORENTINE TRAGEDY
(A fragment of one act)

THIS fragmentary piece was an attempt by Wilde to make a play out of one of the paradoxical stories with which he loved to entertain his friends at a restaurant table or on some such social occasion. He refers in *De Profundis* to having written it in 1893, while Alfred Douglas was in Egypt. Early in 1895 he wrote to George Alexander, the actor-manager, promising to send him the 'vital parts' within a few days. This is no doubt the moment that the play came closest to being written in full. With *The Importance of Being Earnest*, *An Ideal Husband* and *A Woman of No Importance* all running in London, he was at his pinnacle of theatrical fame, and it would only have needed Alexander's encouragement, and promise of money, to spur him on. But within a few days the Marquis of Queensberry had left his infamous message at the Albemarle Club, and precipitated Wilde into his nightmare.

Nearly two years later, struggling to write something, anything, in the solitariness of his cell in Reading Gaol, Wilde tried to return to the piece, but found he could remember only scraps of it and could invent no more. At Berneval-sur-Mer, a few weeks after his release, he was trying to convince himself that he would soon have the play completed and get £500 for it, possibly from some American source. Later that year he was telling Robert Ross that he was going to Rouen to 'rewrite my *Love and Death – Florentine Tragedy*', but in another month's time he was writing from Naples, 'Tomorrow I begin the *Florentine Tragedy*.' Hesketh Pearson, dealing with Wilde's creditors' sale of his effects on 24 April 1895, while he was in Holloway Prison awaiting his first trial, says that amongst the many items stolen in the disorderly proceedings was 'the complete form of *A Florentine Tragedy*'. If such a thing ever existed, only a fragment remains. It was first printed in the Collected Edition of 1908. It had been performed at last in

June 1906, as a curiosity, alongside *Salomé*, by the Literary Theatre Society in London. The poet, playwright and critic, T. Sturge Moore, had supplied a scene to replace the missing opening.

. . . .

Simone, a merchant of Florence, returns home at night, footsore and weighed down by his heavy pack, from which he has sold only one item all day. He finds his young wife, Bianca, entertaining a gentleman, whom he takes to be some visiting kinsman of hers. The man introduces himself as Sir Guido Bardi, son of the ruler of Florence. Simone is much flattered to meet so noble a person in his home, and hopes his wife has not been wearying him with the mindless chattering which, he implies, is her wont. Guido assures him this is far from the case:

GUIDO: Your gracious lady,
      Whose beauty is a lamp that pales the stars
      And robs Diana's quiver of her beams,
      Has welcomed me with such sweet courtesies
      That if it be her pleasure, and your own,
      I will come often to your simple house.
      And when your business bids you walk abroad
      I will sit here and charm her loneliness
      Lest she might sorrow for you overmuch.
      What say you, good Simone?

Simone is even more flattered and proceeds to put the occasion to good mercantile use, insisting on showing Guido some of the finest clothes from his pack. The prince has no eyes for anything but Bianca, however, and tries to silence her husband's tedious salesmanship by offering to send his servant round in the next morning with orders to pay double the price for the goods. Simone tactlessly presses him further:

SIMONE: I have a curious fancy
      To see you in this wonder of the loom
      Amidst the noble ladies of the court,
      A flower among flowers.
      They say, my lord,
      These highborn dames do so affect Your Grace

That where you go they throng like flies around you,
Each seeking for your favour.
I have heard also
Of husbands that wear horns, and wear them bravely,
A fashion most fantastical.

Guido silences these unwelcome references and says his servant will bring a hundred thousand crowns. Simone is overjoyed, to the point of promising his benefactor anything it is in his power to give:

GUIDO: What if I asked
For white Bianca here?

Simone thinks this a great joke, and tells his wife rudely to get on with her spinning, which is all she is fit for, while he harangues Guido about the injustices the Italian merchants are suffering from English competition. Bianca tries to silence him and apologizes for him to the visitor. While Simone's back is turned, Bianca tells Guido her contempt for her husband, wishing 'Oh, would that Death might take him where he stands!'

Simone overhears the reference to death and makes some pointed references to the punishment of adultery. He suddenly turns honey-sweet as he catches sight of a lute with which Guido had doubtless been serenading Bianca before his return. He presses the prince to play. When he refuses, Simone offers him drink, but, noting that wine has already been spilt on the tablecloth, suddenly loses his own appetite for festivity.

Guido is now impatient to leave, and whispers to Bianca that he will come back at dawn to take her away. He bids them farewell. As he gets their visitor's cloak and sword for him, Simone pauses to admire the fine quality of the Ferrara blade. He recalls that he too has a sword somewhere, an old, somewhat rusty one, and proposes that they test one another's skill. Guido, surprised, sees at once his chance of lawfully getting rid of this impediment to his desires, and agrees to the contest. Simone's sword is found, and with Bianca holding a flaming torch the two combatants fall to.

Almost instantly Simone is pinked, but it is only a slight wound. He attacks Guido again and disarms him. He throws his own sword away and they draw their daggers. Bianca urges Guido to kill Simone, who orders her to extinguish the torch. In what light is left the men grapple with one another, until Guido is forced onto the table on his back. Simone seizes him by the throat. Sensing that his opponent is in earnest, Guido manages to plead that his death would end the ruling line and leave Florence open to her enemies. Simone presses harder. Guido gasps for a priest:

SIMONE: What wouldst thou have a priest for? Tell thy sins
   To God, whom thou shalt see this very night
   And then no more for ever.

He kills Guido, rises, and looks for Bianca, prepared to deal with her. But she is moving slowly towards him, as though dazed, and with outstretched arms:

BIANCA: Why
   Did you not tell me you were so strong?
SIMONE: Why
   Did you not tell me you were beautiful?
   He kisses her on the mouth.

LA SAINTE COURTISANE

or

The Woman Covered in Jewels

(One Act, uncompleted)

LIKE *A Florentine Tragedy*, *La Sainte Courtisane* derives from Wilde's table-talk. Friends seem to have heard him tell it in varying styles, and it appears from *De Profundis* that he began to write it down in December 1893, during the brief period of respite while Alfred Douglas was in Egypt. Asked in 1895 how it was progressing, he turned the question aside with a jest. It was amongst the works considered for completion and publication after his release from prison when the need to raise money was imperative, but having retrieved the manuscript from Ada Leverson, who had been keeping it for him, he left it in a cab in Paris. In any case, he was by then beyond writing 'beautiful, coloured, musical things', such as he had described *Salomé* and *La Sainte*. 'Alas! she no longer says marvellous things; the robbers have buried her white body and carried away her jewels', he told Charles Ricketts. *La Sainte Courtisane* has never been performed on the stage: it was first published by Ronald Ross in *Miscellanies*, Vol. XIV of the Collected Edition, 1908.

· · · ·

Oscar Wilde sets the scene as follows:

A corner of a valley in the Thebaid. On the right hand of the stage is a cavern. In front of the cavern stands a great crucifix. On the left, sand dunes. The sky is blue like the inside of a cup of lapis lazuli. The hills are of red sand. Here and there on the hills there are clumps of thorns.

Two men speak of a beautiful, luxuriously clad woman, who is approaching. She has hair 'like threads of gold' and a purple robe. One has heard talk that she is the Emperor's daughter; the other thinks she may be one of the gods, come from Nubia. Goddess or princess, they determine not to speak to her, but she addresses them:

MYRRHINA: Where does he dwell, the beautiful young hermit who will not look on the face of woman? Has he a house of reeds or a house of burnt clay or does he lie on the hillside? Or does he make his bed in the rushes?

FIRST MAN: He dwells in that cavern yonder.

MYRRHINA: What a curious place to dwell in.

FIRST MAN: Of old a centaur lived there. When the hermit came the centaur gave a shrill cry, wept and lamented, and galloped away.

SECOND MAN: No. It was a white unicorn who lived in the cave. When it saw the hermit coming the unicorn knelt down and worshipped him. Many people saw it worshipping him.

FIRST MAN: I have talked with people who saw it.

Myrrhina questions them closely about the hermit: does he raise crops, or fish, or weave, or plough? If he does none of these, as they say, where does he get his food? They answer that they give it him, because he is a holy man. Intrigued that any man should prove worth doing something for without profit, she orders them to go and tell him that one has come from Alexandria to speak with him. They say they dare not. She herself calls into the cave tempting him with seductive phrases and accounts of her desirability in all men's eyes. Honorius, the hermit, replies:

HONORIUS: The body is vile, Myrrhina. God will raise thee up with a new body which will not know corruption, and thou wilt dwell in the Courts of the Lord and see Him whose hair is like fine wool and whose feet are of brass.

A gap occurs in the work, during the course of which Honorius has evidently come out of his cave and reached the point of succumbing to Myrrhina's lures. But she too has undergone change:

HONORIUS: Myrrhina, the scales have fallen from my eyes and I see now clearly what I did not see before. Take me to Alexandria and let me taste of the seven sins.

MYRRHINA: Do not mock me, Honorius, nor speak to me with such bitter words. For I have repented of my sins and I am seeking a cavern in this desert where I too may dwell so that my soul may become worthy to see God.

It is now he who begs her to go with him to Alexandria, and she who refuses. He cries out in despair:

HONORIUS: Why didst thou come to this valley in thy beauty?

MYRRHINA: The God whom thou worshipped led me here that I might repent of my iniquities and know Him as the Lord.

HONORIUS: Why didst thou tempt me with words?

MYRRHINA: That thou shouldst see Sin in its painted mask and look on Death in its robe of Shame.

SALOMÉ
(One Act)

It seems that *Salomé* was completed in Paris in a few weeks before Christmas 1891. How long it had been in preparation is not known. In October Wilde had told friends that he was writing a play in French and hoped to be elected to the Academic Française. There is a story that, returning to his Paris lodgings one day, he chanced to notice a blank manuscript book lying on the table, and immediately began to write *Salomé* in it. 'If the blank book had not been there on the table I should never have dreamed of doing it, I should not have sent out to buy one' are his reported words.

Hesketh Pearson suggests that, although *Salomé* was written in French, this first draft, in the heat of inspiration, would have been in English. At any rate, by the year's end Wilde had completed the full version in his excellent French and given it to several French friends, including Pierre Louÿs and André Gide, who ironed out some anglicisms and made other corrections and grammatical suggestions. He then read it to Sarah Bernhardt, who declared at once that she wished to play the nubile Salomé. The fact that she was nearly fifty would not have deterred her for one moment, and her slim and sensuous beauty and passionate style of acting were ideally suited to the role: nearly a decade later Wilde was still able to declare, 'The only person in the world who could act Salomé is Sarah Bernhardt, that "serpent of old Nile," older than the Pyramids.'

The play was to be presented in London, in French. The Palace Theatre, which Richard D'Oyly Carte had opened only two years earlier for the purpose of establishing 'English Grand Opera', had already become available for any takers, English opera having failed to materialize on the grand scale, and this fine, big theatre was leased for *Salomé*. Graham Robertson, currently in vogue as a stage designer, was engaged to do the décor and costumes, both of

which were to be exotic and extravagant, with at Wilde's suggestion, everyone on the stage in yellow, and, at Robertson's, 'a pale
ivory terrace against a great empty sky of deepest violet'. Wilde
also wanted, in place of an orchestra, braziers of burning perfume:
'a new perfume for each new emotion'.

Albert Darmont was engaged to play opposite Bernhardt as
Herod, and rehearsals began in the summer of 1892 at a time when
all London knew Oscar Wilde as the brilliant author of *Lady
Windermere's Fan*. It was not until they had been in progress for
some weeks that it occurred to anyone to submit a copy of the play
to the Lord Chamberlain for scrutiny under the Theatres Act
1843, which required all new plays for public performance to be
granted a licence, or refused one in the interests of 'the preservation
of good manners, decorum, or of the public peace'. (This censorship of plays in Great Britain, which had its origins several centuries earlier, was not ended until 1968. Only a month before the
Salomé application a Parliamentary committee had reconsidered
it and decided to perpetuate it.) It was open to the Lord Chamberlain to allow certain controversial plays to go forward provided
stipulated cuts or alterations were made; but *Salomé* was beyond
the pale. The Examiner of Plays refused to permit a licence to a
piece portraying biblical characters.

The argument that biblical figures had been shown in medieval
mystery plays carried no weight. There was no alternative to
abandoning the project. Outraged and financially damaged,
Sarah Bernhardt stormed back to France. Wilde spoke hysterically of following in her footsteps, taking French nationality, and
turning his back on philistine England for good. The noted dramatic critic William Archer – the only witness connected with the
stage who had addressed the Parliamentary committee in favour
of the ending of censorship – asked him in the *Pall Mall Gazette*
to reconsider: 'It is surely unworthy of Mr. Wilde's lineage to
turn tail and run away from a petty tyranny which lives upon the
disunion and apathy of English dramatic authors. Paris does not
particularly want Mr. Wilde. There he would be one talent
among many, handicapped moreover, in however a slight degree,

by having to use an acquired idiom. I am not aware that anyone has produced work of the highest artistic excellence in a living language which was not his mother tongue. Here, on the other hand, Mr. Wilde's talent is unique. We require it and we appreciate it – those of us, at any rate, who are capable of any sort of artistic appreciation. And especially we require it to aid in the emancipation of art from the stupid meddling of irresponsible officialdom.'

It is a curious parallel of opposites, as it were, with the situation two years later when those closest to Wilde were urging him to 'turn tail and run away' to France from persecution under an anachronistic law, and he would not. One cannot help wondering whether the earlier occasion recalled itself to his mind then, and influenced him at all; though it is unlikely.

Salomé was first published in France in February of the following year, 1893, and a number of copies of the edition were simultaneously sold in London and duly reviewed there. *The Times* was scathing: 'It is an arrangement in blood and ferocity, morbid, *bizarre*, repulsive, and very offensive in its adaptation of scriptural phraseology to situations the reverse of sacred. It is not ill-suited to some of the less attractive phases of Mme Bernhardt's dramatic genius.' The *Pall Mall Gazette* commented: 'So long as the State maintains such an officer, it would be hard to see how the Examiner of Plays could have acted otherwise.' It was especially censorious on the subject of the play's heavy derivation from Flaubert and several other writers, adding, 'Mr. Wilde resembles some traveller who contents himself with making a dissected map at home when he might be exploring the Land East of the Sun, West of the Moon, or sailing to the Islands of Felicity. For it can be in no sense admitted as a proof of Mr. Wilde's originality that he has written his *Salomé* in French. That may be a success in linguistics, that may be a proof of elegance and taste, but it does not add one jot either to the merits or to the defects of *Salomé*. It has no more to do with any possible value that the piece may have as a work of art than would the fact that Mr. Wilde had written *Salomé* while standing on one leg . . .'

The two who spoke out most strongly in *Salomé*'s favour were Lord Alfred Douglas, in a review in an Oxford University magazine, *The Spirit Lamp*, and William Archer, in the journal *Black and White*. An interesting remark emerges *en passant* from each of these writings. Alfred Douglas says: 'One thing strikes one very forcibly in the treatment, the musical form of it. Again and again it seems to one that in reading one is *listening*; listening, not to the author, not to the direct unfolding of a plot, but to the tones of different instruments, suggesting, suggesting, always indirectly, till one feels that by shutting one's eyes one can best catch the suggestion.' Archer's complementary phrase is: 'There is at least as much musical as pictorial quality in *Salomé*. It is by methods borrowed from music that Mr. Wilde, without sacrificing its suppleness, imparts to his prose the firm texture, so to speak, of verse.' The analogy with music occurs in other reviews, at other times, of *Salomé*, and in critical discussions of Wilde's work; and I venture to think it demonstrates the very essence of the 'play'. *Salomé* is pure opera, in its artificiality of conception, shape and language, and it is no fluke that the form in which it has come to the notice of the widest public has been through Richard Strauss's operatic version, which caused a sensation when it was first performed at Dresden in 1905. Curiously enough, the story of Wilde's having suddenly been inspired to write it continued that, late that evening, he went out to a restaurant for something to eat and asked the leader of the orchestra to play something suggestive of 'a woman dancing with her bare feet in the blood of a man she has craved for and slain'. The resulting music is said to have silenced the other diners and caused them to look at each other 'with blanched faces'; so, if this is true, this work which has become so linked with music was to some extent conceived to music.

Sarah Bernhardt did at length present *Salomé*, opening at the Théâtre de l'Œuvre, Paris, on 11 February 1896, but the result seems to have been disastrously bad. In 1899 Wilde saw her act at Naples, went round to see her, and they wept together. It was their last encounter.

He also tried the great Italian actress Eleanora Duse, who read the play, admired it, but declined to play in it. *Salomé*'s success as a stage play was to come, however, but not until after its author's death, when it was presented in 1902 at the Kleines Theater, Berlin. Max Reinhardt sprang to fame as its director, and some of Wilde's immense posthumous reputation in Europe dates from this production.

Salomé's publishing history in England is similarly chequered. In 1893 Wilde allowed Alfred Douglas to make an English translation: a task for which he himself was the best equipped person in the world, though no doubt he sought to help further the career of the young man with whom he was by now infatuated. His critical faculties prevailed when he saw the result, which he corrected a good deal, and for this Douglas paid him out in his characteristic way, according to a passage in *De Profundis*: '. . . new scenes occurred, the occasion of them being my pointing out the schoolboy faults of your attempted translation of *Salomé*. You must by this time be a fair enough French scholar to know that the translation was as unworthy of you, as an ordinary Oxonian, as it was of the work it sought to render.' The published work was nevertheless dedicated to 'my friend Lord Alfred Bruce Douglas, the translator of my play', but Douglas's name did not appear on the title page, and he never subsequently acknowledged the translation as his.

There was trouble also over the illustrations. Aubrey Beardsley, aged twenty-two, precocious, effete, and feverishly anxious to make his name before tuberculosis inevitably claimed him, had also submitted a translation, which Wilde rejected utterly. But, through the intervention of Robert Ross, he consented to Beardsley's illustrating the volume. He did not care for the results, perhaps because he found their decadence too brilliantly achieved to stand alongside his text without somewhat over-shadowing his own effects: 'They are cruel and evil', he said, adding 'and so like dear Aubrey.' But he admitted the drawings, insisting only on the removal of two or three which clearly carica-tured himself, and they have come to be regarded as amongst Beardsley's finest work.

London publication of *Salomé* in English was on 9 February 1894, and it appeared in the U.S.A. that same year. Its reception in America was not good, either in print or when it was first performed, in November 1905, by a New York group, the Progressive Stage Society. After its first professional performance in America at the Astor Theatre, New York, in November 1906, the *New York Tribune* reviewer wrote it off as 'decadent stuff, and unworthy of notice'. The first London performance, necessarily a private one, was at the Bijou, Bayswater, on 10 May 1905.

. . . .

On a moonlit terrace of Herod's palace in Judea some attendants and soldiers lean on the balcony. The thoughts of one of them, Narraboth, the young Syrian captain of the guard, are on the Princess Salomé, daughter of their Queen Herodias and stepdaughter of Herod.

THE YOUNG SYRIAN: How beautiful is the Princess Salomé to-night!

THE PAGE OF HERODIAS: Look at the moon! How strange the moon seems! She is like a woman rising from a tomb. She is like a dead woman. You would fancy she was looking for dead things.

THE YOUNG SYRIAN: She has a strange look. She is like a little princess who wears a yellow veil, and whose feet are of silver. She is like a princess who has little white doves for feet. You would fancy she was dancing.

THE PAGE OF HERODIAS: She is like a woman who is dead. She moves very slowly.

From the banqueting hall below comes a babble of Jewish voices arguing about religion. This provokes some desultory discussion amongst the idlers, which is interrupted by a voice issuing from an old cistern, surrounded by green bronze.

After me shall come another mightier than I. I am not worthy so much as to unloose the latchet of his shoes. When he cometh, the solitary places shall be glad. They shall blossom like the lily. The eyes of the blind shall see the day, and the ears of the deaf shall be opened. The new-born child shall put his hand upon the dragon's lair, he shall lead the lions by their manes.

It is the voice of Jokanaan (John the Baptist), a prophet who had come with disciples from the desert. Herod had imprisoned his own elder brother in that same cistern for twelve years in order to possess Herodias, his brother's wife, and had eventually had him executed. Jokanaan denounced them both for their incestuous relationship and has consequently been imprisoned in the cistern, with orders that no one is to speak to him. It does not stop him using his own voice, however, and his foretellings of divine retribution are beginning to affect the conscience-troubled Herod.

The bewitching Salomé comes on to the terrace from the heat and noise of the banqueting hall. She hears the voice of Jokanaan and is at once curious to see him. The soldiers dare not let her, but Salomé is adept at getting what she wants and addresses the captain of the guard:

SALOMÉ: You will do this thing for me, Narraboth. You know that you will do this thing for me. And to-morrow when I pass in my litter by the bridge of the idol-buyers, I will look at you through the muslin veils, I will look at you, Narraboth, it may be I will smile at you. Look at me, Narraboth, look at me. Ah! you know that you will do what I ask of you. You know it well . . . I know that you will do this thing.

Virtually hypnotized, he orders Jokanaan to be brought out. There follows a tussle of wills, the prophet upbraiding Salomé and she determined to prove the supremacy of sexual desire. Again and again she demands: 'Let me kiss thy mouth, Jokanaan.' Unable to bear any more of it, the captain of the guard kills himself and falls between them. He lies unnoticed:

SALOMÉ: Let me kiss thy mouth.
JOKANAAN: Cursed be thou! Daughter of an incestuous mother, be thou accursed!
SALOMÉ: I will kiss thy mouth, Jokanaan.

Unvanquished, Jokanaan returns to his cistern. The king enters with Herodias and their courtiers. He slips in the dead man's blood and interprets it, as he does most things, as an evil omen.

Nevertheless it does not deter him from his transparent lust for his
stepdaughter, and he tries to tempt her with wine, fruits, and the
promise of her mother's throne. But she is pale and brooding, and
refuses all these. It is only when he supports his plea with a new
promise that she suddenly shows interest:

HEROD: Dance for me, Salomé, I beseech you. If you dance for me
you may ask of me what you will, and I will give it you, even unto
the half of my kingdom.

SALOMÉ: Will you indeed give me whatsoever I shall ask, Tetrarch?

HERODIAS: Do not dance, my daughter.

HEROD: Everything, even the half of my kingdom.

SALOMÉ: You swear it, Tetrarch?

HEROD: I swear it, Salomé.

HERODIAS: Do not dance, my daughter.

SALOMÉ: By what will you swear, Tetrarch?

HEROD: By my life, by my crown, by my gods. Whatsoever you desire
I will give it you, even to the half of my kingdom, if you will but
dance for me. O, Salomé, Salomé, dance for me!

SALOMÉ: You have sworn, Tetrarch.

HEROD: I have sworn, Salomé.

Salomé sends her slaves for perfumes and her seven veils, and has
her sandals removed. Then she performs the sensuous dance of the
seven veils. Herod is transported:

HEROD: Ah! Wonderful! Wonderful! You see that she has danced for
me, your daughter. Come near, Salomé, come near, that I may give
you your reward. Ah! I pay the dancers well. I will pay thee royally.
I will give thee whatsoever thy soul desireth. What wouldst thou have?

SALOMÉ: I would that they presently bring me in a silver charger. . .

HEROD: In a silver charger? Surely yes, in a silver charger. She is
charming, is she not? What is it you would have in a silver charger,
O, sweet and fair Salomé, you who are fairer than all the daughters
of Judea? What would you have them bring thee in a silver charger?
Tell me. Whatsoever it may be, they shall give it to you. My treasures
belong to thee. What is it, Salomé?

SALOMÉ: The head of Jokanaan.

Horrified, Herod refuses, but is reminded of his oath. He begs her to accept something else – jewels, peacocks, half his kingdom – rather than the head of the holy man whom he has dared to imprison but dare not put to death. It is of no avail: Salomé, supported by her mother, has set her mind upon her reward. Herod reluctantly takes from his finger the ring of death and hands it to a soldier to convey to Naaman, the huge executioner. The executioner enters the cistern. Lasciviously, Salomé leans over the side and peers in, jeering at the executioner for hesitating to strike, lamenting because Jokanaan utters no sound of fear. She urges soldiers to go down and finish the task, but they recoil. At length the executioner's arm rises above the cistern's rim, bearing, on a silver shield, the head of Jokanaan. Salomé seizes it. Herod hides his face with his cloak. Herodias smiles and fans herself.

SALOMÉ: Ah! thou wouldst not suffer me to kiss thy mouth, Jokanaan. Well! I will kiss it now. I will bite it with my teeth as one bites a ripe fruit. Yes, I will kiss thy mouth, Jokanaan. I said it. Did I not say it? I said it. Ah! I will kiss it now. . . . But wherefore dost thou not look at me, Jokanaan? Thine eyes that were so terrible, so full of rage and scorn, are shut now. Wherefore are they shut? Open thine eyes! Lift up thine eyelids, Jokanaan! Wherefore dost thou not look at me? Art thou afraid of me, Jokanaan, that thou wilt not look at me . . .? And thy tongue, that was like a red snake darting poison, it moves no more, it says nothing now, Jokanaan, that scarlet viper that spat its venom upon me. It is strange, is it not? How is it that the red viper stirs no longer . . .? Thou wouldst have none of me, Jokanaan. Thou didst reject me. Thou didst speak evil words against me. Thou didst treat me as a harlot, as a wanton, me, Salomé, daughter of Herodias, Princess of Judea! Well, Jokanaan, I still live, but thou, thou art dead, and thy head belongs to me. I can do with it what I will. I can throw it to the dogs and to the birds of the air. That which the dogs leave, the birds of the air shall devour . . . Ah, Jokanaan, Jokanaan, thou wert the only man that I have loved. All other men are hateful to me. But thou, thou wert beautiful! Thy body was a column of ivory set on a silver socket. It was a garden full of doves and of silver lilies. It was a tower of silver decked with shields of ivory. There was nothing in the world so white as thy body. There was nothing in the world so black as thy hair. In the whole world there was nothing so red as thy mouth. Thy voice was a censer that scattered strange perfumes, and when I looked on thee I heard a strange music. Ah, wherefore didst thou not look at me, Jokanaan? Behind thine hands and thy curses thou didst hide thy face. Thou didst put upon thine eyes the covering of him who would see his God. Well, thou hast seen thy God, Jokanaan, but me, me, thou didst never see. If thou hadst seen me thou wouldst have loved me. I, I saw thee, Jokanaan, and I loved thee. Oh, how I loved thee! I love thee yet, Jokanaan, I love thee only . . . I am athirst for thy beauty; I am hungry for thy body; and neither wine nor fruits can appease my desire. What shall I do now, Jokanaan? Neither the floods nor the great waters can quench my passion. I was a princess, and thou didst scorn me. I was a virgin, and thou didst take my virginity from me. I was chaste, and thou didst fill my veins with fire . . . Ah! ah! wherefore didst thou not look at me, Jokanaan? If thou hadst looked at me thou hadst loved me. Well I know that thou wouldst have loved me, and the mystery of love is greater than the mystery of death. Love only should one consider.

Fearful of the outcome, Herod prepares to hide himself away in the palace. The slaves put out their torches; the stars disappear; a great black cloud obliterates the moon. From the darkness the voice of Salomé is heard exulting: 'I have kissed thy mouth, Jokanaan.' A single moonbeam bathes her in silver light. Herod turns and orders her to be killed. Upon the word, his soldiers crush her with their shields.

LADY WINDERMERE'S FAN
A Play about a Good Woman

'It was the best of times, it was the worst of times, it was the age of
wisdom, it was the age of foolishness, it was the epoch of belief, it was
the epoch of incredulity, it was the season of Light, it was the season of
Darkness, it was the spring of hope, it was the winter of despair, we
had everything before us, we had nothing before us, we were all going
direct to Heaven, we were all going direct the other way. . . .'

THE quotation, of course, is not from Oscar Wilde – it is the opening of Charles Dickens's *A Tale of Two Cities* – but it is an apt
foreshadowing in print of the course of Wilde's life during the
years 1892–5. In that time he rose to the peak of artistic and commercial success, won the large sums of money for which he had so
long craved, gained widespread admiration hitherto withheld by
members of the public, found himself the most talked-of playwright in London, able to indulge himself in every luxurious
habit . . . and moved inexorably into disaster, disgrace and ruin.

The prologue to this tragi-comedy period opened late in 1890
when George Alexander, the young actor-manager who had
recently taken over the St James's Theatre, had the perception to
invite Wilde to write a modern comedy. Wilde agreed amiably
and pocketed £100 advance against royalties. Occasional remind-
ers from Alexander produced assurances that, though nothing
tangible had been achieved, cerebral processes were in motion.
Late in the summer Wilde rented a cottage near Lake Windermere; here, with no fleshpots to distract him, he got down to hard
work and in two or three weeks completed the play, which he
entitled *A Good Woman*. He sent it to Alexander who read it once
and immediately offered its author £1,000 for an outright sale.
Wilde replied, 'I have so much confidence in your excellent
judgment, my dear Alex, that I cannot but refuse your generous
offer.' It proved the excellence of his own judgment: *Lady Windermere's Fan*, as the piece was to be re-titled, earned him many
times the amount offered him by Alexander.

Lady Windermere is as artificial as anything else he ever wrote; but in a different way. Instead of pursuing aesthetic or sensual effect, Wilde let his sense of humour have its head. To say that the protagonists would scarcely have behaved in real life as he made them behave on the stage, and so would not have found themselves in their various predicaments, is to put it mildly; but although *Lady Windermere* is partially about blackmail and the redemption of a wicked woman through motherly love, Wilde was essentially writing society comedy. Upper class or dandified though his characters in his four society comedies are, their behaviour is, for the most part, well removed from that of their contemporary counterparts in real life; but again, it is the illusion that counts. People in Wilde's time who had never moved in such circles believed it was how such people did behave and speak; those who were acquainted with the real thing saw the joke and read their own friends and enemies into Wilde's characters; while today we easily accept those languid young noblemen, formidable dowagers and cynical old clubmen as the epitome of a vanished breed, lucky enough always to have moved, without visible means of support, in luxurious surroundings, wherein witty epigrams flowed as abundantly as the hock and seltzer.

Various real-life models from Wilde's own acquaintances have been acknowledged amongst his characters; and there is always an internal clue as to where the pieces, all dashed off at high speed, were composed: e.g. *Lady Windermere's Fan* at Windermere; *A Woman of No Importance* in Norfolk (Hunstanton Chase, the main setting, is named from the Norfolk coastal resort of Hunstanton); *An Ideal Husband* at Goring-on-Thames (Viscount Goring); and *The Importance of Being Earnest* at Worthing, Sussex (John Worthing). But the principal character of them all is Oscar Wilde. Facets of the lighthearted side of himself glitter in many of his people, whose talk, epigrammatic, paradoxical and irresponsible, echoes his own: literally does so, for many of his best lines of dialogue were already familiar to those who were accustomed to hearing his table-talk. In short, nothing so scintillatingly witty as *Lady Windermere's Fan* had been seen on the London stage since

Sheridan's three great comedies of the 1770s, and the first night audience, on 20 February 1892, recognized as much. Incurably *provocateur*, however, Wilde damaged himself in some critics' eyes when, called for by an ecstatic audience after the final curtain, he strolled on to the stage with a lit cigarette in his fingers, and said: 'Ladies and gentlemen, I have enjoyed this evening immensely. The actors have given us a charming rendering of a delightful play, and your appreciation has been most intelligent. I congratulate you on the great success of your performance, which persuades me that you think almost as highly of the play as I do myself.' The audience may have frowned at the cigarette a bit, but they appreciated the speech hugely and gave Wilde a further ovation. The critics found both in bad taste.

'*Lady Windermere's Fan* is not really a play; it is a pepperbox of paradoxes', wrote one of them. The influential and incensed Clement Scott pictured Wilde saying to himself, 'I will show you and prove to you to what an extent bad manners are not only recognized but endorsed in this wholly free and unrestrained age. I will do on the stage of a public theatre what I should not dare do at a mass meeting in the Park. I will uncover my head in the presence of refined women, but I refuse to put down my cigarette.' The equally influential A. B. Walkley, writing in the *Speaker*, saw the cigarette and curtain-speech in perspective: 'Here is a gentleman who devotes brilliant talents, a splendid audacity, an agreeable charlatanry and a hundred-Barnum-power of advertisement, to making a change in old customs and preventing life from being monotonous. He does this in innumerable ways – by his writings, his talk, his person, his clothes, and everything that is his. He has aimed at doing it in his play, *Lady Windermere's Fan*, and has been, to my mind, entirely successful.'

Nevertheless, with Alexander as Lord Windermere, Marion Terry as Mrs Erlynne and Lily Hanbury as Lady Windermere, the play ran to packed houses for five months, was toured with equal success in the autumn, and brought back to the St James's in October. Its first American production opened in New York on 6 February 1893. Critical opinion was not enthusiastic, but, again, the public differed and there followed a highly successful run of several months. First publication of the text was by Mathews & Lane, London, in November 1893. When Wilde was bankrupted in 1895, Alexander bought the rights, subsequently made some voluntary payments to the author, and, at his own death in 1918, bequeathed the rights to Wilde's son, Vyvyan Holland.

· · · ·

First Act

It is the afternoon of Lady Windermere's twenty-first birthday and she is arranging the flowers for the party she is giving that evening at her London home. A visitor, Lord Darlington, is announced. Lady Windermere is a prim, almost puritanical, young woman, married only two years and with a child of six months. She chides Darlington for attempting to return to the extravagant compliments he had paid her at a Foreign Office function on the previous evening. Darlington's reply is characteristically flippant – 'Nowadays we are all of us so hard up, that the only pleasant things to pay *are* compliments. They're the only things we *can* pay' – but she is made curious by his implication that before long she will view him differently, since she will find herself in need of a true friend. He puts to her the hypothetical case of a husband who within two years of marriage suddenly becomes preoccupied with a woman of doubtful character, and suggests that, in such an instance, his wife is entitled to console herself with another man. Lady Windermere rejects the notion emphatically:

LORD DARLINGTON: Ah, what a fascinating Puritan you are, Lady Windermere!
LADY WINDERMERE: The adjective was unnecessary, Lord Darlington.
LORD DARLINGTON: I couldn't help it. I can resist everything except temptation.

Lady Windermere's self-assurance is soon to be shattered. The visitors who follow Lord Darlington are the Duchess of Berwick and her daughter Agatha. Having dispatched the girl to the terrace to contemplate the sunset, the Duchess discloses that Lord Windermere has taken to paying almost daily visits to a house in Curzon Street occupied by a Mrs Erlynne who had arrived in London with little to her name beyond a reputation scandalous enough to debar her from all society, yet is now wealthy. The Duchess advises Lady Windermere to pursue the classic remedy for such a case: take her husband abroad for a time and let separation rid him of a habit about which it would be a mistake to make a dramatic fuss:

DUCHESS OF BERWICK: These wicked women get our husbands away from us, but they always come back, slightly damaged, of course. And don't make scenes, men hate them!

LADY WINDERMERE: It is very kind of you, Duchess, to come and tell all this. But I can't believe that my husband is untrue to me.

DUCHESS OF BERWICK: Pretty child! I was like that once. Now I know that all men are monsters. The only thing to do is to feed the wretches well. A good cook does wonders, and that I know you have. My dear Margaret, you are not going to cry?

LADY WINDERMERE: You needn't be afraid, Duchess, I never cry.

DUCHESS OF BERWICK: That's quite right, dear. Crying is the refuge of plain women but the ruin of pretty ones.

When her callers have departed Lady Windermere tries to assure herself that what she has been told cannot be true; but conviction will not come. She is drawn to the bureau where her husband's bank book is kept. She examines the book and finds nothing to suggest that he has been paying large sums to any individual; but as she is replacing it with relief she sees another book. It has a lock. She cuts off its cover with a paper-knife and is horrified to read a series of entries: 'Mrs Erlynne – £600 – Mrs Erlynne – £700 – Mrs Erlynne – £400.' With a cry, she throws the bank book to the floor: a moment later Lord Windermere enters, sees at once what has happened and earnestly tries to reassure his outraged wife that she, like everyone else, is misinterpreting his relationship with Mrs Erlynne. She is a woman whose husband had died many years before, who has lost everything – 'threw it away, if you like' – and whom he wishes to help regain her place in society. He will give his wife no further details about Mrs Erlynne, and outrages her by asking her to help him in the task he has undertaken by sending her an invitation to the party that evening. She refuses: he insists that in that case he will invite Mrs Erlynne himself. Lady Windermere picks up the beautiful fan that has been his birthday present to her and warns him that if Mrs Erlynne crosses her threshold that evening she will strike her across the face with the fan:

LADY WINDERMERE: If you wish to avoid a public scandal, write at once to this woman, and tell her that I forbid her to come here!

LORD WINDERMERE: I will not – she must come!

LADY WINDERMERE: Then I shall do exactly as I have said. You leave me no choice.

LORD WINDERMERE: (*calling after her*): Margaret! Margaret! (*A pause.*) My God! What shall I do? I dare not tell her who this woman really is. The shame would kill her. (*Sinks down into a chair and buries his face in his hands.*)

Second Act

Late that evening Lady Windermere stands in the drawing-room to receive her guests before they pass into the adjoining ballroom, where a band is playing dance music. Lord Darlington hovers close to her as she fingers her fan and listens attentively to the guests' names being called. At the name of Mrs Erlynne the fan falls from Lady Windermere's hand. Lord Darlington restores it to her, but she has lost the chance to make her threatened gesture, for the elegant, beautifully dressed Mrs Erlynne has made her bow to her and swept on into the room, where she is eagerly monopolized by an older friend of Lord Windermere's, Lord Augustus ('Tuppy') Lorton, the Duchess of Berwick's brother. When at length Mrs Erlynne comes over to try to converse with Lady Windermere the latter merely bows curtly and allows Lord Darlington to escort her out to the terrace. Lord Darlington proceeds to make the most of her distress:

LORD DARLINGTON: If I know you at all, I know that you can't live with a man who treats you like this! What sort of life would you have with him? You would feel that he was lying to you every moment of the day. You would feel that the look in his eyes was false, his voice false, his touch false, his passion false. He would come to you when he was weary of others; you would have to comfort him. He would come to you when he was devoted to others; you would have to charm him. You would have to be to him the mask of his real life, the cloak to hide his secret.

LADY WINDERMERE: You are right – you are terribly right. But where am I to turn? You said you would be my friend, Lord Darlington. – Tell me, what am I to do? Be my friend now.

LORD DARLINGTON: Between men and women there is no friendship possible. There is passion, enmity, worship, love, but no friendship. I love you.

He asks her to leave the house with him that night. She says she has not the courage. He begs her. She wavers, and he threatens that she must agree at once or he will leave England and she will never see him again. She refuses, and Lord Darlington leaves the house.

To Lady Windermere's distress is added the annoyance of being told by some of her guests that they have been chatting with Mrs Erlynne and have been captivated by her beauty and charm. Then, her presence unnoticed, she overhears a conversation between Mrs Erlynne and Lord Windermere. Mrs Erlynne tells him she has decided to accept Lord Augustus Lorton's proposal of marriage, and wants Windermere to settle a discreet annual allowance of £2,500 on her, as if from some distant relative. This is the last straw for Lady Windermere: she determines to go at once to Lord Darlington. She scribbles a note, seals it in an envelope, and, putting on her cloak, goes out hurriedly.

Mrs Erlynne re-enters alone in search of Lady Windermere. Parker, the butler, tells her that his mistress has just left the house. Puzzled at this behaviour, and seeing the envelope which is addressed to Lord Windermere, Mrs Erlynne opens the letter, reads it, and sinks down in anguish:

MRS ERLYNNE: Oh, how terrible! The same words that twenty years ago I wrote to her father! and how bitterly I have been punished for it! No; my punishment, my real punishment is to-night, is now!

Lord Augustus finds her. He is astonished to be instructed to take Lord Windermere down to his club at once and to keep him there for the rest of the night at all costs. She hurries purposefully away.

Third Act

Lady Windermere is waiting impatiently in Lord Darlington's rooms, for he has not yet returned there. Instead, Mrs Erlynne enters, telling Lady Windermere to go home immediately. She discloses that she had read the note, kept it from Lord Windermere and told him that his wife had gone to bed. Lady Windermere swears she will never return to him, and listens with contemptuous disbelief to Mrs Erlynne trying to persuade her that Lord Windermere's love is for his wife alone, that there is no romantic attachment between herself and him, and that Lady Windermere is in danger of ruining her life in the way that she had ruined hers. Her final appeal is to Lady Windermere's love for the child she is proposing to abandon: Lady Windermere bursts into tears and helplessly asks the older woman to take her home.

They are about to leave when they hear men's voices. Mrs Erlynne pushes Lady Windermere behind one of the curtains, and herself goes into an adjoining room. The men who enter are Lord Darlington, Lord Windermere, Lord Augustus and two other club-mates. They settle down to an epigrammatic discussion of marriage, in which Lord Darlington emerges as curiously changed from his former cynical self, for which he accounts by telling them that he is in love with the only good woman he has met in his life, but that his love is not returned and he is going away. One of his hearers, Cecil Graham, is amused by Darlington's moralizing, which he takes to be hypocritical, for he has caught sight of a

fan lying on the sofa. He draws the fan to the attention of
Windermere, who at once recognizes his own present to his wife
and accuses Darlington of having Lady Windermere concealed
on the premises. Darlington, realizing that Lady Windermere
must have come to him in his absence, refuses to let her husband
search his rooms. Windermere notices a movement behind the
curtain and is just going towards it when the door to the adjoining
room opens. The men turn, to see Mrs Erlynne there, and Lady
Windermere takes her chance to slip from behind the curtain
and out of the room. Mrs Erlynne blandly explains that she must
have taken Lady Windermere's fan in mistake for her own. In the
words of the stage direction, Lord Windermere looks at her in
contempt, Lord Darlington in mingled astonishment and anger.
Lord Augustus turns away. The other men smile at each other.

Fourth Act

When they meet again in their home next morning, Lord and
Lady Windermere are each troubled in a different way. She is full
of remorse for having gone to Lord Darlington, and certain that
Mrs Erlynne will have put her own reputation first and told the
truth to the men after her own escape. She does not know that
Mrs Erlynne had done nothing of the sort, but had let the men
think the worst about her own presence in Lord Darlington's
rooms; she is therefore astonished to hear her husband disavow
the woman for whose sake he had put his marriage to such considerable risk:

LORD WINDERMERE: Margaret, I thought Mrs Erlynne was a woman
more sinned against than sinning, as the phrase goes. I thought she
wanted to be good, to get back into a place that she had lost by a
moment's folly, to lead again a decent life. I believed what she told
me – I was mistaken in her. She is bad – as bad as a woman can be.
LADY WINDERMERE: Arthur, Arthur, don't talk so bitterly about any
woman. I don't think now that people can be divided into the good

and the bad as though they were two separate races or creations. What are called good women may have terrible things in them, mad moods of recklessness, assertion, jealousy, sin. Bad women, as they are termed, may have in them sorrow, repentance, pity, sacrifice. And I don't think Mrs Erlynne a bad woman – I know she's not.

Lord Windermere is on the point of telling her where Mrs Erlynne had been discovered the previous evening when the butler enters, carrying on a salver Lady Windermere's fan and Mrs Erlynne's card. Windermere begs his wife not to receive the visitor, but she asks Mrs Erlynne up. She has come to take her leave: the English climate does not suit her, she has decided. But she would like to take with her a photograph of Lady Windermere, preferably with her infant son. Lady Windermere goes to fetch one. Now that they are alone, the secret shared by Windermere and Mrs Erlynne emerges in their conversation:

LORD WINDERMERE: Rather than my wife should know – that the mother whom she was taught to consider as dead, the mother whom she has mourned as dead, is living – a divorced woman, going about under an assumed name, a bad woman preying upon life, as I know you now to be – rather than that, I was ready to supply you with money to pay bill after bill, extravagance after extravagance, to risk what occurred yesterday, the first quarrel I have ever had with my wife. You don't understand what that means to me. How could you? But I tell you that the only bitter words that ever came from those sweet lips of hers were on your account, and I hate to see you next her. You sully the innocence that is in her. And then I used to think that with all your faults you were frank and honest. You are not.

MRS ERLYNNE: Why do you say that?

LORD WINDERMERE: You made me get you an invitation to my wife's ball.

MRS ERLYNNE: For my daughter's ball – yes.

LORD WINDERMERE: You came, and within an hour of your leaving the house you are found in a man's rooms – you are disgraced before every one.

MRS ERLYNNE: Yes.

She admits that she had been content to live for twenty years without thought of the illegitimate child she had borne another man, until she had learnt that her daughter had married a rich man and had seen her chance to win money by blackmail. But now that she has met her daughter and realized how close she had come to ruining her life for her, she is conscious of a mother's feelings for the first time. The role of a married woman's mother is not to her taste, however – 'I have never admitted that I am more than twenty-nine, or thirty at the most. Twenty-nine when there are pink shades, thirty when there are not' – so she has decided to leave her daughter with her illusions of a supposedly dear, dead mother. Mistrusting her, Windermere threatens to tell his wife the truth. Mrs Erlynne counters that if anyone does so, it will be herself – before she leaves the house, or never at all.

When Lady Windermere returns with the photograph, Mrs Erlynne asks Lord Windermere to go and see if her carriage has arrived. Reluctantly he does so. Mrs Erlynne does not broach her secret to her daughter; she merely advises her not to yield to the temptation she feels to confess to having gone to Lord Darlington's and ask forgiveness. Windermere returns uneasily to say that the carriage has not arrived. Mrs Erlynne makes one final request of Lady Windermere: that she will let her keep the fan she had returned. It bears a name they share – Margaret.

Parker enters to announce the simultaneous arrival of the carriage and Lord Augustus Lorton. The latter greets Mrs Erlynne coldly, but she persuades him to escort her to her carriage. With a last look from the doorway at her daughter, she goes, leaving the Windermeres alone:

LADY WINDERMERE: You will speak against Mrs Erlynne again, Arthur, will you?

LORD WINDERMERE: She is better than one thought her.

LADY WINDERMERE: She is better than I am.

LORD WINDERMERE: Child, you and she belong to different worlds. Into your world evil has never entered.

LADY WINDERMERE: Don't say that, Arthur. There is the same world for all of us, and good and evil, sin and innocence, go through it hand in hand. To shut one's eyes to half of life that one may live securely is as though one blinded oneself that one might walk with more safety in a land of pit and precipice.

They are interrupted by the hurried return of Lord Augustus, blurting out that Mrs Erlynne has explained everything. For a moment both are horror-stricken, until he adds what 'everything' means: that Mrs Erlynne had merely gone to Lord Darlington's rooms in search of himself, Lord Augustus, having called at his club in vain. They are to be married after all, Mrs Erlynne's only condition being that they go to live out of London.

LORD WINDERMERE: Well, you are certainly marrying a very clever woman!

LADY WINDERMERE: Ah, you're marrying a very good woman!

A WOMEN OF NO IMPORTANCE

THE exhilaration of *Lady Windermere*'s success was soon to be tempered by the banning of *Salomé*, described earlier in this book. Distressed and hurt, Wilde retired to the spa town of Homburg, near Frankfurt, and submitted to a health cure which occupied the greater part of July 1892. When he returned to England it was to a rented house at Felbrigg, near Cromer, Norfolk, where he began work on another play in his more acceptable vein. This was *A Woman of No Importance*, which he finished later at Babbacombe Cliff, Torquay, a house he rented from November 1892 until March 1893.

The new play was not written for George Alexander, but for a rival actor-manager, Herbert Beerbohm Tree. Tree had been acquainted with Wilde for some time and admired his personal flair and social gifts. For his part, Wilde respected Tree's intelligence as an actor more highly than he did Alexander's – Alexander was the 'romantic lead' type, Tree the character man, calling for more versatility as distinct from handsome looks – but he did not see Tree in the sort of dandified role that Alexander was playing so successfully in *Lady Windermere*. However, Tree was successfully established at one of London's leading and historic theatres, the Haymarket, and Wilde agreed to his request for another society comedy. In the event, he provided Tree with a role, Lord Illingworth, which suited him perfectly and which, it is said, he made a detectable part of his own character in private life for the rest of his days.

Rehearsals with Alexander had not always run smoothly: of the actor's art Wilde had his own ideas, which were not necessarily shared by the professionals; and there had been dispute as to whether Mrs Erlynne's secret should or should not be disclosed to the audience early in the play. With Tree everything proceeded much more easily and *A Woman of No Importance* opened on 19 April 1893 to a distinguished audience and an excellent reception. In addition to Tree as Lord Illingworth, Mrs Bernard Beere played Mrs Arbuthnot, with Fred Terry as Gerald Arbuthnot, Julia Neilson as Hester Worsley, Mrs Tree as Mrs Allonby, and Rose Leclercq as Lady Hunstanton.

Again, Wilde had a curtain-gesture for his audience. In response to calls for 'Author!' he stood up in his box, unmistakably recognizable, and announced, 'Ladies and gentlemen, I regret to inform you that Mr Oscar Wilde is not in the house.' He had already cocked a snook at the critics. In answer to complaints by some of them that *Lady Windermere* lacked action, he had ensured that the first act of *A Woman of No Importance* should contain no action at all, merely a coruscation of epigrams. Audiences were duly convulsed, but the plot was flimsy and a relentless succession of laughs tends to pall, so that although the play did good business its run was shorter by some weeks than that of *Lady Windermere*.

The critics were tolerant enough, but again it was left to A. B. Walkley in the *Speaker* to give Wilde his due: 'A dramatic critic of credit and renown made a confession to me the other day. "I have been spending the morning", said he, "in trying to write my notice of Oscar's new play, and I have found it jolly tough work. It's easy enough to point out scores of faults, and one has to point them out; but, hang it all, one can't help feeling that there is more in the fellow than in all the other beggars put together." That happens to be precisely my own experience. I feel that the "other beggars" can, many of them, give Mr Oscar Wilde points and a beating at the mere cat's-cradle game of dramatic intrigue-weaving, and yet in point of intellect none of them can touch him. Nine English playwrights out of ten, with all their technical skill, their knowledge of "the sort of thing the public want, my boy," strike one as naïve persons; they accept current commonplaces, they have no power of mental detachment, of taking up life betwixt finger and thumb, and looking at it as a queer ironic game. But Mr Wilde is the tenth man, sceptic, cynic, sophist, as well as artist, who moves at ease amid philosophical generalizations, and is the dupe of nothing – except a well-turned phrase.

This temperament is common enough among the bookmen, but among the playwrights it is exceedingly rare.'

The play was received less than rapturously in New York when it opened on 11 December 1893: perhaps not unnaturally, in view of some of the dialogue concerning the American Hester Worsley and her countrywomen. Publication in book form was by Mathews & Lane, London, in October 1894.

. . . .

First Act

On the terrace of Hunstanton Chase, Lady Hunstanton's country home, Lady Caroline Pontefract quizzes Hester Worsley, an orphaned American heiress visiting England for the first time. Hester proves to be outspoken, puritanical, and scornful of England's out-dated institutions and attitude to women. She is also an ardent admirer of Gerald Arbuthnot:

LADY CAROLINE: Ah, yes! the young man who has a post in a bank. Lady Hunstanton is most kind in asking him here, and Lord Illingworth seems to have taken quite a fancy to him. I am not sure, however, that Jane is right in taking him out of his position. In my young days, Miss Worsley, one never met any one in society who worked for their living. It was not considered the thing.

HESTER: In America those are the people we respect most.

LADY CAROLINE: I have no doubt of it.

HESTER: Mr Arbuthnot has a beautiful nature! He is so simple, so sincere. He has one of the most beautiful natures I have ever come across. It is a privilege to meet *him*.

LADY CAROLINE: It is not customary in England, Miss Worsley, for a young lady to speak with such enthusiasm of any person of the opposite sex. English women conceal their feelings till after they are married. They show them then.

Gerald Arbuthnot arrives to break the news that Lord Illingworth has offered to make him his secretary, which implies a brilliant future. Lady Hunstanton determines to get the withdrawn Mrs Arbuthnot, Gerald's mother, to come over and join her guests that evening. Lord Illingworth, whom the ladies of the house-party clearly admire for his reputation as cynic and amorist, engages another guest, Mrs Allonby, in conversation, about the attitude of men to puritan-minded women, and upon his declaring that any woman will succumb to flattery and love-making he is challenged to kiss Miss Worsley.

A reply has been brought from Mrs Arbuthnot to Lady Hunstanton's invitation, to say that she will come over after dinner. Lord Illingworth catches sight of the handwriting: it reminds him of that of a woman he had known years before. When Mrs Allonby asks him who she was, he replies simply, 'Oh! no one. No one in particular. A woman of no importance.'

Second Act

In the drawing-room after dinner that evening, the ladies await the arrival of the men and discuss the husband's role in marriage:

LADY CAROLINE: It is much to be regretted that in our rank of life the wife should be so persistently frivolous, under the impression apparently that it is the proper thing to be. It is to that I attribute the unhappiness of so many marriages we all know of in society.

MRS ALLONBY: Do you know, Lady Caroline, I don't think the frivolity of the wife has ever anything to do with it. More marriages are ruined nowadays by the common sense of the husband than by anything else. How can a woman be expected to be happy with a man who insists on treating her as if she was a perfectly rational being?

LADY HUNSTANTON: My dear!

MRS ALLONBY: Man, poor, awkward, reliable, necessary man belongs to a sex that has been rational for millions and millions of years. He can't help himself. It is in his race. The History of Woman is very different. We have always been picturesque protests against the mere existence of common sense. We saw its dangers from the first.

LADY STUTFIELD: Yes, the common sense of husbands is certainly most, most trying. Do tell me your conception of the Ideal Husband. I think it would be so very, very helpful.

MRS ALLONBY: The Ideal Husband? There couldn't be such a thing. The institution is wrong.

LADY STUTFIELD: The Ideal Man, then, in his relations to *us*.

LADY CAROLINE: He would probably be extremely realistic.

MRS ALLONBY: The Ideal Man! Oh, the Ideal Man should talk to us as if we were goddesses, and treat us as if we were children. He should refuse all our serious requests, and gratify every one of our whims. He should encourage us to have caprices, and forbid us to have missions. He should always say much more than he means, and always mean much more than he says.

LADY HUNSTANTON: But how could he do both, dear?

MRS ALLONBY: He should never run down other pretty women. That would show he had no taste, or make one suspect that he had too much. No; he should be nice about them all, but say that somehow they don't attract him.

LADY STUTFIELD: Yes, that is always very, very pleasant to hear about other women.

MRS ALLONBY: If we ask him a question about anything, he should give us an answer all about ourselves. He should invariably praise us for whatever qualities he knows we haven't got. But he should be pitiless, quite pitiless, in reproaching us for the virtues that we have never dreamed of possessing. He should never believe that we know the use of useful things. That would be unforgivable. But he should shower on us everything we don't want.

LADY CAROLINE: As far as I can see, he is to do nothing but pay bills and compliments.

MRS ALLONBY: He should persistently compromise us in public, and treat us with absolute respect when we are alone. And yet he should be always ready to have a perfectly terrible scene, whenever we want one, and to become miserable, absolutely miserable, at a moment's notice, and to overwhelm us with just reproaches in less than twenty minutes, and to be positively violent at the end of half an hour, and to leave us for ever at a quarter to eight, when we have to go and dress for dinner. And when, after that, one has seen him for really the last time, and he has refused to take back the little things he has given one, and promised never to communicate with one again, or to write one any foolish letters, he should be perfectly broken-hearted, and telegraph to one all day long, and send one little notes every half-hour by a private hansom, and dine quite alone at the club, so that every one should know how unhappy he was. And after a whole dreadful week, during which one has gone about everywhere with one's husband, just to show how absolutely lonely one was, he may be given a third last parting, in the evening, and then, if his conduct has been quite irreproachable, and one has behaved really badly to him, he should be allowed to admit that he has been entirely in the wrong, and when he has admitted that, it becomes a woman's duty to forgive, and one can do it all over again from the beginning, with variations.

Hester Worsley, who has been sitting alone with a book, castigates them for the artificiality of their views and dilates upon the shallowness of English society as compared with American idealism.

Mrs Arbuthnot arrives. She is curious to know something of the Lord Illingworth who has offered her son his secretaryship, and by degrees it emerges that he is a former George Harford, who had succeeded to his late father's title after his elder brother's death in a hunting accident. Mrs Arbuthnot shows some agitation and says she must speak to her son at once. Lady Hunstanton is about to send a servant for him, but at that moment the gentlemen come in. Lord Illingworth does not notice Mrs Arbuthnot, whose eyes never leave him as he crosses the room to address gallant remarks to Lady Stutfield and Mrs Allonby; the latter teasingly offers him a week in which to 'convert' the American girl.

Gerald Arbuthnot comes over and asks Lord Illingworth to meet his mother. On seeing her, Illingworth is clearly shaken, but he recovers his poise at once. When a general move is made towards the music-room he stays behind with Mrs Arbuthnot, and it is at once revealed that Gerald is their illegitimate son, and that Illingworth, then George Harford, had refused to marry her before the birth, as a result of which she had left him and has kept their son to herself during twenty years of country seclusion. Illingworth is glad to have found his son by such a chance, but Mrs Arbuthnot tells him firmly that she will not allow Gerald to be associated with him. Illingworth argues that she is speaking selfishly, and that, whatever their past circumstances, what now matters is their son's chance of advancement from clerk in a small-town bank to a position in the world of diplomacy. She begs him not to take Gerald away. He answers that it is for Gerald to decide.

Gerald returns. Without telling him the truth of his birth, his mother puts it to him that he is happy living with her, and does not possess the qualifications for his new work. Lord Illingworth intervenes to say that he is the best judge of that, and frankly invites her to speak out any real objection she has to Gerald's going to work for him. She says she has none.

Third Act

A little later, in the picture-gallery opening on to the terrace, Lord Illingworth congratulates Gerald on his mother's good sense, and his own at not wishing to remain in obscurity.

LORD ILLINGWORTH: To be modern is the only thing worth being nowadays. You want to be modern, don't you, Gerald? You want to know life as it really is. Not to be put off with any old-fashioned theories about life. Well, what you have to do at present is simply to fit yourself for the best society. A man who can dominate a London dinner-table can dominate the world. The future belongs to the dandy. It is the exquisites who are going to rule.

GERALD: I should like to wear nice things awfully, but I have always been told that a man should not think so much about his clothes.

LORD ILLINGWORTH: People nowadays are so absolutely superficial that they don't understand the philosophy of the superficial. By the way, Gerald, you should learn how to tie your tie better. Sentiment is all very well for the buttonhole. But the essential thing for a necktie is style. A well-tied tie is the first serious step in life.

GERALD: I might be able to learn how to tie a tie, Lord Illingworth, but I should never be able to talk as you do. I don't know how to talk.

LORD ILLINGWORTH: Oh! talk to every woman as if you loved her, and to every man as if he bored you, and at the end of your first season you will have the reputation of possessing the most perfect social tact.

GERALD: But it is very difficult to get into society, isn't it?

LORD ILLINGWORTH: To get into the best society, nowadays, one has either to feed people, amuse people, or shock people – that is all!

GERALD: I suppose society is wonderfully delightful!

LORD ILLINGWORTH: To be in it is merely a bore. But to be out of it simply a tragedy. Society is a necessary thing. No man has any real success in this world unless he has got women to back him, and women rule society. If you have not got women on your side you are quite over. You might just as well be a barrister or a stockbroker, or a journalist at once.

GERALD: It is very difficult to understand women, is it not?

LORD ILLINGWORTH: You should never try to understand them. Women are pictures. Men are problems. If you want to know what a woman really means – which, by the way, is always a dangerous thing to do – look at her, don't listen to her.

GERALD: But women are awfully clever, aren't they?

LORD ILLINGWORTH: One should always tell them so. But, to the philosopher, my dear Gerald, women represent the triumph of matter over mind – just as men represent the triumph of mind over morals.

GERALD: How then can women have so much power as you say they have?

LORD ILLINGWORTH: The history of women is the history of the worst form of tyranny the world has ever known. The tyranny of the weak over the strong. It is the only tyranny that lasts.

GERALD: But haven't women got a refining influence?

LORD ILLINGWORTH: Nothing refines but the intellect.

GERALD: Still, there are many different kinds of women, aren't there?

LORD ILLINGWORTH: Only two kinds in society: the plain and the coloured.

GERALD: But there are good women in society, aren't there?

LORD ILLINGWORTH: Far too many.

GERALD: But do you think women shouldn't be good?

LORD ILLINGWORTH: One should never tell them so, they'd all become good at once. Women are a fascinatingly wilful sex. Every woman is a rebel, and usually in wild revolt against herself.

GERALD: You have never been married, Lord Illingworth, have you?

LORD ILLINGWORTH: Men marry because they are tired; women because they are curious. Both are disappointed.

GERALD: But don't you think one can be happy when one is married?

LORD ILLINGWORTH: Perfectly happy. But the happiness of a married man, my dear Gerald, depends on the people he has not married.

GERALD: But if one is in love?

LORD ILLINGWORTH: One should always be in love. That is the reason one should never marry.

GERALD: Love is a very wonderful thing, isn't it?

LORD ILLINGWORTH: When one is in love one begins by deceiving oneself. And one ends by deceiving others. That is what the world calls a romance. But a really *grande passion* is comparatively rare nowadays. It is the privilege of people who have nothing to do.

The rest of the party return, and Mrs Arbuthnot tries to persuade Gerald that it is time for them to leave. He is reluctant to go, and reveals what he believes will be a pleasant surprise for her – he is to accompany Lord Illingworth to India at the end of the month. She inists on their going home, and he goes off to say good-night to Lord Illingworth. Hester Worsley finds Mrs Arbuthnot, recognizes her sorrow at the thought of losing her son, and goes to fetch Gerald to her, for her to make one more effort to dissuade him from leaving her. Gerald comes in, and his mother, speaking in the third person, tells him of Lord Illingworth's past treachery to a young woman who had been going to bear his child. Gerald's response is unwittingly cruel:

GERALD: My dear mother, it all sounds very tragic, of course. But I dare say the girl was just as much to blame as Lord Illingworth was. – After all, would a really nice girl, a girl with any nice feelings at all, go away from her home with a man to whom she was not married, and live with him as his wife? No nice girl would.

At this, Mrs Arbuthnot tells him she withdraws her objection to his taking the post. He is just thanking her when Hester Worsley runs in, terrified, crying out that Lord Illingworth has just 'insulted' her. Gerald leaps to his feet, threatening to kill the man who has defiled the girl he loves. Mrs Arbuthnot restrains him with the cry, 'Stop, Gerald, stop! He is your own father!'

Fourth Act

Next morning Lady Hunstanton and Mrs Allonby call at Mrs Arbuthnot's to inquire after her: she had had to be taken home in distress the previous evening. Gerald tells them that she is resting, and that he has given up the intention of becoming Lord Illing-worth's secretary, because he does not feel himself capable and does not wish to leave his mother. Advising him that he is acting foolishly, they leave. Mrs Arbuthnot comes in. Gerald tells her his decision, adding that he has written a letter, which he had been about to seal, asking Lord Illingworth to come there and make his atonement by asking Mrs Arbuthnot to be his wife. She replies that marriage would be simply a hideous mockery.

Gerald continues to urge her. Hester, who had left the scene with horror the previous evening, has arrived and overheard them, and now she supports Mrs Arbuthnot in her refusal and offers to marry Gerald in spite of having learnt of his illegitimacy and his mother's shame. She and Gerald go out to the garden. A visitor is announced to Mrs Arbuthnot: it is Lord Illingworth, who inists on being received. He has come to apologize for his behaviour towards Hester and to try to make amends by making Gerald legal heir to his estates and property, provided that he lives half of every year with each parent. Mrs Arbuthnot declines the arrangement. Illingworth sees Gerald's unsealed letter addressed to him and reads it. Condescendingly, he offers marriage, in order to get back his son. He is refused, and rises to take up his hat and gloves:

LORD ILLINGWORTH: Quarter to two! Must be strolling back to Hunstanton. Don't suppose I shall see you there again. I'm sorry, I am, really. It's been an amusing experience to have met amongst people of one's own rank, and treated quite seriously too, one's mistress and one's . . .

She strikes him across the face with one of his gloves. Control-ling himself, he goes to the window for one last look at his son, then leaves. A little later Gerald and Hester enter from the garden. Gerald notices one of Lord Illingworth's gloves lying on the floor. He picks it up:

GERALD: Hullo, mother, whose glove is this? You have had a visitor, Who was it?

MRS ARBUTHNOT: Oh! no one. No one in particular. A man of no importance.

AN IDEAL HUSBAND

IT is a tragically ironical title for a play which opened only a matter of weeks before its author's exposure as anything but the ideal husband himself. In *De Profundis*, Wilde blamed Lord Alfred Douglas's demands upon his time and purse for the fact that the play had to be wrung out, rather than dashed off as a quick successor to *A Woman of No Importance*; but there is no doubt that his own growing indolence and high living and the amount of time he spent with other young men besides Douglas dissipated his creative energies during 1893–4. He seems to have begun to tinker with the play during a stay at Goring-on-Thames in the summer of 1893 and to have written virtually all of it that October in chambers at 10 and 11 St James's Place, London, which he had taken specially for the purpose of disciplining himself into some sort of writing routine; but he was still terming it 'a little incomplete' in February 1894.

Not wishing to return to George Alexander, and with Beerbohm Tree away in America, Wilde sent *An Ideal Husband* to another actor-manager, John Hare, who had had the Garrick Theatre built for him by W. S. Gilbert. Hare did not like the way the play reached its ending and declined it. It finished up in the hands of Lewis Waller, who, with H. H. Morell, had taken the Haymarket in Tree's absence, and when the curtain went up on it there for the first time on 3 January 1895 it was with Waller as Lord Chiltern, Julia Neilson as Lady Chiltern, Charles Hawtrey as Lord Goring, and Florence West as Mrs Cheveley.

Since *A Woman of No Importance* in the spring of 1893 Wilde had given the public no substantial work other than the printed English version of *Salomé* (February 1894) and the juvenile, highly perfumed poem, *The Sphinx* (June 1894), neither of which had done anything to enhance his name. *An Ideal Husband*, by contrast, was received with great enthusiasm by the first-night audience.

It is longer than any of the other plays, and less witty, though there were enough epigrams to please those who went hoping for them. What they found was an essentially dramatic story of blackmail, with a number of twists of plot, and with a use of wit as leavening rather than as *raison d'être*. As always with Wilde, the plot was recognized by critics and informed playgoers as derivative and artificial in its logic of character and occurrence at several points; but it established itself at once as a success and had run for 111 performances when it was taken off on the day after Wilde's arrest. It was to have ended its run at about that time in any case, but when it was revived some days later at another theatre it stood no chance in the face of the opprobrium which now besmirched his name, and it came off after a matter of days.

As usual, the critics were grudging with praise. Clement Scott, in the *Illustrated London News*, was as patronizing towards Wilde as ever: 'Oscar Wilde is the fashion. His catch and whimsicality of dialogue tickle the public. Just now the whole of society is engaged in inventing Oscar Wildeisms, just as a few months ago they were employed in discovering the missing word in competitions. It is the easiest thing in the world. All you have to do is to form an obvious untruth into a false epigram. Cleverness nowadays is nothing but elaborate contradiction, and the man or woman who can say that black is white or white is black in a fanciful fashion is considered a genius. There is scarcely one Oscar Wildeism uttered in the new Haymarket play that will bear one minute's analysis, but for all that they tickle the ears of the groundlings, and are accepted as stage cleverness.' The usually friendly A. B. Walkley ended his piece in the *Speaker*: 'In sum, though it has to be said that Mr. Wilde's piece, by dint of sheer cleverness, keeps one continually amused and interested; that it presents at least one pleasant and human character, everybody's friend save his own – the fact remains that Mr. Wilde's work is not only poor and sterile, but essentially vulgar.'

The most interesting review in retrospect is by the newly-appointed drama critic of the *Saturday Review*, George Bernard Shaw, who recognized in Wilde a fellow assailant of the stuffy

English theatre and its critics, with whom he himself would have so much grappling to do. He wrote: 'Mr. Oscar Wilde's new play at the Haymarket is a dangerous subject, because he has the property of making his critics dull. They laugh angrily at his epigrams, like a child who is coaxed into being amused in the very act of setting up a yell of rage and agony. They protest that the trick is obvious, and that such epigrams can be turned out by the score by anyone light-minded enough to condescend to such frivolity. As far as I can ascertain, I am the only person in London who cannot sit down and write an Oscar Wilde play at will. The fact that his plays, though apparently lucrative, remain unique under these circumstances, says much for the self-denial of our scribes.'

An Ideal Husband was given its first American presentation in New York on 12 March 1895 and gained Wilde his best press and most appreciative audiences in that country so far. First printed publication was by Leonard Smithers, London, in 1899, in a limited edition of signed copies.

．　．　．　．

First Act

A reception is in progress at the Grosvenor Square house of Sir Robert Chiltern, a rising politician, and his wife Gertrude. One of the guests, Lady Markby, has brought a friend, Mrs Cheveley, whom Lady Chiltern recognizes at once as a disliked former schoolfellow. Mrs Cheveley is introduced to Robert Chiltern, who compliments her on the brilliant reputation she has acquired in society in Vienna, where she has lived for several years, and asks why she has chosen to return to London:

CHILTERN: May I know if it is politics or pleasure?

MRS CHEVELEY: Politics are my only pleasure. You see, nowadays it is not fashionable to flirt till one is forty, or to be romantic till one is forty-five, so we poor women who are under thirty, or say we are, have nothing open to us but politics or philanthropy. And philanthropy seems to me to have become simply the refuge of people who wish to annoy their fellow-creatures. I prefer politics. I think they are more . . . becoming!

CHILTERN: A political life is a noble career!

MRS CHEVELEY: Sometimes. And sometimes it is a clever game, Sir Robert.

He reminds her that she has not answered his question. Mrs Cheveley replies that she has come to London to meet him and ask him to do something for her. On the advice of a mutual friend of theirs, the late Baron Arnheim, she has invested heavily in a grandiose political and financial scheme to construct a canal in the Argentine. Chiltern assures her that she has involved herself in a worthless project which is, in fact, nothing more than a deliberate Stock Exchange swindle. He himself is going to attend the House of Commons next evening and present the damning report of a Foreign Office commission of inquiry into it. Mrs Cheveley coolly requests him to withdraw the report, on the grounds that the commissioners have been mistaken or misinformed, and tell the House that the Government is going to reconsider the question in the light of the canal's potentially great importance. If he will do this, she adds, she will pay him handsomely. He is outraged:

MRS CHEVELEY: My dear Sir Robert, you are a man of the world, and you have your price, I suppose. Everybody has nowadays. The drawback is that most people are so dreadfully expensive. I know I am. I hope you will be more reasonable in your terms.

CHILTERN: If you will allow me, I will call your carriage for you. You have lived so long abroad, Mrs Cheveley, that you seem to be unable to realise that you are talking to an English gentleman.

MRS CHEVELEY: I realise that I am talking to a man who laid the foundation of his fortune by selling to a Stock Exchange speculator a Cabinet secret.

She confronts him with her knowledge that when he had been new to Parliament and without money and position he had sold to Baron Arnheim a Cabinet secret that had enabled the Baron and his associates to achieve a great financial *coup*, for which he had been rewarded with a fortune. Mrs Cheveley, who had been the Baron's last mistress before his death, now possesses the letter in which Chiltern had conveyed the secret, and threatens to ruin him with it if he will not do as she wishes. Chiltern offers her money instead. She refuses, and tells him he must give his immediate undertaking to co-operate with her so that she may telegraph her associates in Vienna, or she will give the letter to the Press. He cannot hold out against her, and consents. She sends him to call her carriage. While he is gone, his wife approaches Mrs Cheveley and asks what her business with her husband has been. Without revealing the weapon she has used, Mrs Cheveley answers frankly that she has persuaded Chiltern to drop his opposition to the Argentine Canal scheme.

Mrs Cheveley goes. The dandified bachelor Lord Goring, a close friend of Robert Chiltern's, enters with Chiltern's sister Mabel. They find a diamond brooch that has been dropped on the sofa. Goring tells her he recognizes it as one he gave to someone years before and takes charge of it, strangely requesting Mabel Chiltern not to tell anyone that it has been found. The other guests have departed and Mabel goes off to bed. Before Lord Goring goes, Lady Chiltern tells him briefly of what Mrs Cheveley had told her. As soon as he has gone she startles her husband by telling him too, adding a warning that even in their schooldays the future Mrs Cheveley had been untruthful, dishonest and an evil influence on others. He insists that he himself has come to the conclusion that the Argentina Canal scheme has been condemned too hastily. His wife does not believe him, and warns him that if he is about to tell her anything to his dishonour it will split them apart.

He assures her that there is nothing in his past or present that she may not know. In that case, she replies, he must write at once to Mrs Cheveley refusing to support her scheme. He attempts to procrastinate by offering to go and tell her himself next day, but his wife is insistent. He writes the letter and, although it is midnight, it is dispatched by hand to Mrs Cheveley's hotel.

Second Act

The following morning Chiltern is visited by Lord Goring, to whom he tells the whole story, confessing how he had succumbed to Baron Arnheim's calculated corruption of his principles for a reward of £110,000. Both agree that, though this had happened eighteen years before, it would still bring ruin upon Chiltern's career, and Goring wonders how a man of such moral tone could have allowed himself to be suborned:

CHILTERN: Weak! Do you really think, Arthur, that it is weakness that yields to temptation? I tell you that there are terrible temptations that it requires strength, strength and courage, to yield to. To stake all one's life on a single moment, to risk everything on one throw, whether the stake be power or pleasure, I care not – there is no weakness in that. There is a horrible, a terrible courage.

Chiltern adds that he has since tried to silence his conscience by paying twice the sum Arnheim gave him into charities. Yet, this would not be enough to mitigate his crime in the public eye if it were to be revealed either through Mrs Cheveley's disclosure or his own confession. Goring advises him to confide in his wife, but he refuses. Chiltern asks Goring about Mrs Cheveley's past and discovers that it includes an engagement to Goring, which had very quickly been broken off. Chiltern drafts a telegram to the British Embassy in Vienna, asking for any details of Mrs Cheveley that he might be able to use as a counter-weapon.

Lady Chiltern comes in and her husband goes to attend to some work. She tries to prise out of Goring anything he may know about Robert Chiltern's past; but while evading her question he tries to prepare the way for an eventual disclosure:

LORD GORING: I think that in practical life there is something about success, actual success, that is a little unscrupulous, something about ambition that is unscrupulous always. Once a man has set his heart and soul on getting to a certain point, if he has to climb the crag, he climbs the crag; if he has to walk in the mire . . .

LADY CHILTERN: Well?

LORD GORING: He walks in the mire. Of course I am only talking generally about life.

LADY CHILTERN (*gravely*): I hope so. Why do you look at me so strangely, Lord Goring?

LORD GORING: Lady Chiltern, I have sometimes thought that . . . perhaps you are a little hard in some of your views on life. I think that . . . often you don't make sufficient allowances. In every nature there are elements of weakness, or worse than weakness. Supposing, for instance, that – that any public man, my father, or Lord Merton, or Robert, say, had years ago, written some foolish letter to some one . . .

LADY CHILTERN: What do you mean by a foolish letter?

LORD GORING: A letter gravely compromising one's position. I am only putting an imaginary case.

LADY CHILTERN: Robert is as incapable of doing a foolish thing as he is of doing a wrong thing.

LORD GORING (*after a long pause*): Nobody is incapable of doing a foolish thing. Nobody is incapable of doing a wrong thing.

LADY CHILTERN: Are you a Pessimist? What will the other dandies say? They will all have to go into mourning.

LORD GORING (*rising*): No, Lady Chiltern, I am not a Pessimist. Indeed I am not sure that I quite know what pessimism really means. All I do know is that life cannot be understood without much charity, cannot be lived without much charity. It is love, and not German philosophy, that is the true explanation of this world, whatever may be the explanation of the next. And if you are ever in trouble, Lady Chiltern, trust me absolutely, and I will help you in every way I can. If you ever want me, come to me for my assistance, and you shall have it. Come at once to me.

To hear the ever-flippant Lord Goring speaking so seriously is a surprise to Lady Chiltern. Before leaving he asks for a copy of her guest-list for the previous evening. She sends him for it to one of her husband's secretaries, Tommy Trafford, with whom, as it happens, her sister Mabel is conducting a teasing flirtation, in the hope of provoking Lord Goring into renouncing bachelorhood for her.

Lady Markby and Mrs Cheveley arrive to inquire whether a diamond brooch Mrs Cheveley had been wearing the previous evening had been found. Mason, the butler, confirms that none of the servants has reported it. Lady Chiltern persuades Mrs Cheveley to stay a little longer while Lady Markby goes to another engagement. She tells her bluntly that it was she who had made her husband write to withdraw his promise. Mrs Cheveley replies that she had better make him reconsider; and when Lady Chiltern refuses contemptuously she angrily reveals the extent of her hold over him. Robert Chiltern has entered the room just in time to hear this last exchange. Lady Chiltern summons Mason to show her visitor out, then Lady Chiltern challenges her husband to confirm or deny the accusation. He confesses and tries to justify his motives. She will not listen, which incenses him to accuse her bitterly of false idealism:

CHILTERN: You made your false idol of me, and I had not the courage to come down, show you my wounds, tell you my weaknesses. I was afraid that I might lose your love, as I have lost it now. And so, last night you ruined my life for me – yes, ruined it! What this woman asked of me was nothing compared to what she offered to me. She offered security, peace, stability. The sin of my youth, that I had thought was buried, rose up in front of me, hideous, horrible, with its hands at my throat. I could have killed it for ever, sent it back into its tomb, destroyed its record, burned the one witness against me. You prevented me. No one but you, you know it. And now what is there before me but public disgrace, ruin, terrible shame, the mockery of the world, a lonely dishonoured life, a lonely dishonoured death, it may be, some day? Let women make no more ideals of men! let them not put them on altars and bow before them or they may ruin other lives as completely as you – you whom I have so wildly loved – have ruined mine!

Third Act

Late that evening Lord Goring is preparing to leave his house in full evening dress for a social engagement when his butler, Phipps, hands him a note from Lady Chiltern. It reads 'I want you. I trust you. I am coming to you.' He has no sooner read it than a visitor is announced, his elderly father Lord Caversham, who has called to make yet another of his hitherto fruitless efforts to persuade his son to mend his indolent ways:

LORD CAVERSHAM: Want to have a serious conversation with you, sir.

LORD GORING: My dear father! At this hour?

LORD CAVERSHAM: Well, sir, it is only ten o'clock. What is your objection to the hour? I think the hour is an admirable hour!

LORD GORING: Well, the fact is, father, this is not my day for talking seriously. I am very sorry, but it is not my day.

LORD CAVERSHAM: What do you mean, sir?

LORD GORING: During the Season, father, I only talk seriously on the first Tuesday in every month, from four to seven.

LORD CAVERSHAM: Well, make it Tuesday, sir, make it Tuesday.

LORD GORING: But it is after seven, father, and my doctor says I must not have any serious conversation after seven. It makes me talk in my sleep.

LORD CAVERSHAM: Talk in your sleep, sir? What does that matter? You are not married.

LORD GORING: No, father, I am not married.

LORD CAVERSHAM: Hum! That is what I have come to talk to you about, sir. You have got to get married, and at once. Why, when I was your age, sir, I had been an inconsolable widower for three months, and was already paying my addresses to your admirable mother. Damme, sir, it is your duty to get married. You can't be always living for pleasure. Every man of position is married nowadays. Bachelors are not fashionable any more. They are a damaged lot. Too much is known about them. You must get a wife, sir. Look where your friend Robert Chiltern has got by probity, hard work, and a sensible marriage with a good woman. Why don't you imitate him, sir? Why don't you take him for your model?

LORD GORING: I think I shall, father.

LORD CAVERSHAM: I wish you would, sir. Then I should be happy. At present I make your mother's life miserable on your account. You are heartless, sir, quite heartless.

LORD GORING: I hope not, father.

LORD CAVERSHAM: And it is high time for you to get married. You are thirty-four years of age, sir.

LORD GORING: Yes, father, but I only admit to thirty-two – thirty-one and a half when I have a really good buttonhole. This buttonhole is not . . . trivial enough.

Unable to drive his despairing parent away, Goring murmurs to Phipps that he is expecting a lady to call: he is to show her into the drawing-room and ask her to wait, while he concludes his conversation with Lord Caversham in the library. No sooner has the library door closed on them than the lady arrives; but it is not Lady Chiltern – it is Mrs Cheveley. Gathering at once from Phipps's manner that a lady had been expected, she determines to find out who she can be. She sends Phipps on a brief errand and examines the correspondence on Lord Goring's desk. She recognizes the handwriting of Lady Chiltern's note and reads it. She is about to steal it when Phipps returns, and she has only time to hide it under the blotter. The butler shows her through to the drawing-room and closes the door, as Goring and his father emerge from the library.

Defeated yet again, the old man leaves, but no sooner has he gone than there is another visitor – Robert Chiltern. Goring is anxious to get rid of him, and even more disconcerted when he quietly ascertains from Phipps that 'the lady' is already in the drawing-room. Chiltern has come to report that nothing has been discovered in Vienna with which to discredit Mrs Cheveley. Goring decides to address Chiltern in terms that his wife will overhear and which may move her to forgiveness, but as he is doing so there is the sound of a chair falling in the next room. Chiltern demands to know who is there, listening to this intimate discussion. Goring, believing it to be Lady Chiltern, tries to prevent him from going so see for himself. Robert Chiltern opens the drawing-room door, returns angrily and, flinging an accusation of treachery at his friend, leaves the house. Lord Goring is astonished to see Mrs Cheveley emerge from the drawing-room, radiant and amused.

Mrs Cheveley has brought Goring an ultimatum: if he will marry her, as had once been intended, and thereby enable her to re-establish herself in London society, she will give him back the letter compromising Robert Chiltern. Goring declines to make this self-sacrificial act and condemns her for having gone to the Chilterns' house that morning and exposed Chiltern's secret to his wife. She protests that she had actually gone to inquire for her missing brooch:

LORD GORING: A diamond snake-brooch with a ruby?

MRS CHEVELEY: Yes. How do you know?

LORD GORING: Because it is found. In point of fact, I found it myself, and stupidly forgot to tell the butler anything about it as I was leaving. It is in this drawer. No, that one. This is the brooch, isn't it?

MRS CHEVELEY: Yes, I am so glad to get it back. It was . . . a present.

LORD GORING: Won't you wear it?

MRS CHEVELEY: Certainly, if you pin it in. (*Lord Goring suddenly clasps it on her arm.*) Why do you put it on as a bracelet? I never knew it could be worn as a bracelet.

LORD GORING: Really?

MRS CHEVELEY: No; but it looks very well on me as a bracelet, doesn't it.

LORD GORING: Yes; much better than when I saw it last.

MRS CHEVELEY: When did you see it last?

LORD GORING: Oh, ten years ago, on Lady Berkshire, from whom you stole it.

MRS CHEVELEY: What do you mean?

LORD GORING: I mean that you stole that ornament from my cousin, Mary Berkshire, to whom I gave it when she was married. Suspicion fell on a wretched servant, who was sent away in disgrace. I recognized it last night. I determined to say nothing about it till I had found the thief. I have found the thief now, and I have heard her own confession.

MRS CHEVELEY: It is not true.

LORD GORING: You know it is true. Why, thief is written across your face at this moment.

MRS CHEVELEY: I will deny the whole affair from beginning to end. I will say that I have never seen this wretched thing, that it was never in my possession. (*Mrs Cheveley tries to get the bracelet off her arm, but fails. Lord Goring looks on amused. Her thin fingers tear at the jewel to no purpose. A curse breaks from her.*)

LORD GORING: The drawback of stealing a thing, Mrs Cheveley, is that one never knows how wonderful the thing that one steals is. You can't get that bracelet off, unless you know, where the spring is. And I see you don't know where the spring is. It is rather difficult to find.

She is unable to unclasp the bracelet. Goring calmly tells her that unless she hands over Chiltern's letter he will send his servant

for the police and ensure that his cousin prosecutes her for the theft
of the bracelet. She gives him the letter, which he burns. Her eye
falls on the blotter on his desk. She begs him for a glass of water,
and as he fetches it she snatches up Lady Chiltern's note:

MRS CHEVELEY: I am never going to try to harm Robert Chiltern
again.

LORD GORING: Fortunately you have not the chance, Mrs Cheveley.

MRS CHEVELEY: Well, if even I had the chance, I wouldn't. On the
contrary, I am going to render him a great service.

LORD GORING: I am charmed to hear it. It is a reformation.

MRS CHEVELEY: Yes. I can't bear so upright a gentleman, so honourable
an English gentleman, being so shamefully deceived and so . . .

LORD GORING: Well?

MRS CHEVELEY: I find that somehow Gertrude Chiltern's dying
speech and confession has strayed into my pocket.

LORD GORING: What do you mean?

MRS CHEVELEY: I mean that I am going to send Robert Chiltern the
love-letter his wife wrote to you to-night.

LORD GORING: Love-letter?

MRS CHEVELEY (*laughing*): 'I want you. I trust you. I am coming to
you. Gertrude.'

LORD GORING: You wretched woman, must you always be thieving?
Give me back that letter. I'll take it from you by force. You shall not
leave my room till I have got it. (*He rushes towards her, but Mrs Cheveley
at once puts her hand on the electric bell that is on the table. The bell sounds
with shrill reverberations, and Phipps enters.*)

MRS CHEVELEY: Lord Goring merely rang that you should show me
out. Good-night, Lord Goring.

Fourth Act

The following morning Lord Goring calls at the Chilterns' house.
He encounters his father, who tells him that, the previous even-
ing, Robert Chiltern had made a brilliant speech in the House of
Commons denouncing the Argentine Canal scheme. Lord Caver-
sham goes off to Downing Street to see the Prime Minister, leaving
Goring alone with Mabel Chiltern, to whom at last he proposes.

She accepts immediately. Lady Chiltern enters, and at Goring's request Mabel goes off into the conservatory, leaving them alone. He tells her of his retrieval and destruction of her husband's letter, but of Mrs Cheveley's theft of her own, which must be prevented from reaching her husband. She is about to go and instruct her husband's secretary that any letter that might arrive for him enclosing a note written on her own pink notepaper must be intercepted and brought to her, when, to their horror, Robert Chiltern enters with the note itself in his hands:

CHILTERN: 'I want you. I trust you. I am coming to you. Gertrude.' Oh, my love! Is this true? Do you indeed trust me, and want me? If so, it was for me to come to you, not for you to write of coming to me. This letter of yours, Gertrude, makes me feel that nothing that the world may do can hurt me now. You want me, Gertrude. (*Lord Goring, unseen by Sir Robert Chiltern, makes an imploring sign to Lady Chiltern to accept the situation and Sir Robert's error.*)

LADY CHILTERN: Yes.

CHILTERN: You trust me, Gertrude?

LADY CHILTERN: Yes.

CHILTERN: Ah! why did you not add you loved me?

LADY CHILTERN: Because I loved you.

Lord Goring quietly moves away into the conservatory, and Lady Chiltern gives her husband the news that he is safe from scandal. His relief is tempered by his principles, which are so strong that he declares his intention of retiring from public life. She ardently supports him, and they speak of an idealized life together away from London. At this point, however, Lord Caversham returns from Downing Street with a letter from the Prime Minister offering Chiltern a seat in the Cabinet, his reward for the high character and moral tone demonstrated in his last night's speech. The old politician is horrified to find the Chilterns united in the decision to refuse the offer. Chiltern goes off to write a letter of resignation for Lord Caversham to take back to Downing Street, and Lord Goring, who has overheard the conversation, takes the opportunity to intervene yet again. Sending his father into the conservatory to talk to Mabel Chiltern, he charges Lady Chiltern with unthinkingly completing Mrs Cheveley's evil scheme for her. Mrs Cheveley had given Robert Chiltern the alternative of acting dishonestly or being forced out of public life. The former possibility has now been averted, but the latter is being thrust upon him by Lady Chiltern, since he has taken his decision in order to regain her respect and secure her love.

Sir Robert Chiltern returns with the completed letter. His wife reads it, and tears it up. He sees the influence of Lord Goring behind her gesture and thanks him warmly for helping him once more; yet, a moment later, he is refusing Goring's request for permission to marry Mabel, who is under her brother's guardianship. His objection arises from the discovery of Mrs Cheveley in Goring's rooms, which Goring is in no position to explain. Lady Chiltern speaks out:

LADY CHILTERN: Robert, it was not Mrs Cheveley whom Lord Goring expected last night.

CHILTERN: Not Mrs Cheveley! Who was it then?

LORD GORING: Lady Chiltern!

LADY CHILTERN: It was your own wife. Robert, yesterday afternoon Lord Goring told me that if ever I was in trouble I could come to him for help, as he was our oldest and best friend. Later on, after that terrible scene in this room, I wrote to him telling him that I trusted him, that I had need of him, that I was coming to him for help and advice. Yes, that letter. I didn't go to Lord Goring's, after all. I felt that it is from ourselves alone that help can come. Pride made me think that. Mrs Cheveley went. She stole my letter and sent it anonymously to you this morning, that you should think . . . Oh! Robert, I cannot tell you what she wished you to think. . .

CHILTERN: What! Had I fallen so low in your eyes that you thought that even for a moment I could have doubted your goodness? Gertrude, Gertrude, you are to me the white image of all good things, and sin can never touch you. Arthur, you can go to Mabel, and you have my best wishes!

Lord Caversham returns with Mabel, to receive the double news that she and his son are to be married and that Chiltern will join the Cabinet. Caversham addresses his son:

LORD CAVERSHAM: If you don't make this young lady an ideal husband, I'll cut you off with a shilling.

MABEL: An ideal husband! Oh, I don't think I should like that. It sounds like something in the next world.

THE IMPORTANCE OF BEING EARNEST

IN the summer of 1894, dwelling in the artistic and social waste-land between *A Woman of No Importance* and *An Ideal Husband* when his expenses were far in excess of his means, Wilde turned once more to George Alexander. They had not always seen eye to eye artistically, but had had a successful commercial relationship over *Lady Windermere's Fan*, and now Wilde asked for an advance of £150 against a comedy to be written, the money to be repay-able if Alexander did not like the finished product. He paid the money, but, in the event, did not care for the play. He passed it to another actor-manager; but Henry James's play *Guy Domville* which had opened at the St James's Theatre at the same time as Wilde's *An Ideal Husband* at the Haymarket, was quickly seen to be destined for a short life (it ran for only 31 performances: James had seen *An Ideal Husband*, he wrote to his brother, and been suddenly 'paralyzed' by the thought: 'How *can* my piece do any-thing with a public with whom *that* is a success?). Alexander hastily retrieved Wilde's new play and announced that it would replace Henry James's. It did so on 14 February 1895: the new play was *The Importance of Being Earnest*.

The play was mostly written during three weeks of a retreat Wilde had spent with his wife, their two children and 'a horrid ugly Swiss governess' at 'The Haven', No. 5, The Esplanade, Worthing, Sussex. 'My play is really very funny,' he wrote to Alfred Douglas; 'I am quite delighted with it.' His delight was not mistaken and has been shared by the world ever since. To employ the old phrase, he took wings to write it, casting aside pretentious-ness and any attempt to be serious, and surrendering himself entirely to the kind of artificiality that can only be sustained by wit. When he read it to them, the actors were convulsed, but feared the whole thing might fly over the audiences' heads, a doubt reflected sardonically by Wilde in a newspaper interview shortly before the opening night when he was asked whether the play would be a success: 'My dear fellow, you have got it all wrong. The play *is* a success. The only question is whether the first night's audience will be one.' The reaction of that audience on 14 February 1895 at the St James's Theatre was subsequently described to Hesketh Pearson by Allan Aynesworth, who played Algernon Moncrieff: 'In my fifty-three years of acting, I never remember a greater triumph. . . . The audience rose in their seats and cheered and cheered again.'

Alexander himself played Jack Worthing, Gwendolen Fairfax was played by Irene Vanbrugh, Cecily Cardew by Evelyn Millard, Lady Bracknell by Rose Leclercq, Miss Prism by Mrs George Cumminge, and Dr Chasuble by H. H. Vincent. Several leading critics who had previously been hostile to Wilde, or had held reservations about him, were at least partly won over, among them H. G. Wells, who wrote in the *Pall Mall Gazette:* 'On the last production of a play by Mr Oscar Wilde we said it was fairly bad, and anticipated success. This time we must congratulate him unreservedly on a delightful revival of theatrical satire. . . . But we could pray for the play's success, else we fear it may prove the last struggle of its author against the growing seriousness of his dramatic style.' William Archer wrote in the *World*: 'It is delightful to see, it sends wave after wave of laughter curling and foaming round the theatre; but as a text for criticism it is barren and delusive. It is like a mirage-oasis in the desert, grateful and comforting to the weary eye – but when you come close up to it, behold! it is intangible, it eludes your grasping. What can a poor critic do with a play which raises no principle, whether of art or morals, creates its own canons and conventions, and is nothing but an absolutely wilful expression of an irrepressibly witty personality?'

The answer, of course, is, capitulate and laugh with the rest, and admit it; but Archer was not that sort of man. George Bernard Shaw was one, within limits, but the new critic was perhaps too busy trying to demonstrate that he was not so easily taken in as his fellow audience members: 'It amused me, of course; but unless comedy touches me as well as amuses me, it leaves me with a sense of having wasted my evening. I go to the theatre to be moved to laughter, not to be tickled or bustled into it; and that is why, though I laugh as much as anybody at a farcical comedy, I am out of spirits before the end of the second act, and out of temper before the end of the third. . . .' Hesketh Pearson reminds us that Shaw attended the second night, when anti-climatic reaction often sets in amongst actors and things tend to fall rather flat; but he records that Shaw never altered his opinion.

The verdict of contemporary audiences and of posterity has been that there is as much to compel helpless laughter in the second and third acts as in the first. *The Importance of Being Earnest* is one of the funniest plays ever written, and its wit is of a kind that does not pall through sheer relentlessness or surfeit. It is a series of brilliant set-piece scenes connected by a thread of irresistible absurdity and peopled by as memorable a set of characters as ever a playwright created. Its first American production, which opened in New York on 22 April 1895, was not much of a success – perhaps the piece was too out-and-out English; but the play has come to be appreciated there as it has in most parts of the world, owing in no small measure, in more recent years, to the sparkling English filmed version directed by Anthony Asquith with Michael Redgrave, Michael Denison, Edith Evans, Dorothy Tutin, Joan Greenwood, Miles Malleson and Margaret Rutherford in roles which might have been created for them alone.

The Importance of Being Earnest had been playing to full houses for less than a month when Wilde was arrested on 5 April 1895. Alexander kept it on for another month, with the author's name removed from the bills and programmes as a sop to prudery. He had to take it off after only 81 performances and lost money on it. A revival in 1902 was only moderately successful, but another one in 1909, with Alexander and Aynesworth in their original roles, made him over £21,000 profit. 'How this would have pleased him!' Alexander was able to write to Robert Ross; but Oscar Wilde was nearly a decade beyond pleasing by then. At least, Alexander, who had bought the rights when Wilde was bankrupted, had made some voluntary payments to him in his last days and, as with *Lady Windermere's Fan*, bequeathed the rights to Wilde's son.

. . . .

First Act

At his London flat Algernon Moncrieff receives a visit from his friend from the country, John Worthing. The fact that Algernon's manservant, Lane, announces the caller as Mr *Ernest* Worthing is explained by Worthing's habit of calling himself John in the country and Ernest in town and professing to be two brothers, the country one worthy and responsible, the town one younger and profligate. Algernon has discovered something of this secret through Worthing's having left his cigarette case behind on an earlier visit, and now that Worthing is expressing a wish to marry Algernon's first cousin, Gwendolen Fairfax, he taxes him with the subject of the inscription in the case:

JACK: You have no right whatsoever to read what is written inside. It is a very ungentlemanly thing to read a private cigarette case.

ALGERNON: Oh! it is absurd to have a hard and fast rule about what one should read and what one shouldn't. More than half of modern culture depends on what one shouldn't read.

JACK: I am quite aware of the fact, and I don't propose to discuss modern culture. It isn't the sort of thing one should talk of in private. I simply want my cigarette case back.

ALGERNON: Yes; but this isn't your cigarette case. This cigarette case is a present from some one of the name of Cecily, and you said you didn't know any one of that name.

JACK: Well, if you want to know, Cecily happens to be my aunt.

ALGERNON: Your aunt!

JACK: Yes. Charming old lady she is, too. Lives at Tunbridge Wells. Just give it back to me, Algy.

ALGERNON: But why does she call herself little Cecily if she is your aunt and lives at Tunbridge Wells? 'From little Cecily with her fondest love.'

JACK: My dear fellow, what on earth is there in that? Some aunts are tall, some aunts are not tall. That is a matter that surely an aunt may be allowed to decide for herself. You seem to think that every aunt should be exactly like your aunt! That is absurd! For Heaven's sake give me back my cigarette case.

ALGERNON: Yes. But why does your aunt call you her uncle? 'From little Cecily, with her fondest love to her dear Uncle Jack.' There is no objection, I admit, to an aunt being a small aunt, but why an aunt, no matter what her size may be, should call her own nephew her uncle, I can't quite make out.

Worthing is compelled to confess to his dual identity and to reveal that Mr Thomas Cardew, an old gentleman who had adopted him as an infant orphan, had made him in his will guardian to his grand-daughter, Miss Cecily Cardew, who lives at Worthing's country place under the charge of her governess, Miss Prism. He refuses to reveal the location of his country home, since he has no intention of permitting Algernon, the man-about-town, to meet his ward. Algernon, too, maintains a fictional character to provide him with excuses for escaping from town whenever convenient: a permanent invalid named Bunbury, living at an undisclosed country place, whom Algernon frequently finds it his duty to visit whenever Bunbury's complaint takes a turn for the worse. He terms this process 'Bunburying', and accuses Worthing of being an advanced practitioner of it. Worthing replies that he is nothing of the sort, for if Gwendolen accepts him he intends to 'kill off' his Ernest identity.

Gwendolen arrives, escorted by her formidable mother, Algernon's Aunt Augusta, Lady Bracknell, who carries Algernon off into the music-room to arrange the music for a reception she is about to give. Worthing and Gwendolen are left alone:

JACK: Charming day it has been, Miss Fairfax.

GWENDOLEN: Pray don't talk to me about the weather, Mr Worthing. Whenever people talk to me about the weather, I always feel quite certain that they mean something else. And that makes me so nervous.

JACK: I do mean something else.

GWENDOLEN: I thought so. In fact, I am never wrong.

JACK: And I would like to be allowed to take advantage of Lady Bracknell's temporary absence. . .

GWENDOLEN: I would certainly advise you to do so. Mamma has a way of coming back suddenly into a room that I have often had to speak to her about.

JACK: Miss Fairfax, ever since I met you I have admired you more than any girl . . . I have ever met since . . . I met you.

GWENDOLEN: Yes, I am quite well aware of the fact. And I often wish that in public, at any rate, you had been more demonstrative. For me you have always had an irresistible fascination. Even before I met you I was far from indifferent to you. We live, as I hope you know, Mr Worthing, in an age of ideals. The fact is constantly mentioned in the more expensive monthly magazines, and has now reached the provincial pulpits, I am told; and my ideal has always been to love some one of the name of Ernest. There is something in that name that inspires absolute confidence. The moment Algernon first mentioned to me that he had a friend called Ernest, I knew I was destined to love you.

JACK: You really love me, Gwendolen?

GWENDOLEN: Passionately!

JACK: Darling! You don't know how happy you've made me.

GWENDOLEN: My own Ernest!

JACK: But you don't really mean to say that you couldn't love me if my name wasn't Ernest?

GWENDOLEN: But your name is Ernest.

He confesses that he is not particularly fond of the name of Ernest, which he feels does not suit him, and suggests that Jack, for instance, might be preferable. She answers that she finds no charm in that name, and even less in its formal origin, John. Privately determining to get himself christened Ernest at once, he asks her to marry him, and is accepted. They are interrupted by the return of Lady Bracknell:

LADY BRACKNELL: Mr Worthing! Rise, sir, from this semi-recumbent posture. It is most indecorous.

GWENDOLEN: Mamma! I must beg you to retire. This is no place for you. Besides, Mr Worthing has not quite finished yet.

LADY BRACKNELL: Finished what, may I ask?

GWENDOLEN: I am engaged to Mr Worthing, mamma.

LADY BRACKNELL: Pardon me, you are not engaged to any one. When you do become engaged to some one, I, or your father, should his health permit him, will inform you of the fact. An engagement should come on a young girl as a surprise, pleasant or unpleasant, as the case may be. It is hardly a matter that she could be allowed to arrange for herself. . . . And now I have a few questions to put to you, Mr Worthing. While I am making these inquiries, you, Gwendolen, will wait for me below in the carriage.

GWENDOLEN: Mamma!

LADY BRACKNELL: In the carriage, Gwendolen! Gwendolen, the carriage!

GWENDOLEN: Yes, mamma. (*Goes out, looking back at Jack.*)

LADY BRACKNELL: You can take a seat, Mr Worthing.

JACK: Thank you, Lady Bracknell, I prefer standing.

LADY BRACKNELL: I feel bound to tell you that you are not down on my list of eligible young men, although I have the same list as the dear Duchess of Bolton has. We work together, in fact. However, I am quite ready to enter your name, should your answers be what a really affectionate mother requires. Do you smoke?

JACK: Well, yes, I must admit I smoke.

LADY BRACKNELL: I am glad to hear it. A man should always have an occupation of some kind. There are far too many idle men in London as it is. How old are you?

JACK: Twenty-nine.

LADY BRACKNELL: A very good age to be married at. I have always been of opinion that a man who desires to get married should know either everything or nothing. Which do you know?

ACK: I know nothing, Lady Bracknell.

LADY BRACKNELL: I am pleased to hear it. I do not approve of anything that tampers with natural ignorance. Ignorance is like a delicate exotic fruit; touch it and the bloom is gone. The whole theory of modern education is radically unsound. Fortunately in England, at any rate, education produces no effect whatsoever. If it did, it would prove a serious danger to the upper classes, and probably lead to acts of violence in Grosvenor Square. What is your income?

JACK: Between seven and eight thousand a year.

LADY BRACKNELL: In land, or in investments?

JACK: In investments, chiefly.

LADY BRACKNELL: That is satisfactory. What between the duties expected of one during one's lifetime, and the duties exacted from one after one's death, land has ceased to be either a profit or a pleasure. It gives one position, and prevents one from keeping it up. That's all that can be said about land.

JACK: I have a country house with some land, of course, attached to it, about fifteen hundred acres, I believe; but I don't depend on that for my real income. In fact, as far as I can make out, the poachers are the only people who make anything out of it.

LADY BRACKNELL: A country house! How many bedrooms? Well, that point can be cleared up afterwards. You have a town house, I hope? A girl with a simple, unspoiled nature, like Gwendolen, could hardly be expected to reside in the country.

JACK: Well, I own a house in Belgrave Square, but it is let by the year to Lady Bloxham. Of course, I can get it back whenever I like, at six months' notice.

LADY BRACKNELL: Lady Bloxham? I don't know her.

JACK: Oh, she goes about very little. She is a lady considerably advanced in years.

LADY BRACKNELL: Ah, nowadays that is no guarantee of respectability of character. What number in Belgrave Square?

JACK: 149.

LADY BRACKNELL: The unfashionable side. I thought there was something. However, that could easily be altered.

JACK: Do you mean the fashion, or the side?

LADY BRACKNELL: Both, if necessary, I presume. What are your politics?

JACK: Well, I am afraid I really have none. I am a Liberal Unionist.

LADY BRACKNELL: Oh, they count as Tories. They dine with us. Or come in the evening, at any rate. Now to minor matters. Are your parents living?

JACK: I have lost both my parents.

LADY BRACKNELL: To lose one parent, Mr Worthing, may be regarded as a misfortune; to lose both looks like carelessness. Who was your father? He was evidently a man of some wealth. Was he born in what the Radical papers call the purple of commerce, or did he rise from the ranks of the aristocracy?

JACK: I am afraid I really don't know. The fact is, Lady Bracknell, I said I had lost my parents. It would be nearer the truth to say that my parents seem to have lost me . . . I don't actually know who I am by birth. I was . . . well, I was found.

LADY BRACKNELL: Found!

JACK: The late Mr Thomas Cardew, an old gentleman of a very charitable and kindly disposition, found me, and gave me the name of Worthing, because he happened to have a first-class ticket for Worthing in his pocket at the time. Worthing is a place in Sussex. It is a seaside resort.

LADY BRACKNELL: Where did the charitable gentleman who had a first-class ticket for this seaside resort find you?

JACK: In a hand-bag.

LADY BRACKNELL: In a hand-bag?

JACK: Yes, Lady Bracknell, I was in a hand-bag – a somewhat large, black leather hand-bag, with handles to it – an ordinary hand-bag in fact.

LADY BRACKNELL: In what locality did this Mr James, or Thomas, Cardew come across this ordinary hand-bag?

JACK: In the cloak-room at Victoria Station. It was given to him in mistake for his own.

LADY BRACKNELL: The cloak-room at Victoria Station?

JACK: Yes. The Brighton line.

LADY BRACKNELL: The line is immaterial. Mr Worthing, I confess I feel somewhat bewildered by what you have just told me. To be born, or at any rate bred, in a hand-bag, whether it had handles or not, seems to me to display a contempt for the ordinary decencies of family life that reminds one of the worst excesses of the French Revolution. And I presume you know what that unfortunate movement led to? As for the particular locality in which the hand-bag was found, a cloak-room at a railway station might serve to conceal a social indiscretion – has probably, indeed, been used for that purpose before now – but it could hardly be regarded as an assured basis for a recognised position in good society.

JACK: May I ask you then what you would advise me to do? I need hardly say I would do anything in the world to ensure Gwendolen's happiness.

LADY BRACKNELL: I would strongly advise you, Mr Worthing, to try and acquire some relations as soon as possible, and to make a definite effort to produce at any rate one parent, of either sex, before the season is quite over.

JACK: Well, I don't see how I could possibly manage to do that. I can produce the hand-bag at any moment. It is in my dressing-room at home. I really think that should satisfy you, Lady Bracknell.

LADY BRACKNELL: Me, sir! What has it to do with me? You can hardly imagine that I and Lord Bracknell would dream of allowing our only daughter – a girl brought up with the utmost care – to marry into a cloak-room, and form an alliance with a parcel. Good-morning, Mr Worthing!

She sweeps imperiously from the room. Algernon returns, having overheard it all, and endeavours to gain further information about Cecily Cardew, but can learn nothing beyond the facts that she is excessively pretty and only just eighteen. He is unexpectedly assisted by the return of Gwendolen, to tell Worthing that, despite her mother's refusal to let them marry, she will remain eternally devoted to him, and to ask for his country address, which the listening Algernon secretly notes on his shirt-cuff.

Second Act

In the garden of the Manor House, Woolton, Hertfordshire, Cecily Cardew is reluctantly undergoing her German lesson from the elderly Miss Prism. She is only too relieved to be able to distract her governess into talking about the literary aspirations of that lady's youth, when she had written a three-volume novel, the manuscript of which had been lost before it could be published; and even more pleased to see Miss Prism's undeclared admirer, the Rev Dr Chasuble, approaching. Without much difficulty, Cecily persuades Miss Prism to go off for a stroll with the Rector. In their absence, the butler, Merriman, informs her that her Uncle Jack's brother Ernest has arrived, is evidently disappointed to find that his brother is away, and would like to speak to her. She sends Merriman to fetch him and to give the housekeeper instructions to prepare a room for him, reflecting to herself that she has never met a really wicked person before and fears that he will turn out to look like everyone else.

He is, of course, Algernon Moncrieff, looking his usual gay, debonair self and anything but wicked:

ALGERNON (*raising his hat*): You are my little cousin, Cecily, I'm sure.

CECILY: You are under some strange mistake. I am not little. In fact, I believe I am more than usually tall for my age. But I am your cousin Cecily. You, I see from your card, are Uncle Jack's brother, my cousin Ernest, my wicked cousin Ernest.

ALGERNON: Oh! I am not really wicked at all, cousin Cecily. You mustn't think that I am wicked.

CECILY: If you are not, then you have certainly been deceiving us all in a very inexcusable manner. I hope you have not been leading a double life, pretending to be wicked and being really good all the time. That would be hypocrisy.

ALGERNON: Oh! Of course I have been rather reckless.

CECILY: I am glad to hear it.

ALGERNON: In fact, now you mention the subject, I have been very bad in my own small way.

CECILY: I don't think you should be so proud of that, though I am sure it must have been very pleasant.

ALGERNON: It is much pleasanter being here with you.

CECILY: I can't understand how you are here at all. Uncle Jack won't be back till Monday afternoon.

ALGERNON: That is a great disappointment. I am obliged to go up by the first train on Monday morning. I have a business appointment that I am anxious . . . to miss!

CECILY: Couldn't you miss it anywhere but in London?

ALGERNON: No: the appointment is in London.

CECILY: Well, I know, of course, how important it is not to keep a business engagement, if one wants to retain any sense of the beauty of life, but still I think you had better wait till Uncle Jack arrives. I know he wants to speak to you about your emigrating.

ALGERNON: About my what?

CECILY: Your emigrating. He has gone up to buy your outfit.

ALGERNON: I certainly wouldn't let Jack buy my outfit. He has no taste in neckties at all.

CECILY: I don't think you will require neckties. Uncle Jack is sending you to Australia.

ALGERNON: Australia! I'd sooner die.

CECILY: Well, he said at dinner on Wednesday night, that you would have to choose between this world, the next world, and Australia.

ALGERNON: Oh, well! The accounts I have received of Australia and the next world, are not particularly encouraging. This world is good enough for me, cousin Cecily.

CECILY: Yes, but are you good enough for it?

ALGERNON: I'm afraid I'm not that. That is why I want you to reform me. You might make that your mission, if you don't mind, cousin Cecily.

CECILY: I'm afraid I've no time, this afternoon.

ALGERNON: Well, would you mind my reforming myself this afternoon?

CECILY: It is rather Quixotic of you. But I think you should try.

ALGERNON: I will. I feel better already.

CECILY: You are looking a little worse.

ALGERNON: That is because I am hungry.

CECILY: How thoughtless of me. I should have remembered that when one is going to lead an entirely new life, one requires regular and wholesome meals. Won't you come in?

ALGERNON: Thank you. Might I have a buttonhole first? I never have any appetite unless I have a buttonhole first.

CECILY: A Maréchal Niel?

ALGERNON: No, I'd sooner have a pink rose.

CECILY: Why?

ALGERNON: Because you are like a pink rose, cousin Cecily.

CECILY: I don't think it can be right for you to talk to me like that. Miss Prism never says such things to me.

ALGERNON: Then Miss Prism is a short-sighted old lady. You are the prettiest girl I ever saw.

CECILY: Miss Prism says that all good looks are a snare.

ALGERNON: They are a snare that every sensible man would like to be caught in.

CECILY: Oh, I don't think I would care to catch a sensible man. I shouldn't know what to talk to him about.

Cecily gives him the buttonhole and they go into the house as Miss Prism and Dr Chasuble return, exchanging sententious allusions to celibacy. They look for Cecily and do not see her, but notice instead a funereally clad male figure approaching. It is Jack Worthing, who gives them the woeful news that his brother

Ernest has passed away at the Grand Hotel in Paris. He follows this, somewhat surprisingly, by asking the Rector if he could manage to christen him later that afternoon, since he cannot recall ever having been baptized. An appointment is made. Cecily comes hurrying from the house and after making a disparaging remark about her guardian's sombre attire gives him the news that his brother Ernest is in the dining-room. She goes back, to return hand in hand with Algernon, in whom, she says, she has discovered more credit than he has ever been given, in view of the tender concern he has been expressing for his invalid friend Bunbury. She goes off with Miss Prism and the Rector. Jack insists that Algernon leave that same afternoon. Algernon consents, but intends to see Cecily again before he goes. She comes back to water the roses, and he tells her that he has been ordered to leave:

ALGERNON: I hope, Cecily, I shall not offend you if I state quite frankly and openly that you seem to me to be in every way the visible personification of absolute perfection.

CECILY: I think your frankness does you great credit, Ernest. If you will allow me, I will copy your remarks into my diary.

ALGERNON: Do you really keep a diary? I'd give anything to look at it. May I?

CECILY: Oh, no. You see, it is simply a very young girl's record of her own thoughts and impressions, and consequently meant for publication. When it appears in volume form I hope you will order a copy. But pray, Ernest, don't stop. I delight in taking down from dictation. I have reached 'absolute perfection'. You can go on. I am quite ready for more.

ALGERNON: Ahem! Ahem!

CECILY: Oh, don't cough, Ernest. When one is dictating one should speak fluently and not cough. Besides, I don't know how to spell a cough.

ALGERNON: Cecily, ever since I first looked upon your wonderful and incomparable beauty, I have dared to love you wildly, passionately, devotedly, hopelessly.

CECILY: I don't think that you should tell me that you love me wildly, passionately, devotedly, hopelessly. Hopelessly doesn't seem to make much sense, does it?. . .

ALGERNON: I love you, Cecily. You will marry me, won't you?

CECILY: You silly boy! Of course. Why, we have been engaged for the last three months.

ALGERNON: For the last three months?

CECILY: Yes, it will be exactly three months on Thursday.

ALGERNON: But how did we become engaged?

CECILY: Well, ever since dear Uncle Jack first confessed to us that he had a younger brother who was very wicked and bad, you, of course, have formed the chief topic of conversation between myself and Miss Prism. And, of course, a man who is much talked about is always very attractive. One feels there must be something in him, after all. I dare say it was foolish of me, but I fell in love with you, Ernest.

ALGERNON: Darling. And when was the engagement actually settled?

CECILY: On the 14th of February last. Worn out by your entire ignorance of my existence, I determined to end the matter one way or the other, and after a long struggle with myself I accepted you under this dear old tree here. The next day I bought this little ring in your name, and this is the little bangle with the true lovers' knot I promised you always to wear.

ALGERNON: Did I give you this? It's very pretty, isn't it?

CECILY: Yes, you've wonderfully good taste, Ernest. It's the excuse I've always given for your leading such a bad life. And this is the box in which I keep all your dear letters.

ALGERNON: My letters! But, my own sweet Cecily, I have never written you any letters.

CECILY: You need hardly remind me of that, Ernest. I remember only too well that I was forced to write your letters for you. I wrote always three times a week, and sometimes oftener.

ALGERNON: Oh, do let me read them, Cecily?

CECILY: Oh, I couldn't possibly. They would make you far too conceited. The three you wrote me after I had broken off the engagement are so beautiful, and so badly spelled, that even now I can hardly read them without crying a little.

ALGERNON: But was our engagement ever broken off?

CECILY: Of course it was. On the 22nd of last March. You can see the entry if you like. 'To-day I broke off my engagement with Ernest. I feel it is better to do so. The weather still continues charming.'

ALGERNON: But why on earth did you break it off? What had I done?

I had done nothing at all. Cecily, I am very much hurt indeed to hear you broke it off. Particularly when the weather was so charming.

CECILY: It would hardly have been a really serious engagement if it hadn't been broken off at least once. But I forgave you before the week was out.

ALGERNON: What a perfect angel you are, Cecily.

CECILY: You dear romantic boy. (*He kisses her, she puts her fingers through his hair*.) I hope your hair curls naturally, does it?

ALGERNON: Yes, darling, with a little help from others.

CECILY: I am so glad.

ALGERNON: You'll never break off our engagement again, Cecily?

CECILY: I don't think I could break it off now that I have actually met you.

Besides, she adds, there is the additional matter of his name. It has always been her ambition to marry someone named Ernest: 'There is something in that name that seems to inspire absolute confidence. I pity any poor married woman whose husband is not called Ernest.' His suggestion that Algernon, for instance, might be an acceptable alternative is brushed aside. He hurries away to see the Rector, and has barely disappeared before Merriman announces that a Miss Fairfax has arrived, wishing to consult Mr Worthing on important business. Assuming 'Mr Worthing' to refer to her Uncle Jack, Cecily tells the butler to invite Miss Fairfax out to the lawn, and to serve tea.

The two girls take to one another immediately; but their affection is short-lived when they discover that each of them considers Ernest Worthing to be her fiancé. Tea is taken to the accompaniment of catty exchanges:

GWENDOLEN: Are there many interesting walks in the vicinity, Miss Cardew?

CECILY: Oh! yes! a great many. From the top of one of the hills quite close one can see five counties.

GWENDOLEN: Five counties! I don't think I should like that; I hate crowds.

CECILY (*sweetly*): I suppose that is why you live in town?

GWENDOLEN (*looking round*): Quite a well-kept garden this is, Miss Cardew.

CECILY: So glad you like it, Miss Fairfax.

GWENDOLEN: I had no idea there were any flowers in the country.

CECILY: Oh, flowers are as common here, Miss Fairfax, as people are in London.

GWENDOLEN: Personally I cannot understand how anybody manages to exist in the country, if anybody who is anybody does. The country always bores me to death.

CECILY: Ah! This is what the newspapers call agricultural depression, is it not? I believe the aristocracy are suffering very much from it just at present. It is almost an epidemic amongst them, I have been told. May I offer you some tea, Miss Fairfax?

GWENDOLEN: Thank you.

CECILY: Sugar?

GWENDOLEN: No, thank you. Sugar is not fashionable any more. (*Cecily looks angrily at her, takes up the tongs and puts four lumps of sugar into the cup.*)

CECILY: Cake or bread and butter?

GWENDOLEN: Bread and butter, please. Cake is rarely seen at the best houses nowadays.

CECILY (*cuts a very large slice of cake and puts it on the tray*): Hand that to Miss Fairfax.

GWENDOLEN: You have filled my tea with lumps of sugar, and though I asked most distinctly for bread and butter, you have given me cake. I am known for the gentleness of my disposition, and the extraordinary sweetness of my nature, but I warn you, Miss Cardew, you may go too far.

CECILY (*rising*): To save my poor, innocent, trusting boy from the machinations of any other girl there are no lengths to which I would not go.

GWENDOLEN: From the moment I saw you I distrusted you. I felt that you were false and deceitful. I am never deceived in such matters. My first impressions of people are invariably right.

CECILY: It seems to me, Miss Fairfax, that I am trespassing on your valuable time. No doubt you have many other calls of a similar character to make in the neighbourhood.

Jack Worthing enters. Gwendolen greets him as *her* Ernest. Algernon joins them and the truth is out: Jack is Gwendolen's, Algernon is Cecily's – and neither can claim the essential name of

Ernest. This reunites the girls at once and they withdraw into the house in affronted sisterhood.

Third Act

In the drawing-room Gwendolen and Cecily watch the two men's tentative approach and agree to receive them:

GWENDOLEN: There are principles at stake that one cannot surrender. Which of us should tell them? The task is not a pleasant one.

CECILY: Could we not both speak at the same time?

GWENDOLEN: An excellent idea! I always speak at the same time as other people. Will you take the time from me?

CECILY: Certainly.

GWENDOLEN AND CECILY: Your Christian names are still an insuperable barrier. That is all!

JACK AND ALGERNON: Our Christian names! Is that all? But we are going to be christened this afternoon.

GWENDOLEN: For my sake you are prepared to do this terrible thing?

JACK: I am.

CECILY: To please me you are ready to face this fearful ordeal?

ALGERNON: I am!

GWENDOLEN: How absurd to talk of the equality of the sexes! Where questions of self-sacrifice are concerned, men are infinitely beyond us.

JACK: We are.

CECILY: They have moments of physical courage of which we women know absolutely nothing.

There is mutual and ecstatic reconciliation, cut short by the arrival of Lady Bracknell. Having reaffirmed her objection to Jack's suitability for Gwendolen, she is now confronted with her nephew Algernon's announcement that he is engaged to Cecily. She embarks upon another of her interrogations:

LADY BRACKNELL: Mr Worthing, is Miss Cardew at all connected with any of the larger railway stations in London? I merely desire information. Until yesterday I had no idea that there were any families or persons whose origin was a Terminus.

JACK: Miss Cardew is the grand-daughter of the late Mr Thomas Cardew of 149 Belgrave Square, S.W.; Gervase Park, Dorking, Surrey; and the Sporran, Fifeshire, N.B.

LADY BRACKNELL: That sounds not unsatisfactory. Three addresses always inspire confidence, even in tradesmen. But what proof have I of their authenticity?

JACK: I have carefully preserved the Court Guides of the period. They are open to your inspection, Lady Bracknell.

LADY BRACKNELL: I have known strange errors in that publication.

JACK: Miss Cardew's family solicitors are Messrs Markby, Markby and Markby.

LADY BRACKNELL: Markby, Markby and Markby? A firm of the very highest position in their profession. Indeed I am told that one of the Mr Markbys is occasionally to be seen at dinner parties. So far I am satisfied.

JACK: How extremely kind of you, Lady Bracknell! I have also in my possession, you will be pleased to hear, certificates of Miss Cardew's birth, baptism, whooping cough, registration, vaccination, confirmation, and the measles; both the German and the English variety.

LADY BRACKNELL: Ah! A life crowded with incident, I see; though perhaps somewhat too exciting for a young girl. I am not myself in favour of premature experiences. Gwendolen! the time approaches for our departure. We have not a moment to lose. As a matter of form, Mr Worthing, I had better ask you if Miss Cardew has any little fortune?

JACK: Oh! about a hundred and thirty thousand pounds in the Funds. That is all. Goodbye, Lady Bracknell. So pleased to have seen you.

LADY BRACKNELL: A moment, Mr Worthing. A hundred and thirty thousand pounds! And in the Funds! Miss Cardew seems to me a most attractive young lady, now that I look at her. Few girls of the present day have any really solid qualities, any of the qualities that last, and improve with time. We live, I regret to say, in an age of surfaces.

Cecily is declared acceptable and Lady Bracknell decrees an early marriage, but Jack intervenes, as Cecily's guardian, to refuse his consent. Lady Bracknell reminds him that it will not be long, in any case, before Cecily is of age, but he informs her that under her grandfather's will she does not come legally of age until she is thirty-five. Lady Bracknell is compelled, against her nature, to appeal to Jack to withdraw his objection. He says he will gladly do so if she will let him marry Gwendolen. Lady Bracknell rises:

LADY BRACKNELL: You must be quite aware that what you propose is out of the question.

JACK: Then a passionate celibacy is all that any of us can look forward to.

LADY BRACKNELL: That is not the destiny I propose for Gwendolen. Algernon, of course, can choose for himself. Come, dear – we have already missed five, if not six, trains. To miss any more might expose us to comment on the platform.

Dr Chasuble enters to announce that everything is ready for the christenings and is dismayed to be told that his services will not be needed. He happens to let drop the name of Miss Prism: Lady Bracknell gives a start and requires Miss Prism to be produced. She is, and grows pale at the sight of Lady Bracknell, who confronts her with the dreadful details of her past:

LADY BRACKNELL: Twenty-eight years ago, Prism, you left Lord Bracknell's house, Number 104, Upper Grosvenor Street, in charge of a perambulator that contained a baby of the male sex. You never returned. A few weeks later, through the elaborate investigations of the Metropolitan police, the perambulator was discovered at midnight standing by itself in a remote corner of Bayswater. It contained the manuscript of a three-volume novel of more than usually revolting sentimentality. But the baby was not there. Prism! Where is that baby?

MISS PRISM: Lady Bracknell, I admit with shame that I do not know. I only wish I did. The plain facts of the case are these. On the morning of the day you mention, a day that is for ever branded on my memory, I prepared as usual to take the baby out in its perambulator. I had also with me a somewhat old, capacious hand-bag in which I had intended to place the manuscript of a work of fiction that I had written during my few unoccupied hours. In a moment of mental abstraction, for which I never can forgive myself, I deposited the manuscript in the basinette, and placed the baby in the hand-bag.

JACK: But where did you deposit the hand-bag?

MISS PRISM: Do not ask me, Mr Worthing.

JACK: Miss Prism, this is a matter of no small importance to me. I insist on knowing where you deposited the hand-bag that contained the infant.

MISS PRISM: I left it in the cloak-room of one of the larger railway stations in London.

JACK: What railway station?

MISS PRISM: Victoria. The Brighton line.

Jack rushes from the room, returning soon afterwards with a black leather hand-bag. From her initials on it and a stain caused by the explosion of a temperature beverage at Leamington, Miss Prism identifies the bag as hers. Jack informs her that he is the former baby she had placed in it, and tries to embrace her as his mother. She recoils, and Lady Bracknell explains that he is the son of her own sister, Mrs Moncrieff, and therefore is Algernon's elder brother. He asks urgently by what name he had been christened. Lady Bracknell is unsure, except that, as the eldest son, he would have been called after his father, whose name she cannot remember either. However, he had been a General, and Jack conveniently happens to possess the Army Lists of the last forty years. A hasty search through them takes place:

JACK: . . . Mallam, Maxbohm, Magley, what ghastly names they have – Markby, Migsby, Mobbs, Moncrieff! Lieutenant 1840, Captain, Lieutenant-Colonel, Colonel, General 1869, Christian names, Ernest John. I always told you, Gwendolen, my name was Ernest, didn't I? Well, it is Ernest after all. I mean it naturally is Ernest.

LADY BRACKNELL: Yes, I remember now that the General was called Ernest. I knew I had some particular reason for disliking the name.

GWENDOLEN: Ernest! My own Ernest! I felt from the first that you could have no other name!

JACK: Gwendolen, it is a terrible thing for a man to find out suddenly that all his life he has been speaking nothing but the truth. Can you forgive me?

GWENDOLEN: I can. For I feel that you are sure to change.

JACK: My own one!

CHASUBLE (*to Miss Prism*): Laetitia!

MISS PRISM: Frederick! At last!

ALGERNON: Cecily! At last!

JACK: Gwendolen! At last!

LADY BRACKNELL: My nephew, you seem to be displaying signs of triviality.

JACK: On the contrary, Aunt Augusta, I've now realised for the first time in my life the vital Importance of Being Earnest.

Discography

(N.B. By no means all the recordings listed below are currently available. I have not shown details of recording companies or serial numbers, since reissues often appear under different labels bearing different numbers.)

POEMS

'The Sea' ('La Mer' – 'A white mist drifts across the shrouds'): read by Michael Bawtree with works by other authors. (1 l.p. entitled *Blackwell's Junior Poetry*.)

'Symphony in Yellow' ('An omnibus across the bridge'): read by Colin Bailey, with 'A Foreign Ruler' by W. S. Landor. (1 l.p., *The Pattern of Poetry, No. 7*.)

'To L. L.' ('Could we dig up this long-buried treasure'): see MISCELLANIES, *The Importance of Being Oscar*.

'The Harlot's House' ('We caught the tread of dancing feet'): see MISCELLANIES, *The Importance of Being Oscar*.

'The Ballad of Reading Gaol': read (slightly abridged) by Frank Duncan, with works by Francis Thompson and Wilfred Owen. (1 l.p., *Late Victorian Poetry*.)

'The Ballad of Reading Gaol': read by Elsa Maxwell, with harp accompaniment, with works by other authors. (1 l.p., *Speaking Lyrics*.)

'The Ballad of Reading Goal': see MISCELLANIES, *The Importance of Being Oscar*.

FAIRY TALES

Basil Rathbone reading 'The Selfish Giant', 'The Nightingale and the Rose' and 'The Happy Prince'. (1 l.p.)

Rex Palmer reading 'The Selfish Giant'. (1 '78'.)

Frank Phillips reading 'The Happy Prince', adapted by Minnie Lake, with orchestral music by Leslie Bridgewater. (1 '78'.)

Orson Welles narrating, with Bing Crosby as the Prince, cast and orchestra, in a dramatization by Orson Welles of 'The Happy Prince', with music by Bernard Herrmann. (1 l.p. side, or 2 sides of 1 '45'.)

'The Happy Prince', an opera for children in one act, music and libretto by Malcolm Williamson, commissioned for the 1965 Farnham Festival. Pauline Stevens as the Swallow and April Cantelo as the Prince, with other singers, and orchestra conducted by Marcus Dods. (1 l.p.)

See also MISCELLANIES, *The Importance of Being Oscar*.

THE PICTURE OF DORIAN GRAY

An adaptation by Howard Rose from an edited version by Launce Maraschal of Constance Cox's stage dramatization. Lord Henry, Ian Hunter; Dorian Gray, David Enders; Basil Hallward, Ralph Michael; Sibyl, Betty Linton; narrator, Lewis Stringer. Produced by Howard Rose. (1 l.p.)

Abridged version read by Hurd Hatfield. (1 l.p.)

See also MISCELLANIES, *The Importance of Being Oscar*.

LADY WINDERMERE'S FAN

Extracts: see MISCELLANIES, *Co-Star*.

THE IMPORTANCE OF BEING EARNEST

Full version directed by Peter Wood. John Worthing, Richard Johnson; Algernon Moncrieff, Alec McCowen; Lady Bracknell, Gladys Cooper; Gwendolen Fairfax, Joan Greenwood; Cecily Cardew, Lynn Redgrave; Miss Prism, Irene Handl; Dr Chasuble, Robertson Hare. (2 l.ps.)

Full version directed by John Gielgud. John Worthing, John Gielgud; Algernon Moncrieff, Roland Culver; Lady Bracknell, Edith Evans; Gwendolen Fairfax, Pamela Brown; Cecily Cardew, Celia Johnson; Miss Prism, Jean Cadell; Dr Chasuble, Aubrey Mather. (2 l.ps.)

Extract: Lady Bracknell interviews John Worthing: Edith Evans and John Gielgud. (1 '78.')

Extract: Proposal scene between John Worthing and Gwendolen Fairfax: John Barton and Dorothy Tutin, with works by other authors. (1 l.p. entitled *Now What is Love*.)

Extract: see MISCELLANIES, *The Importance of Being Oscar*.

Extracts: see MISCELLANIES, *Co-Star*.

Mein Freund Bunbury: a musical based on the play, music by Gerd Natschinski, libretto by Helmut Bez and Jürgen Degenhardt, first performed at the Berlin Metropol Theater 2 October 1964. (Recorded on 1 l.p., conducted by the composer, with Maria Alexander, Margot Dörr, Bob Benny and Horst Schulze. Its relevance to the play can perhaps be gauged by the titles of some of the numbers: 'Charleston', 'Black Bottom', 'Sunshine Girl'.)

MISCELLANIES

The Importance of Being Oscar: Micheál MacLiammoir on 2 l.ps. (1) Poem 'To L.L.'; extract from 'An Ideal Husband'; poem 'The Harlot's House'; extract from 'The Picture of Dorian Gray'; extract from 'Salomé', read in French; (2) Extracts from 'De Profundis' and a reading of 'The Ballad of Reading Gaol'.

Frank Pettingell reading 'The Selfish Giant'; witticisms; trial; a talk; 'The Remarkable Rocket'. (1 l.p.)

Martyn Green reading aphorisms, with works by other authors, on 1 l.p. entitled *Libertine Limericks and other Ribaldries, Bawdries and Conceits*.

Co-Star: a series of l.ps. in which the listener is able to 'co-star' with well-known actors and actresses who play parts of scenes from celebrated plays and leave pauses for the listener to speak the part of the other character involved, using a script supplied with the disc. (N.B. The scripts are heavily adapted and have had material added, and by no means correspond with the original texts.) Oscar Wilde extracts in the series are: *The Importance of Being Earnest*: Tallulah Bankhead as Lady Bracknell in her interview with John Worthing; Vincent Prince as John Worthing in the Act 1 scene with Algernon Moncrieff; June Havoc as Gwendolen in the proposal scene with John Worthing; Vincent Price as John in the proposal scene. *Lady Windermere's Fan*: Tallulah Bankhead in extracts.

SALOMÉ

Music drama in one act by Richard Strauss (opus 54), libretto by Hedwig Lachmann. First produced Dresden, 9 December 1905. I list only complete versions, though there are numerous recordings of extracts, in particular 'The Dance of the Seven Veils'.

2 l.ps. in German: Caballe, Milnes, Lewis, Resnik; London Symphony Orchestra, cond. Leinsdorf.

2 l.ps. in German: Goltz, Gutstein, Melchert, Ericsdotter; Saxon State Opera Orchestra, cond. Suitner.

2 l.ps. in German: Nilsson, Wächter, Stolze, Hoffman; Vienna Philharmonic Orchestra, cond. Solti.

2 l.ps. in German: Goltz, Braun, Patzak, Kenney; Vienna Philharmonic Orchestra, cond. Krauss. (Highlights from this recording available on 1 l.p.)

2 l.ps. in German: Wegner, Metternich, Szemere, von Milinkovic; Vienna Philharmonic Orchestra, cond. Moralt.

2 l.ps. in German: Jones, Fischer-Dieskau, Cassilly, Dunn; Hamburg State Opera Orchestra, cond. Böhm. Recorded live at the premiere of a new production at the Hamburg State Opera, 1971.

Selected Bibliography

THE first complete edition of Oscar Wilde's works was edited by Robert Ross and published in 1908 in 15 volumes. A single-volume collection, edited by G. F. Maine (Collins, London), omits the unfinished plays. A good short-list of books about Wilde might be: *Bibliography of Oscar Wilde* compiled by Stewart Mason, first published in 1914 and reissued 1967; *The Autobiography of Lord Alfred Douglas*, 1929; *The Life of Oscar Wilde* by Hesketh Pearson, 1946; *The Trials of Oscar Wilde* by H. Montgomery Hyde, 1948 ('Notable British Trials' series); *The Letters of Oscar Wilde* edited by Rupert Hart-Davis, 1962; *Oscar Wilde*, a biography, by Philippe Jullian, 1969; and *Oscar Wilde*, edited by Karl Beckson, in the series 'The Critical Heritage', 1970.

Of the dozens of others written about him, or into which he enters substantially, the following is a brief selection:

Croft-Cooke, Rupert: *Bosie*, 1963.

Croft-Cooke, Rupert: *The Unrecorded Life of Oscar Wilde*, 1972.

Douglas, Lord Alfred: *Oscar Wilde and Myself*, 1914.

Ellmann, Richard: *Oscar Wilde*, a selection of critical essays, 1969.

Ellmann, Richard: *The Artist as Critic*, critical writings of Oscar Wilde, 1969.

Ervine, St. John: *Oscar Wilde, a present time appraisal*, 1951.

Harris, Frank: *Oscar Wilde: His Life and Confessions*, 1930.

Holland, Vyvyan: *Son of Oscar Wilde*, 1954.

Hyde, H. Montgomery: *Oscar Wilde, The Aftermath*, 1963.

Leverson, Ada: *Letters to the Sphinx from Oscar Wilde*, 1930.

Lewis and Smith: *Oscar Wilde Discovers America*, 1936.

Mason, Stewart: *Oscar Wilde: Art and Morality*, 1908.

O'Sullivan, Vincent: *Aspects of Oscar Wilde*, 1936.

Queensberry and Colson: *Oscar Wilde and the Black Douglas,*
    1949.
Ricketts, Charles: *Recollections of Oscar Wilde,* 1932.
Robertson, W. Graham: *Time Was,* 1931.
San Juan, Epifanio, Jnr: *The Art of Oscar Wilde,* 1967.
Sherard, Robert: *Life of Oscar Wilde,* 1906.
Sherard, Robert: *The Real Oscar Wilde,* 1911.
White, Terence de Vere: *The Parents of Oscar Wilde,* 1967.
Wyndham, Horace: *Speranza,* 1951.
Wyndham, Violet: *The Sphinx and Her Circle,* 1963.